LAST ONE C

LAST ONE OUT...

When Hull Invaded Wembley

Vince Groak

Scratching Shed Publishing Ltd

Dedicated to the players, who made it all happen.
And in memory of Roger and Clive, Ronnie and Paul.

Wednesday morning.
Rovers' team bus is mobbed as it pulls out of Craven Park.

Contents

The Author

VINCE GROAK began writing about sport in the late 1990s with ground-breaking Hull FC fanzine *In Any Kind of Weather*.

His first published work as a ghost-writer followed a chance encounter with Lee Crooks, whose autobiography *From Hull to Hell and Back* came out in 2011.

As well as a devoted black and white, Vince is a school teacher at Hessle High School in East Yorkshire. He lives in Willerby with wife, Claire, and children, Dylan and Ebony.

Foreword

The Rt Hon Lord Prescott

NOTHING CAPTURES THE spirit of Hull like rugby league. Hull people are straightforward, honest, resilient and blessed with enormous creative instincts – just like the game itself.

It came as no surprise to me when I recently discovered that Hull's local rugby teams were the first amateur clubs to apply to join the Northern Union just weeks after rugby's great split of 1895. When something important is at stake, Hull people are not slow to stand up for what is right.

As Vince Groak shows, the 1980 Challenge Cup final highlighted all of these qualities and much more besides. It was the first time that two clubs from the same city outside of London had ever played against each other at Wembley in a major rugby or football final. And it was probably the first time in history that a city had been so empty on a Saturday afternoon – it was estimated that well over a quarter of Hull's population travelled down to Wembley for the match.

For so long ignored or maligned, our city was on the national stage at last. The teams did us proud, both sets of supporters were magnificent and an indelible new page was written in the history of Hull.

Last One Out...

Some of the greatest rugby players ever seen were on display that day. Rovers' Roger Millward played most of the match with a broken jaw and would be acclaimed as one of the greatest of all time when he was inducted into the Hall of Fame. Steve Norton, Hull's great ball-handling forward terrorised defences across Britain and Australia alike.

Clive Sullivan, who graced both clubs, made history when he became the first black player to captain a British national team in any sport in the 1972 World Cup. Like me, Clive was an adopted Welsh son of Hull and, although he played for Rovers that day, he was loved equally on both sides of the river, a shining example of the welcome this city has for newcomers.

But it wasn't just the players who made an indelible mark on our city. Colin Hutton kicked the last-minute goal that won Hull the Championship in 1956. Then he moved to East Hull to coach Rovers and transformed them into one of the teams of the 1960s. In his sixty years at the Robins, no-one was more responsible for making Rovers the great club they are today.

Over 35 years after it took place, people still ask me about the 1980 final. It often crops up in conversations about what makes Hull such a unique city. And now, thanks to Vince Groak's painstaking research, I can tell them there's a book that reveals everything they need to know.

But it also preserves the memories and stories of the people who made May 3rd so important for our great city. Although my fellow Rovers fans might disagree, it shows that the most important thing was not that Rovers won the bragging rights, but that the city of Hull itself was the winner.

And I for one can't wait for the next all-Hull rugby league cup final.

The Rt Hon Lord Prescott, April 2017

Prologue

CLIVE SULLIVAN'S ROOM at the Runnymede Hotel. Just after 11pm, May 2nd 1980. All the Rovers players are there.

Except Roger.

"Look lads, whatever it takes, there is no way we can lose tomorrow," says John Millington. "We won't be able to set foot in Hull again if we get beat."

Most of his team-mates, particularly those from Hull, nod and mutter their agreement.

"Listen," chips in Brian Lockwood, "you've got to calm yourselves down. There's no good getting too wound up about it. You've just got to relax and treat it as a normal game."

The Hull resident lads wince and bristle, look at the floor. They know what's coming.

"It's alright for you," barks Millington, "You can just go back home to Castleford. You don't have to live with the bastards." Nobody, but nobody, hated the black and whites as much as Millo.

Last One Out...

"You have to listen to Locky," says Sullivan, "he's been here before, he knows what he's talking about."

Lockwood, the only member of the Rovers starting thirteen to have played in a Challenge Cup final before, did indeed know what he was talking about but his words still rankled with the Hull blokes. Locky was an out-of-towner, a 'Wessie'. He could never fully grasp the importance of tomorrow's game.

How could he?

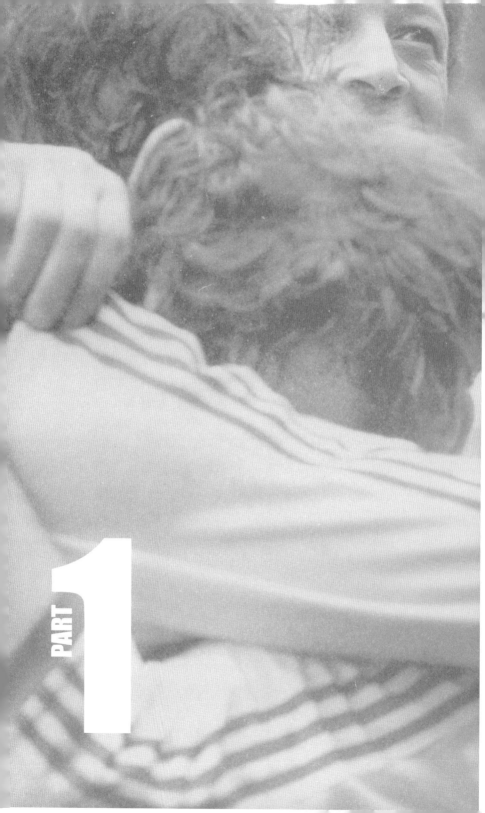

PART 1

A Tatty Fish Town

1

MONDAY NIGHT, JANUARY 1973. The BBC's *Play For Today* is 'Land of Green Ginger', written by Jarrow-born Alan Plater and set amongst the fish docks and derelict streets of Hull, the city he had come to call home. It tells the story of a young woman, Sally, who upon returning there for the weekend tries to persuade her fiancé, Mike, to turn his back on the fishing industry and find a safer job on shore. In return, she will pass up a job abroad that her employers in London have offered her. As they contemplate a future together in Hull, Mike takes Sally to the banks of the Humber and shows her the changes unfolding on the wide open estuary.

"What am I meant to be looking at?" asks Sally.

"What I'm showing you isn't there yet ... it's the bridge I'm talking about," he tells her.

"The Humber Bridge? What'll happen when it's built?"

"I think they're hoping that people will drive across it ... It's going to bring trade and prosperity to Hull. It said so in the paper, must be true. It'll be like the Klondike round here. We're all going to make our fortunes. Ten grand a year. Big houses near Kirkella golf course. Three weeks at Butlin's. Hull's going to beat Kingston Rovers at Wembley, fifty points to nil. City's going to win the European Cup three years running. I'll be Lord Mayor ... And I'll pack in the fishing."

***

WORK BEGAN ON the Humber Bridge in March 1973.

Due to open three years later, it was expected to cost £23m and knock fifty minutes off the travelling time between Hull and Grimsby, two of the UK's biggest fishing ports. In so doing, it would bring prosperity to the whole area, including the new county of Humberside, created on April Fool's Day, 1974.

In 1973, there were few jobs more dangerous or demanding than Mike's. A distant-water fisherman could expect to work 16 hours a day for weeks at a time on vessels hundreds of miles from home, on storm-tossed seas in sub-zero temperatures. They would try to forget the risks: a fatality rate seventeen times that of the average UK male worker. But that wasn't the worst of it. By the mid-1970s, the industry itself was doomed. The EEC and the Common Fisheries Policy, the Cod Wars and the Cold War, all conspired to bring Hull's fishing heritage to its knees. Labour or Conservative, nobody came to help and within a few years it was all over. A way of life changed forever.

By the time the Humber Bridge did finally open in June 1981 – five years late and vastly over-budget – Hull was in the grip of a wider, particularly northern, industrial recession. Unemployment rocketed. No matter how impressive it might be, it was going to take more than a new bridge to revitalise Kingston upon Hull.

***

ON SHORE, SLUMS and streets flattened by the Luftwaffe were still being replaced with industrial zones and discount retail parks, their former residents displaced to sprawling new housing estates in the north of the city. Those who chose to remain were often elderly, vulnerable or infirm, living in sub-standard housing, once proud communities devastated by unemployment, depravation and crime.

The sort of breeding ground, in fact, that produced one Peter Dinsdale, a notorious serial arsonist whose murderous spree began in June 1973 when, as a 12-year-old, he broke into a house in West Hull, poured paraffin about the place, lit it, and killed a six-year-old schoolmate. By the time of his final atrocity in 1979, 'Daft Peter' – as he was commonly known in the Hull FC clubhouse where he occasionally collected glasses – had claimed twenty-six victims; most of them very young, very old or disabled. A common factor in most of the attacks being that doors and windows were left open, a throwback to an era when community spirit was strong.

Having changed his name to Bruce Lee, Britain's then most prolific serial killer set his final blaze on Selby Street, less than one hundred yards from the Boulevard, Hull FC's ground, ending the lives of three more children. The 11,500 crowd that flocked to the semi-final of that night's BBC2 Floodlit Trophy, when Hull faced Leigh, would have passed both the makeshift incident station outside and the seventy or so police officers making door-to-door enquiries.

It was a traumatic period in which spirits in the city were at least briefly lifted by a 9-6 home win, followed, two weeks later, by victory in the final against FC's neighbours to the east, Hull KR. It was the black and whites' first major trophy for over twenty years and a curtain-raiser of sorts for a more glamorous encounter five months later. But back in 1973, when 'Mike' was dreaming on television of putting a half-century on his club's local rivals, a trip to Wembley could not have seemed further away. And even more so when the sport as a whole reorganised itself into two divisions in 1974 with Hull FC in the bottom tier, joined a year later by Rovers. Attendances were low at both clubs, money hard to come by. The best or most ambitious players in East Yorkshire moved west to sign for Leeds or went to play in Australia.

For the city's third professional team, Hull City, football meant soccer, not rugby. But for them too it was a story of perennial struggle, with most of the late 1960s and early 1970s spent in Division Two. Come the '80s, they were in Division Four, decline well and truly set in. In short, interest in sport in Hull had never been lower. Over a single weekend in 1975, the combined home attendances of all three teams numbered less than 10,000 – fewer than one person in twenty-five choosing to watch live professional sport in the city.

But the downturn wasn't confined to Hull; elsewhere too people were turning away from rugby league in droves. In 1971, a three-match Test series with New Zealand drew a total of just 13,351 fans. In 1973, fewer than 10,000 turned up at Wembley to watch Great Britain against Australia, hence the switch to two divisions, a so-called 'last throw of the dice'. In 1974, the value of sponsorship across the game was just £20,000, all of which led Hull KR director Ron Chester to lament: "Rugby league is not dying, it's already dead!"

***

NOT EVERYONE HAD given up. Over a period of years, a few lone voices began to challenge the ambitions of those running Hull's three clubs. Voices were first raised in East

Hull, or rather Paragon Street, where the *Hull Daily Mail* was then published. After a particularly disappointing defeat, Rovers' reporter John Sexton gave vent to the frustrations: "After performances like the one Kingston Rovers turned in last Saturday the time for mincing words has gone. For the good of the club, for the good of the players and for the good of the supporters, harsh things have to be said – and now."

Having set out his stall, Sexton let rip at the players: "Too many lack heart ... Where are the hard men in the side?" And warming to his theme, the reporter then set his sights on the directors, the capital letters Sexton's own: "The Robins have no training pitch and, on dark nights, nowhere can they train except Craven Park. BUT THEY ARE NOT PERMITTED TO USE THE WHOLE PITCH. This is the ridiculous restriction..." But the board were particularly criticised for their involvement in team affairs: "It is also time the team was selected by one man – the coach, Arthur Bunting. Selection by committee is the wrong policy. If you pay the man to coach the team he should be able to pick the team he wants and stand or fall by his decisions."

In August 1974, a Hull City shareholders meeting came to life when one supporter/shareholder stood up and said it was time that Hull City put an end to their "unsuccessful meanderings, got new blood on the board ... and rid the club of the tatty, fish town image of the last seventy-four years," some 34 years before Premier League football was realised. As for Hull FC, equally frustrated reporter Dick Tingle said: "Hull FC have now spent two seasons in Division Two and the fans are not going to wait much longer before even the 1,500 start dwindling away to well under 1,000..."

How, then, did Hull FC and Hull Kingston Rovers rise above such unrest and play beneath Wembley's Twin Towers within half a decade? To answer that, we must return to 1974.

1974/75: A Tale of Two Cities

2

ARTHUR FLETCHER LOVED Hull FC so much he called his cat 'Sully'. But after Clive Sullivan signed for Hull KR in the summer of 1974, the pet mysteriously disappeared. Such was the strength of feeling when the FC legend left the club.

"We used to get all sorts of abuse," recalls Clive's wife, Ros. "We woke in the middle of the night once and someone had vandalised Clive's car. We thought it was red paint they had thrown over it, but it turned out to be tomato ketchup."

Sullivan's spell as player-coach of Hull FC had not gone well. His best players either left or retired and he was given no money to replace them. Finally, in the Spring of '74, after been stiffed over a testimonial deal, he asked to leave.

Colin Hutton, having played for Hull and coached Rovers was by then an influential director at Craven Park. He was also very well acquainted with the Sullivans. He paid a visit to their pub, The Hawthorne Hotel, and within a few days Sullivan became a Robin.

As for the cat, fanatical FC fan Arthur always insisted

that no harm came to it. "I moved house and it preferred to stay put," he said. "But it was true that I went off the animal in such a big way that perhaps the cat got the message."

***

AFTER TASTING SUCCESS in the late '60s, Rovers drifted into the 1970s. Big names like Bill Holliday and Frank Foster weren't replaced and an apparent lack of ambition left players unsettled. Phil Lowe had opted to try his hand in Australia and even Roger Millward had considered leaving in '72.

There was talent – Roy Holdstock, John Millington, Dave Hall, Steve Hartley, Paul Rose – but it was raw. Arthur Bunting, who took over as coach when John Whiteley was sacked in '72, knew it and so did Colin Hutton. If they were to get straight out of Division Two, they would need experience.

After landing Sullivan, they looked even further west, signing veterans Bernard Watson and Neil Fox from Leeds and Wakefield respectively. In the week prior to the season's opener, the Eva Hardaker Trophy clash with Hull FC, *Hull Daily Mail* writer John Sexton was impressed by the facelift and also enhancements made to Rovers' Craven Park home. "Most striking is the completion of the new pebble-dash wall which replaces the corrugated iron fence at the front of the ground," he wrote. Heady days indeed.

Hull FC, meanwhile, turned to Sully's assistant David Doyle-Davidson and suffered another hammer blow when Mick Harrison signed for Leeds. Hull got £10,000 but the coach saw none of it, so 'Doyle' resigned himself to the squad at his disposal; Jimmy Portz, Brian Hancock, Chris Davidson, the two Macklins, Alf and Jim, Alan Wardell, Don Robson, Keith Tindall and Terry Devonshire, among them. Any hope of promotion most likely rested on the shoulders of their best player, Len Casey, at least that was how a loyal support base in the region of a couple of thousand saw it. There was no money in the club and no-one associated with it had any idea of how to generate any.

***

HULL IN THE summer of 1974. The *Gaul* was lost, they'd started building the Bridge and we'd all found ourselves living in 'Humberside'. The recession was biting hard and a strike was never far away. The Locarno had become Tiffany's and everybody was 'Kung Fu Fighting'. As the *Gaul* inquest began, the people of the city were in a familiar position; lied to, excluded and neglected, so few really noticed a new rugby league season.

The Eva Hardaker Trophy was named for the wife of Ernest Hardaker who, as Hull chairman, had presided over FC's most successful era to date; the late '50s and early '60s, when a club powered by Roy Francis's giant pack had won the Championship and been to Wembley twice. Commencing in 1960, the trophy was awarded each year to the winners of the Hull versus Rovers pre-season friendly. But, by the mid '70s there wasn't much interest and only 2,400 turned up on a Sunday afternoon in mid-August to see Rovers win 24-13.

Hull, under new captain Chris Davidson, put up a spirited performance that might have won the game but for a late Rovers try and the skipper's own woeful performance with the boot – two goals from nine attempts. And, finally, for the benefit of the small crowd, both sets of players laid on a mass second-half brawl which saw Ged Dunn and Alan Wardell sent off by referee Fred Lindop.

The derby win augured well for Bunting's men, his controversial signings looked lively. Sullivan scored a couple of early tries while Fox continued to be a one-man points-machine. Rovers' early winning streak also took them to the final of the Yorkshire Cup, where there was the brief but tantalising prospect of an all-Hull final until FC were beaten at home by Wakefield in the semi-finals. Rovers duly beat Wakefield to pick up the trophy and for *Hull Daily Mail* writer Sexton it was a pivotal moment. "Winning the Yorkshire Cup in 1974 was a real breakthrough," he reflected forty years later. "They'd won it in the '60s and in 1971, but had done nothing with the team afterwards. Winning it again changed the mindset of the club and many of its players."

Rovers competed for silverware on five fronts. Along with the Yorkshire Cup and Division Two Championship, there was the Floodlit Trophy, the Players No 6 Trophy and the Challenge Cup to aim for. And they punched above their weight in them all, playing twenty cup ties in total, twelve against top-flight sides of which, remarkably, they won eight. But those cup distractions did have a bearing on their league form and it wasn't until November that their season really clicked into gear. After that, the records began to tumble.

Winger Ged Dunn scored nine tries in his first fourteen appearances and, by late October, hit a rich seam of form to add fifteen more in ten games. When Sully returned from injury in December, he was just as prolific and the wingers' tries helped Rovers put together a run that saw them lose just once in sixteen league games between October and April.

***

IN HIS BOOK *Fever Pitch*, Nick Hornby recounts the trials of an obsessive fan's devotion to Arsenal football club. And, in a manner that will be familiar to all sports fans, he describes the conditions that must be met in order for a game to become truly memorable. Over the years, I have also come to my own set of circumstances that must be in place for a Hull FC game to be etched in the memory bank.

It should be a night game, played midweek. It must be cold, the pitch wet and muddy, me and my dad would arrive early to take up our usual position in the Threepenny Stand on the 25-yard line, opposite the players' entrance. Hull had to be unfancied, the underdogs, preferably playing a side in a higher league or at the top end of the league. Let's be honest, it probably had to be Leeds, with our opponents on an unbeaten run. We must win (of course) in any of the following circumstances: a man down, having had a forward sent off in cruelly unfair fashion; a ridiculous comeback (in those days, five points adrift met this condition); taking the lead early doors before clinging on, backs-to-the-wall.

And on the hooter, me and my dad dashing down the steps at the Airlie Street end to catch the 89F on Boulevard. There, I would listen to all the men talking about the match, as the bus slowly carried us home to North Hull.

It is uncanny how many times those conditions were met under the coaching of David Doyle-Davidson. Take the 1974 Yorkshire Cup fixture with Leeds.

In Hull, there has never been much affection for that West Yorkshire city and its rugby league team in particular. They have greater prominence, money and carry themselves with a little too much confidence. In the parochial 1970s, this was all the motivation players and fans needed to turn every Hull-Leeds encounter into a grudge match, though no-one anticipated the drama that unfolded in this round two fixture on a chilly Tuesday night at the Boulevard.

The Loiners, destined to finish third in Division One, were expected to win with relative ease, so Hull's early 7-0 lead was a shock, not least to the visitors' discipline. But as

Leeds scrum-half Keith Hepworth lashed out at Hull captain Brian Hancock, it was the home side who suffered most. As late as 2014 Hancock maintained his innocence, bristling at the injustice of it all. "It was Don Robson, our second-rower, that smacked Heppy, not me," he said. "Anyway, [Hepworth] was on the floor lashing out and trying to kick me as I stood over him. He kept doing it while others were piling in, so I just gave him a boot up the arse to calm him down and got sent off!" Among his wild-haired, side-burned, socks-rolled-down teammates, Hancock cut an unusual figure with his neatly trimmed moustache and occasional well-groomed beard, shirt tucked in, socks pulled up. If the team he captained had the look of a prison rugby team, he'd be the one in for fraud. And in 411 appearances over thirteen years, this was his only red card. It incensed Hull to the extent that Len Casey was also given his marching orders for dissent.

Down to eleven men, Hull's protests continued before prop Jim Macklin decided to lead the team off the field. As they began to trudge off, Leeds took the tap and proceeded to saunter upfield for an unopposed try, so infuriating Hull that the players then 'walked back on' and just managed to chase down the Leeds player before he could cross the line.

In the second half, the expected Leeds whitewash never materialised, Hull's depleted troops driven to a famous win by the sort of noise and atmosphere for which the Boulevard was famous. Dick Tingle in the following day's *Hull Daily Mail* called it: "...one of Hull's greatest performances in their 109-year history." Leeds' coach Roy Francis, who knew a thing or two about Hull FC, agreed: "What else can anybody say except that it was magnificent."

For Hull, that Yorkshire Cup shock was the highlight of an otherwise desperate season. As 1974 gave way to 1975, the only excitement on the horizon seemed to be the addition of a new clubhouse at the Airlie Street end. "We didn't have much of a clue what we were doing," recalls Tony Roberts who, aged just 20, became the first manager of the Humber Sportsmans Club. "But luckily for us, the Directors were even more clueless and so they just let us get on with it."

Doyle-Davidson did manage to sign some new players: George Clark from Hunslet and Bill Ramsey from Bradford. Clark was a prolific centre and brought much-needed class to a weak back division. Ramsey's impact was even greater, the experienced pack leader the team desperately needed.

By March 1975, sitting ninth in the league, all hope of promotion gone, Hull faced a rare Saturday afternoon fixture, against Huyton. The Merseyside club are sadly long forgotten and, truth be told, few knew much about them then. The reverse fixture in October had attracted 150 spectators, won at a canter by Huyton. Dick Tingle said it was: "The Airlie Birds' worst performance of the season," in a campaign that had plenty of contenders for that particular honour. So when Huyton turned up at the Boulevard on an unseasonably cold, spring day, revenge was on the agenda. Beforehand, Doyle-Davidson raised an eyebrow or two by giving scrum-half Steve Lane his debut at the expense of the more experienced Ken Foulkes. Hull's other scrum-half, Chris Davidson, had been declared unavailable after having gone on a two-week family holiday to Tunisia.

Hull won 17-15 thanks to a late penalty goal by Keith Boxall, prompting Tingle to find a new "worst performance of the season." But it also became one of Hull's most famous fixtures of the decade; just 983 fans rocked up – the lowest attendance in club history. During the salad days yet to come, tens of thousands of supporters keen to demonstrate their hard-won badge of loyalty would claim to have been at the Boulevard that day. Brian Hancock played stand-off and has less than fond memories of such crowds. "Later in my career, I was lucky to play in front of big attendances, but in the mid '70s, players could hear everything the spectators said. Not just songs, but individual comments. They'd tend to start with the fullback, calling him 'effing useless and so on. Then they'd pick on the wingers, then the centres and on it went. I usually played number six so knew when it was going to be my turn. I'd be thinking, 'here it comes, here it comes!'"

"The gatemen almost outnumbered the spectators," reflected journalist Tingle at the end of the decade. "Officials didn't need to bring the attendance figure up to the press box because you only needed a few minutes to count the fans."

Within a week, Hull KR and Hull City would also record season low crowds; Rovers, in spite of their success, attracted just 3,380 to a home game against Doncaster while City mustered 5,248 for Cardiff's visit, this being the weekend when less than 10,000 people from a population of around a quarter of a million collectively turned out.

***

BY EARLY APRIL 1975, leaders Huddersfield had finished the Division Two campaign while Rovers still had three games in hand, five points adrift. If the Robins could maintain their winning run, they would not only be promoted at the first time of asking but would go up as champions.

It wasn't to be. In the first of those fixtures, Rovers lost 16-7 at Workington and, despite winning their last two, had to settle for second place. Nevertheless, it had been a hugely successful season and a record-breaker at that. With 42 tries, Ged Dunn topped the try-scoring lists while Neil Fox, with 146 goals and 333 points, set a further two club records. Yet there were still rumblings of unrest. Bunting and his directors had invested heavily in the likes of Sullivan, Fox and Bernard 'Bobo' Watson, but that rankled with the local boys, several of whom had asked to be transfer-listed. Although the Robins were off back to the top flight, it wouldn't be plain sailing.

Hull FC, on the other hand, finished a disappointing season eighth and in an average gate of 2,001, I may very well have been the one. Finally, my dad had persuaded my mam that her six-year-old son was grown up enough to go to the Boulevard. Setting off from our house on Welbeck Street, we would stop for a drink in Walton club and have a bag of chips from the chippy at the foot of the Walliker Street flyover.

The only memory I have of my very first game was that Len Casey was sent off. I can still see him, stomping from the pitch towards the dressing rooms below us in the Best Stand (relocation to the Threepenny Stand was a few years away). A search of the archives reveals that Casey was sent off three times that year, making it impossible to pinpoint the exact date. And in fact Hull received ten dismissals that season – another unwanted record for arguably the Boulevard's least successful team ever.

In the wider world, life in Hull was changing fast in the spring of 1975. Employment on the eastern docks was in steep decline. By 1974, only twelve firms remained from the 140 that employed over 4,500 registered dockers in 1965. Now it was under two thousand. For decades, trawlers from Hull had fished lucrative Icelandic waters but now the trade was in an irreversible downward spiral and in the west everyone living around Hessle Road, where Hull FC were based, knew and felt it. Life was bewildering. All they had once cherished ... work ... community ... the local rugby league club ... was in freefall. Contemplating a new season ahead and the Airlie Birds' prospects in it, they could not possibly have imagined the astonishing boost that was coming their way.

1975/76: Smoking Gun

3

IT'S SATURDAY NIGHT, just before Christmas, 1975. We are watching *The Generation Game*, waiting for my dad to come home from Salford. The door opens and 'Old Faithful' fills the house as he bounces into the front room.

"You wouldn't believe it, Vince. We beat Salford. Salford! Unbelievable. They were brilliant. Boxall? Couldn't lay a finger on him. Absolutely bloody brilliant. And after the game, all of 'em came straight in the bar, everybody singing 'Old Faithful'. Their hair was still wet! They couldn't wait to get in the bar with the supporters. Their hair was still wet!"

***

THE EXPLOITS OF Hull FC in the Players No.6 Trophy of 1975/76 are indeed scarcely believable. That a Division Two team could make it to the final of a major competition was an achievement in itself, but when you consider who they beat along the way the achievement was all the more remarkable.

After struggling to beat Doncaster in the first round, no one gave Hull a prayer when drawn at home to Leeds. Leeds, with their internationals like Alan Smith, Syd Hynes, Les Dyl, Keith Hepworth, Steve Pitchford, David Ward. Leeds, who'd go on to win the Yorkshire Cup and finish third in Division One. But Hull, as we have seen, revelled in the role of underdog, played the part to perfection. It had become the custom by the mid 1970s for team photos to be taken on the pitch, just before kick-off. Thirteen players huddled together, forwards standing, backs crouched in front. Subs and kitman either side, wearing tracksuits. Not a sponsor's logo in sight.

There they were: Alf Macklin and his wild sideburns, Georgie Clark (already a fans' favourite), Kenny Foulkes, the mighty Bill Ramsey, 'Flash' Flanagan, Alan Wardell, Keith 'White Rhino' Boxall, uncontrollable Mick Crane, leader of men Chris Davidson and the rest. Gazing out in their magnificent, faded, irregular black-and-white-hooped shirts.

The watching six thousand was the biggest attendance the Boulevard had seen in many a year, making the noise of a crowd ten times the size as they encouraged their boys to a magnificent display. Tries from Flanagan and Boxall were matched by two from Leeds and the scores were level at 9-9 when the final hooter went. A draw was more than anyone hoped for, the replay the following Thursday at Headingley.

It helped Hull that it came just two days before Leeds were due to meet Hull KR in the Yorkshire Cup final, but Leeds were still firm favourites to brush Hull aside.

The schedule meant that less than three thousand fans turned up, but over half were from Hull and they witnessed one of the finest performances seen from a Hull side since, well, the previous year against Leeds. Beforehand, Doyle-Davidson played a masterstroke, promoting Boxall to hooker, and the blond forward went on the rampage. Leeds were no match for either him or his teammates, Macklin scoring twice and Hancock contributing likely the best try of his career. In short, Leeds were hammered, 23-11. As a reward, St Helens, the current champions, came next.

Saints would win the Challenge Cup and Premiership at the end of the season, their team boasting such talents as Geoff Pimblett, Les Jones, Roy Matthias, Graham Liptrot, Dave Chisnall and George Nicholls, but Hull were unfazed. "You just want to be drawn at home," Boxall later recalled. "We weren't really that bothered who we played, we were going well so gave ourselves a chance. The draw might have been on the telly but most of the lads wouldn't have seen it because they'd be at work. To be honest, there were that many cup games, you didn't think too much about it."

The BBC decided to televise the game on Saturday afternoon, mid-November. Four days earlier both sides were due to meet in the Floodlit Trophy, also on telly, when Doyle-Davidson, facing five games in a fortnight, rested several players in a side beaten comfortably at Knowsley Road. At the end of that game, Eric Chisnall couldn't resist giving some stick to the Hull players, telling them Saints would give them another hammering at the Boulevard, to which Boxall replied: "We can't wait either. We've got a fourteenth man at home. You think your supporters are good, wait till you hear our lot."

***

THE FRONT PAGE of the *Hull Daily Mail* carried the story of four local girls who skipped school, travelled to Edinburgh and slept in a phone box so they could attend the court trial of Les McKeown, lead singer of the Bay City Rollers, accused of dangerous driving. "We'll stay as long as we need to," one said. On the back, it was all about the Boulevard, where Hull tore into Saints from the start with two tries in the first twelve minutes. The expected fightback arrived but the second half – live on *Grandstand* – was one of the best rear-guard results in ages as the black and whites held on for a 9-8 win. In the semi-final draw on Monday morning, Salford emerged third, Hull FC fourth.

An away tie at Salford in 1976 was tough as they come. By May, the 'Red Devils' were champions, wingers Maurice Richards and Keith Fielding topped the try-scoring charts with 70 tries between them. David Watkins's 175 goals were streets ahead of next placed Sammy Lloyd. Halfbacks Ken Gill and Steve Nash were both internationals. Centre Chris Hesketh, the Great Britain captain, had been given an MBE.

After beating Saints, Hull lost at Batley in the league, then won at York and sat just inside the top half of Division Two as, elsewhere in the city, Ken 'Waggy' Wagstaff was being forced to retire at Boothferry Park. When the Airlie Birds turned up to training on the Tuesday before the big match, 'Doyle' sat them in front of one of those fancy new video recording machines upon which, to much initial amusement, they watched a recording of their victory over St Helens.

Outside, East Yorkshire was hit by atrocious weather, traffic chaos and a spate of accidents. On Friday, a corporation bus collided with a whisky tanker on Leads Road, killing one woman and injuring twenty-eight other passengers, Hull Royal Infirmary's biggest emergency in years. And as the city awoke on Saturday, the rescue was underway of the Hull tug *Norman*, which had sank off Spurn Point in the early hours.

None of which deterred over a thousand Hull FC fans from journeying to Salford for what they hoped would be a spirited performance in gallant defeat, although there was always the fear of humiliation. Hull's forward pack, led by

Bill Ramsey, hadn't read either script. Boxall scored twice and Hull dominated throughout, winning the game 22-14. After an awesome display, dozens of Hull fans crawled around the Willows on hands and knees, kissing the pitch their heroes had just graced, before joining them in the bar to celebrate late into the night, the players' hair still dripping wet.

"That was true," Boxall now confirms. "We didn't have hairdryers and mirrors and all of that stuff then, did we?"

***

"I'LL TAKE YOU to the final," promised my dad. "One way or another, we're going." And we did, six weeks later on a bus trip from Walton club.

We parked on Victoria Road, Headingley, and walked the short distance to the ground, soaking up the atmosphere. Some Hull fans, in their exuberance, spilled onto the pitch, breaking one of the low walls marking its perimeter, but that just added to the sense of occasion. It was my first cup final and the team's first major final in sixteen years. Widnes, our opponents, were 'Cup Kings', the current Challenge Cup holders indeed, with a team full of internationals ... Alan Prescott, 'Mick' George, Eric Hughes, Reg Bowden, Jim Mills, Keith Elwell, Mick Adams. Every one of Hull's team, except Ken Foulkes and Bill Ramsey, were local, no internationals.

In the end, it turned out to be one game too far. Hull's magnificent cup run ended in a 19-13 defeat, but not before Widnes were given an almighty scare. It was the first time a side from rugby league's second flight had negotiated a path to the final of a major cup competition and it had been no fluke. Hull's growing band of supporters had a tantalising glimpse of what might lay ahead.

***

ON THEIR RETURN to Division One, Rovers began the season impressively, winning ten from thirteen and sweeping into the quarter-finals of the Players No.6 Trophy and the final of the Yorkshire Cup. Keeping faith with most of the side that got them promoted, the only notable addition was Len Casey, the latest star to leave Hull FC.

But, just days before Rovers were to meet Leeds in the Yorkshire Cup final, Arthur Bunting dropped a bombshell. Frustration at his lack of control over team affairs proved too much and he resigned as coach.

Born in 1936 in Hemsworth, near Featherstone, Bunting joined Hull KR from Bramley in 1959. He played 237 times for Rovers, including at scrum-half in their only Challenge Cup final, at that time, in 1964. For two years, until he retired in 1968, his halfback partner was a young Roger Millward. On retirement, Bunting joined the coaching staff at Rovers where – upon Johnny Whiteley's sacking in 1972 – he took over the lead role. *Hull Daily Mail* man John Sexton was well aware of Bunting's frustrations.

"Arthur would ring after training on a Tuesday night and ask what team I would pick," he said. "Then he would tell me his own preferred side. Usually, we chose more or less the same team. Later that night, after the board meeting, he would call back with the team the board had chosen. More often than not, it bore no resemblance to either of our sides. That season there were a lot of unhappy players. Rovers had signed older players such as Bernard Watson, Sully, Neil Fox and the young lads felt they weren't going to get their chance. With the board deciding who was signed and who played it was hard for Arthur to keep everyone happy."

Roy Holdstock was one such player. Having made his

debut at seventeen in 1971, he was still battling to hold down a regular place and recalls how difficult the situation was. "The coach used to put his team down and then give it to the board. And one of them might say 'Well, I don't like him' or 'I saw him boozing around town. so he isn't playing.'"

Rovers appointed Bunting's assistant, Harry Poole, as his successor, who asked for – and received – full control over all playing affairs, starting with that Yorkshire Cup final in 1974. And the players soon noticed a difference. "Harry was very strong," said Holdstock. "Harry would tell the directors who was playing. Now we were *his* team."

Under Poole, everyone got a chance, even those that hadn't previously fitted in, as John Millington explains. "Steve Hartley was incredible, like lightning. But he never got a chance until Harry took over. I'd watch some blokes and think, how the hell is he in the team ahead of Steve Hartley?"

The times were changing in West Hull too. While the Rovers directors were relinquishing control, the Hull Board were swept aside entirely. It had been a feature of the mid-1970s, turmoil in the boardroom. Yet, in October 1975, just before the cup run, the rumours had substance. A boardroom coup unfolded, which saw nine new men take control of the club, bursting with energy and ambition.

The players approved. "In the past we had to fight for everything we got," Brian Hancock told the *Hull Daily Mail*. "At times, [it had been] almost a running battle and deadlock over something as small as 50p." Now, they were being treated fairly, the new board having "...gone out of their way to give the players every incentive to do well."

Win bonuses became more generous. They'd travel to away games early, sometimes stay overnight. Professionalism crept in. Buoyed by success in the Players No.6, Hull finished the season strongly and, with eight league games left, there

was still a chance of promotion. Defeats at Bramley and
Rochdale then set them back, but going up remained a
mathematical possibility with three games to go. Hull needed
not onlt to win the lot but win big enough to haul in Leigh's
massive points difference advantage. It led to a bizarre end.
Hull blew away Barrow, Doncaster and Whitehaven, scoring
thirty-five tries in three games. But only thirteen conversions
were kicked, so Hull finished level on points with Leigh and
missed out. Another season in the Second Division lay ahead.

1976/77: FC on the Up; Rovers Come of Age

4

PHIL LOWE AND Steve Norton hug each other in the middle of Sydney Cricket Ground. It's September 1976. They've won the Australian Grand Final. Their team, Manly Warringah, have just beaten Parramatta 13-10 thanks to Lowe's first-half try and five goals from Graham Eadie. In the footsteps of Malcolm Reilly and Brian Lockwood, they are changing the way Australians view English rugby league and, equally ominously, inspiring a young generation of forwards.

In a fortnight, Lowe will be back in England, at Craven Park, scoring a try on second debut as Hull Kingston Rovers beat Workington. Aged 26 and at the peak of his powers, Phil Lowe is the best second row forward in the world.

***

LOWE'S INITIAL DEBUT had been as a 17-year-old in 1967. Soon after, he won his first medal when Rovers beat Hull in the Yorkshire Cup Final. He was Rovers' player of the year in 1968/69 and, in February 1970, was selected by and played for England for the first time. On that year's GB tour of New Zealand, he scored twice on his Lions debut at Carlaw Park. In 1972, he was the sensation of Great Britain's World Cup win in France. He impressed again during the 1973 Ashes series in England and, still just 23, was already ranked among the greats: "But I remember Ken Arthurson telling me that I would only reallyknow if I was the best in the world if I tested myself in Australia." Hence the stint at Manly.

Lowe signed for three years, Rovers got fifteen grand and the promise that he would rejoin them when he'd had enough of Australia. And Lowe was determined to make sure it worked out, heading down to Manly in January to join his new teammates for pre-season training, joining the likes of Reilly, Lockwood, 'Knocker' Norton, Gary Stephens and Cliff Watson in successfully trying their hand down under. In seventy-two games, he scored twenty-five tries and carved his name into Aussie folklore. Up and down the famous Manly Corso, bars still hang his shirts on their walls. "To this day," says Lowe, "I'm welcomed with open arms whenever I go into any bar there."

In Lowe's absence, Rovers brought in Fox, Sullivan, Bernard Watson and Len Casey. Alongside those veterans a generation of Hull-born youngsters were cutting their teeth. "When I left they were all just kids," says Lowe, "but by the time I came back, they were men." With Lowe slotting into the back row alongside Paul Rose and Casey, it was a formidable pack with which Harry Poole hoped to tackle their second season in Division One.

Meanwhile, after three years in Division Two, the men now running Hull FC knew they needed new signings. With Bill Ramsey having gone to Widnes, a pack leader was a priority and the club was constantly linked with anyone and everyone. Some rumoured deals were real, others invented to keep the fans happy. And in the blistering summer of '76, the Airlie Birds came close to pulling off one of their biggest transfer coups ever.

"It was a done deal," said Mike Page, the ex-cricketer who joined the board the year before. "We weren't always popular in Wales and would get chased out of grounds by chairmen, who didn't want us poaching their best players. But I had been down there and spoken to his family. We'd agreed terms and got him a job at Hull Royal Infirmary. He was on his way to Hull to sign a contract but, at some point, stopped and rang his dad, who persuaded him to turn round and drive back to Wales. He ended up signing for Bridgend, so we just missed out on JPR Williams."

Instead, Doyle-Davidson got Keith 'Heppy' Hepworth, not as big a name as JPR or a direct replacement for either the Welshman or Bill Ramsey, but a masterstroke nevertheless.

Along with winger Graham Bray, signed in mid-season from Featherstone, and a resurgent Keith Boxall, the promise of a side that had shown itself only fleetingly in the previous two years was realised when the team got off to a flying start, winning thirteen of their first fifteen games and sitting top of the tree by Christmas. "Around the same time I signed, Dave Marshall and Jimmy Crampton also arrived," Bray says. "The directors wanted to see the club going forward. Some owned clothing companies and provided us with club suits."

***

EVEN WITH LOWE back, it was a frustrating autumn for the Robins, knocked out early in the Floodlit and JP cups and stuck in mid-table at the turn of the year. Then fresh blood arrived in the shape of Allan Agar and David Watkinson.

With the two Hull sides in different divisions, there was no Boxing Day derby. Rovers were playing at home in the afternoon, while Hull had an early kick-off at York, where Colin Hutton and Peter Frankland drove to watch the black and whites. By chance, York were giving a trial to a young forward. David Watkinson takes up the story.

"I'd had a few trials with Wakefield the previous season but had dropped back into the amateur league, playing for Heworth. Then York asked me to go for a trial. I discussed it with my dad, who said I had nothing to lose. I usually played loose forward but their hooker at the time, Ronnie Wileman, was injured so they asked me to play nine instead. I was in the programme as AN Other." Watkinson's one and only game there was a fierce encounter which saw three men sent off including Hull's Keith Boxall – for hitting Watkinson. York won and Watkinson impressed the watching directors.

"It was all very fortunate that Hutton and Frankland were at the game," said Watkinson. "They went away, did some research and a few days later invited me to Craven Park. They offered far more than I had asked from York, so I signed. Within a few weeks I was in the first team."

The main stand of Featherstone Rovers' Post Office Road ground is visible from Allan Agar's kitchen window. He made his debut there as an 18-year-old and retains close ties with a club he coached to Challenge Cup victory in 1983. But it was with Dewsbury that he made his name, winning a Championship winners' medal in 1973. Soon afterwards, he moved to Hunslet and, at 27, his career appeared to be going nowhere. Until another deputation of directors from Hull Kingston Rovers came to watch him play in January, 1977.

"At the time, Hunslet played on the dog track at the back of Elland Road football stadium in Leeds," he says. "We were doing okay and the team ended up getting promoted.

We were at home to Huddersfield and, beforehand, I found out Percy Johnson and Peter Frankland from Hull KR were here. I didn't think too much of it but had a decent game and afterwards they said they wanted to sign me."

Rovers weren't short of halfbacks. Millward, Hartley and Hall shared the six and seven shirts. "I always used to say that I was going to Rovers to wear the number 14 shirt on my back," Agar remembers. "I never, ever took for granted that I had a place in the side. I never had the pace that Roger or Steve had, but Roger knew what I could do. Everybody knew, even then, that Rovers were going to become a really strong team and that meant they would have lots of games. I was always confident I'd play plenty of rugby at Rovers."

A few weeks later, with Agar and Watkinson on board, Harry Poole explained the reason for signing out-of-town men. "Rovers can beat anybody at Craven Park," he told David Watkinson, "but once they go over Boothferry Bridge, their hearts go one way and their heads the other. We need out-of-towners to sort them out." On New Years Day, Rovers lost away yet again, this time at Leeds. With just one away win in nine games, Poole had a point.

***

FOR HULL AND Rovers, 1977 began well. By mid-February, both had progressed to round two of the Challenge Cup. The following Monday, live on *Look North*, the draw was made and for the third time in six years they were drawn together, this time at Craven Park.

Cup derbies had been a rarity during the 1960s. Rovers beat Hull at Headingley in the 1967 Yorkshire Cup Final and that was that. But, at the start of the 1970s, cup competitions repeatedly threw up derby ties. The Boulevard, August 1970, and Hull beat Rovers in the first round of the Yorkshire Cup. In early November, they met again, this time at Craven Park in the Floodlit Trophy and Rovers won 18-8. The following season, drawn together at the Boulevard in the first round of the Challenge Cup, the game was postponed three times due to power cuts caused by the miners' strike. When the game finally went ahead on a Thursday night in early February, Hull won 7-5. Two years later, at the same stage, the Hull teams faced each other yet again. An ill-tempered game at the Boulevard saw fights break out regularly and Millington and Wardell were sent off. This time, Rovers won 13-2.

And so, for the fifth time in seven years, there would be a derby cup tie. Going into it, Hull were unbeaten in five, Rovers in six, and such good form attracted nearly 11,000 spectators. Tensions were high and one surge by fans broke the perimeter fence, causing a spill onto the greyhound track.

The game was just as fraught. Early in the second half it was deadlock, 6-6, with three penalties apiece from Colin Tyrer and David Marshall. Up stepped Lowe. On 65 minutes, a typical barnstorming run saw him score a try converted by Tyrer. A drop-goal from Millward soon after made the score 12-6 and Rovers were through, comfortable enough to hold on, despite a scoreline narrowing late try from Hancock.

The Robins were bobbing along. All the promise of a side moulded over several years was coming to fruition. "We'd grown up together," says Roy Holdstock. "We were all mates doing what we enjoyed most." David Hall, who signed for Rovers in 1970, adds that: "Things were a bit rough for five years or so, but then it clicked and became a rollercoaster for all of us, which lasted a long time."

And they stayed together. Of the side that beat Hull in 1977, nine (Smith, Sullivan, Hartley, Millward, Millington, Rose, Lowe, Casey and Agar) would play at Wembley three years later, while Hall, Watkinson and Holdstock were on the sidelines watching. Only Steve Hubbard, Brian Lockwood and Phil Hogan were still to join the club.

By 1977, the Challenge Cup was close to an obsession for Roger Millward and Clive Sullivan. Neither had played in a cup final despite many, many years in the game and great international achievements. After beating Hull, Rovers beat Castleford to set up a semi-final with Widnes.

Maybe, this would be their year.

***

ROVERS WERE NOT in action on the weekend prior to the Cup semi-final, so Harry Poole went to Wheldon Road to watch Castleford play Widnes, the Robins' cup opponents. He was joined by Millward and Agar, who both lived nearby.

Then tragedy struck. After returning the short distance to his home on the outskirts of Castleford, Poole suffered a heart attack during the night and died. Agar remembers his total shock when the news was delivered by telephone early the next day. "We'd seen him that same night and there was no sign that there was anything wrong with him."

David Watkinson, who Poole signed just a few weeks earlier, recalls: "It knocked the stuffing out of us. He was an influential guy and understood the club completely. He'd say the players didn't believe in themselves enough. But he did."

Rovers' correspondent John Sexton paid a remarkably prescient tribute: "the greatest tragedy is that he has died with the team on the verge of producing all he promised."

That promise would be realised by Roger Millward. At 29, he had already captained Rovers for eight years. Initially on a trial basis, Millward became player-coach. "There was a buzz around the club and that was due to Harry," he said, shortly before sadly passing away himself in 2016. "I had been the only person he would travel with from Castleford and we'd talk about rugby league all the time, sharing ideas. After he'd gone, I made sure his ideas were carried on."

Unsurprisingly in the circumstances, Rovers lost the semi-final the following week. "It really skittled the players," admitted John Millington. "I think we'd have won and gone to Wembley if that hadn't happened."

It was more heartache for Millward. He had the job he'd dreamed of, but not in the circumstances he would have wanted. Partly because of the tragedy, yet another chance at Wembley had slipped by.

***

KNOCKED OUT OF the Cup, Hull turned their sights on the league. And walked it. The nucleus of the side had been together for years, but the signings of Bray – and especially Hepworth – had transformed the team.

The fans loved it and began to return. First in a trickle, then a flood. Home games drew 3,860 on average, which meant crowds had almost doubled in the space of two years. The black and whites lost just one more game and cruised to promotion and the title.

On April 24th, after ten years at the club, captain Brian Hancock was presented with the Division Two trophy by Hull-born comedian Norman Collier and the celebrations began at the Boulevard.

Knocker and Locky

5

IT WAS WITH some trepidation that I set off to Castleford, in the Autumn of 2015, to meet my hero, Steve 'Knocker' Norton. I'd met him twice before. First as a gawky pre-adolescent, when he signed my programme before a game at the Boulevard in the late 1970s, and then many years later at the launch of Lee Crooks's autobiography, *From Hull to Hell and Back*, which I co-authored. It had not gone well. "What you writing Crooksy's book for?" he asked. "He's a cunt. You should have written mine."

This time, I spoke to 'Knocker' on the phone the week before and he'd been in a better mood; generous and funny, plenty of stories to tell. We arranged to meet in The Junction which, like most town centre pubs on a Saturday afternoon, had all the characters. Knocker fit right in. I bought drinks for him, his wife and myself, which seemed to go down well, and we took ourselves off to a quiet corner for a yarn.

His ex-teammate Brian Lockwood, meanwhile, rarely ventures into Cas nowadays. In a converted barn on the outskirts of Methley, south east of Leeds, he is enjoying a comfortable retirement that rarely involves mixing with his former colleagues. But both men were born there and, like most lads of their generation, grew up down t' Lane, idolising the legendary team of the 1950s and '60s ... Keith Hepworth, Alan Hardisty, John Sheridan, Derek Edwards, Dennis Hartley ... before going into the game themselves. Norton made his name with Fryston Juniors, while Lockwood thrilled TV viewers as one of the stars of the Castleford inter-city schoolboys team of the soon-to-be 'swinging sixties'.

As for the big-time, Lockwood first appeared with his hometown club in 1965, Norton five years later. By the early '70s both had progressed to Great Britain selection and, soon afterwards, played club rugby down under where, within a few years, they joined the likes of Stephens, Lowe and Reilly in reaching the Australian Grand Final.

Their return coincided with a memorable year – 1977, the Queen's Jubilee. As the rest of the world got in a lather over the Sex Pistols, John Travolta, *Star Wars* and *Starsky and Hutch*, in Hull it was all about Caesar's Casino, the Trogg Bar and Romeo's and Juliet's. By the end of the summer, Elvis was dead but Lockwood and Norton were back. And soon, having fallen out with their clubs, they were after a move.

***

LOCKWOOD CAME FROM true-blood, rugby league stock. Uncles and cousins played across West Yorkshire for years. Under the tutelage of the ruthless Derek Turner, Lockwood honed his skills as a rugged but uniquely-skilled, ball-playing back row forward. It was a tough apprenticeship.

"I came off the pitch once at Hunslet, after Cas had won by thirty points and I'd been given the man of the match award. As I came up the steps, Turner was stood there, towering over me. I was about 20 and he asked: 'Do you think you've had a good game?' I looked up at him, and didn't know what to say, so said nowt. And he asked me again: 'Do you think you had a good game,' I suppose I probably shrugged or nodded. Next thing, he's punched me on the jaw and knocked me out." But there is no doubt that Turner rated the young forward, putting him in the second row for the 1969 Cup final with Salford. Cas won and Lockwood picked up his first Challenge Cup winners medal. The next May, he had another and, two years later, was a World Cup winner.

By then another Cas man, the aforementioned Malcolm Reilly, was wowing the Aussies and clever, tough forwards of Lockwood's ilk had suddenly become very fashionable.

Sometime around this point, Lockwood left his job as a plumber for the Coal Board and set up his own business. He was just about to walk into a convention in early 1974 when he overhead a conversation between two men in front of him.

"I see Lockwood's off to Australia."

"Aye. Canterbury Bankstown. Two thousand quid."

That was news to him, but it turned out to be true. Cas were indeed prepared to let Lockwood spend the summer down under. The player himself, initially unsure, decided to give it a go and it turned out to be a good decision; not only did it end with Lockwood playing in the Grand Final of 1974 it also whetted his appetite for the Australian lifestyle. The decision to move to Balmain the following season was much easier after a wrangle with Castleford over a benefit season.

"I was heartbroken when they said they were releasing me," recalled Lockwood. "I left the boardroom in tears. When I got home, [wife] Anne could see how upset I was, but told me I'd had a call from Keith Gittings, chairman of Balmain. He was going to ring again an hour later. I asked Anne what she thought about going back and she said it was up to me. The country wasn't in a good way. People were being laid off and struggling to get hold of things like toilet rolls and sugar, so it was tempting. Anyway, I sat down and made a list of all the things I wanted ... an apartment, a couple of return flights, a car, eight thousand dollars, which was more money than I'd ever earned and more than I could imagine. But I thought, well if I don't ask for it, I won't get it. Anyway, on the dot, Keith rang back and I read this list of things. At the end, he just said: 'Okay, that shouldn't be a problem.' And I thought, shit, I could have asked for more.'

The couple spent three years at Balmain.

***

STEVE NORTON WAS just 17 in 1970, when he broke into the Castleford team and was then an unused substitute in the Challenge Cup win that same year. And to begin with he didn't always play loose forward, at centre when Cas beat Hull KR in the 1971 Yorkshire Cup Final. But when Reilly signed for Manly, Norton made the number 13 shirt his own. Still only 21, he was one of the youngest 1974 Lions tourists and made his Test debut against Australia in Sydney.

As with Lockwood, a taste of the Aussie lifestyle left 'Knocker' open to offers and when, in 1976, he received a call from Manly saying they were looking to replace Reilly, he jumped at the chance to join up with a man who'd become a great mate, Frank Stanton. Norton had only been in Australia a few days when Stanton decided to find out a bit more about his new signing.

"So, Steve, are you anything like Malcolm Reilly?"

"I'm twice better than 'im," said Norton.

"Twice better? Why, what can you do?"

"I can do t' lot. Sidestep, swerve. I can use t' ball, tackle. The lot."

"What are you like at fighting?" asked Stanton.

"Average."

"Well stand well back then," said Stanton, before laying down precisely how he wanted Norton to play.

"He told me to get the ball from acting half and pass it," Norton says now. "That's all he asked me to do and that's all I did. 'And then,' he'd tell me, 'just when they think you're going to pass, do something completely different and you've got 'em.' And we won t' premiership. Very simple really."

Norton soon became a favourite in northern Sydney, where old-timers still wax lyrical about 'Knocker' Norton and Phil Lowe. He had a second less successful season in 1977 but, by the start of September, was back in Castleford. But he didn't have a club, having had a row with them over money.

"I hadn't played for Castleford for eighteen months and was never going to play for them again," says Norton. "I had an offer from Leeds and nearly signed for Bradford, but there was no way the chairman was going to sell me to a top club, only a club he thought was going to get relegated. That's how I ended up talking to Hull FC."

Norton is now in his early sixties. The bald head – once likened to a badly dented watering can – still glistens, and the right hand that launched a thousand hand-offs grips a pint of bitter as he leans across the table to share a truth he has been insisting on for thirty years and more. "I knew Hull FC were going to be my club. Immediately. It was when the chairman and director, Charlie Watson and Roy Waudby, turned up to see me. They were eating fish and chips. Out of newspaper! And they brought a box of cream cakes. Cream cakes! I thought these are straight-up, normal people I can play for. But I still told 'em: 'I've got an agreement with Peter

Fox at Bradford and they're offering more money than thee'. Luckily, Mal Reilly wanted to sign Jimmy Crampton from Hull and so the clubs did a deal and I went there."

***

EITHER SIDE OF his final stint at Balmain, Lockwood held the player-coach role at Wakefield, where he had a fraught relationship with the board. The signing in 1977 of rugby union halfback Mike Lampkowski typified the relationship. "I'd never even heard of him," said Lockwood. "They just told me I had a new scrum-half."

By January 1978, relations were at breaking point. "I was told I could either resign or be sacked. They didn't really have much choice after I'd grabbed the vice-chairman by the throat after a game at Warrington. Well I wasn't going to have him coming in the dressing room criticising the players while I was the coach. That was my job."

So Lockwood and Wakefield went their separate ways just as Hull KR were looking for a new forward. Injuries and suspensions had badly depleted Rovers' pack, the season all-but ground to a halt. Rovers not only needed another body, they needed craft, guile; someone with rugby intelligence to lead them around. "A week after I fell out with Wakefield, Roger phoned and asked if I was interested and I said 'aye'."

Millward, chairman Bill Land and Colin Hutton paid a visit to The Sun, Lockwood's pub. Talks went well and the group met up again the next day at the old greyhound stadium at Elland Road, where Rovers were playing Hunslet.

"I hadn't seen anything like it," remembers Lockwood. "Chaos. There were hundreds of Rovers supporters crammed into this little ground, making a right racket and creating a great atmosphere. Rovers absolutely hammered Hunslet and

I said to Roger: 'You've got a great team here, what do you want me for?' But he explained that, as good as Rovers were, they needed someone to settle them down. By then, I knew exactly the kind of role he wanted me to play – pack leader."

"Lockwood was a great signing," said journalist John Sexton. "The missing piece of the jigsaw. Not only was he the ball player Rovers needed but he was a great help to Roger. Bringing Locky in gave him a sounding board. They played together as kids in those inter-city games on telly in the early '60s, hadn't they? Roger was a novice coach who needed someone he could trust and share ideas with."

Lockwood and Millward were also cousins, but they weren't soulmates. Millward knew he needed Lockwood and Lockwood knew that a move to Rovers was the best way to revitalise his career. "I still have ambitions left in rugby league," he told the *Hull Daily Mail*. "I'd like to play for Great Britain again and go on tour." Another goal was to return to Wembley. Although he only spent two and a half seasons at Craven Park, that was enough time to achieve all three.

***

STEVE NORTON WAS Arthur Bunting's first signing at Hull FC. "And the best," said a man who wasn't just getting an international forward, but a character around whom he could build a strong club culture.

"'Knocker' was infectious," Bunting continued. "When I joined Hull, the players went straight home after training, there was no team spirit. I tried to encourage them to have a drink together but no-one was interested. When 'Knocker' arrived, everyone just wanted to be around him."

"The place smelled fusty and mouldy," is how Norton tells it. "I knew they'd good players ... David Marshall, Alf

Macklin, Chris Davidson ... but something vital was missing. None of the players socialised; some were quite aloof. They were good people but very private and a bit sceptical of me at first. They'd heard about all this money that Hull had paid Cas and thought I'd been given some of it. Us players were all dummies back then, we didn't have a clue about money, so I wanted to put them straight. After training I said: 'Right, we're all going to The Clarendon and the drinks are on me'."

The next time he asked, they went again. Then to the Kingfisher... Albion ... Norland ... Top House. Tuesday nights mostly, sometimes Thursdays and definitely, always, after a game. "We always went in the pub with the supporters and didn't leave the last one had gone. That was our strong point. Nowadays players go off to their own pubs, or go home, but we all went together. We were like sheep." And everyone had to join in, whether a drinker or not, routinely sinking ten pints of bitter, sometimes more. He waved around a newspaper cutting and said: "See that headline: 'Norton rules again'. Is there only me playing in this team? It was a joke and taken as one, but it made sure there were no poseurs in the side."

But there was a price to pay. "There must have been twenty-three divorces in my first two years at Hull and I were first. My wife were lovely, by the way. It was a world record, never mind all yer Yorkshire Cups and titles! I'd tell the blokes: 'You're stranded. Tha' can't play for this team and think tha's going to have a nice, happy family life, watching telly. We're going for broke. It's all or nothing. We're here and we're going to every cup final.'" There is a telling pause, before he concludes: "Most of which we lost, by the way."

Norton signed on the last Thursday of January, trained at the Boulevard that same night and made his debut at home to St Helens on Sunday in front of Hull's biggest crowd of the season. Norton was brilliant, mesmerising in defeat. In the weeks to come, Hull fans, hungry for success, starved of glamour, feasted on his talents. He was a typical Hull player from the beginning, a scrapper, a battler, but, boy, could he play. With no rugby under his belt for six months, within weeks he was bewildering second division defences with his running, stepping, offloading. Like water running over glass, he glided, he flowed.

Bunting was delighted to see his players having a drink together, at least in those early years. "That signing was the biggest we ever pulled off. 'Knocker' changed everything."

Norton moved to North Ferriby and was a larger than life figure in East Yorkshire for almost a decade. Supporters, impressed by his obvious talents in drinking and playing, called him 'God'. Lee Crooks would later become his brother-in-law but, by the early 1980s, was another disciple: "I tried for years to live like Knocker did, but learned the hard way that it wasn't possible."

***

WHILE NORTON WAS house-hunting in East Yorkshire, Lockwood was definitely not handing over the keys to his pub. "I had seen what it was like in my early days in Castleford. If I'd played Friday night and we'd got beat, I daren't go out into town the next day. Hull was going to be ten times worse. I stayed in Wakefield."

And so Lockwood, like his cousin, became a traveller, an out-of-towner. And Rovers went from strength to strength, but it wasn't without problems. Midway through the season, amid the interminable grind of playing once or twice a week and driving between Wakefield and Hull, tensions between the two family members erupted. Millward, pushing his men hard in training, was confronted by his cousin.

"Roger, get off my back will you?" said Lockwood. "I'm giving you everything I can. I'm training every session and playing every week. I'm your leading tackler and giving all I've got on the field. But I can't keep up with some of these lads." The man himself he wasn't the best trainer: "...but I had a pub in Wakefield and, after training, still had to drive home and shut the pub up. I wouldn't get to bed until well after midnight and then be working all the next day. There was no way I could keep up with young blokes like Steve Hartley or Mike Smith. Roger was a bit naughty with me at times."

For both men, though, playing in Hull had immediate rewards. By the autumn of 1978, Norton and Lockwood were back in the Great Britain side. The former played in all three Tests while Lockwood, 30, was recalled into the 'Dad's Army' front-row for the second. Both would also tour again in 1979.

Domestically, the 1980 Cup final was Lockwood's last appearance for Rovers. After a short and unhappy time at Oldham, he went to Widnes and twice returned to Wembley in 1981 and '82. His last professional game, fittingly, was the Cup final replay against Hull FC at Elland Road. He coached briefly and continued to run pubs in the Wakefield area. Now aged 69, he retains few links with rugby league, aside from an annual appearance at the Lance Todd dinner in Salford.

Norton meanwhile was devastated by Wembley defeat in 1980 and vowed he would lead the team back, to win. He made three more Wembley appearances in 1982, 1983 and 1985, but none were successful and he left Hull for Wakefield in 1987, but that didn't last long: "I didn't have the love." Nothing could compare to the fans of Hull FC.

Norton lives in Castleford but Hull FC are still his team. He habitually attends player reunions and still reminds his ex-teammates that he was the superstar of the club. Jokingly, of course, but everyone knows he is right.

1977/78: Everything Had to Change

6

THE FEUD BETWEEN Colin Tyrer and Keith Hepworth went all the way back to the 1970 Challenge Cup final. Hepworth, playing scrum-half for Castleford, thumped the Wigan fullback off the ball, breaking his jaw. Tyrer was carried from the field and Hepworth played on. Wigan, bereft of their goalkicker, lost 7-2 and Cas retained the Cup.

Eight years later, Hepworth and Tyrer faced each other again, this time in a Hull derby; the second round of the Challenge Cup. Before the game, Hepworth led a bemused Steve Norton out of the Hull dressing room to meet Rovers' team bus as it arrived at The Boulevard.

"He dragged me out of the dressing room. It was very strange," Norton remembers. "'What's thee doing?' I asked him. And, when Tyrer got off the bus, Heppy pushed his way through the supporters and got right in his face, bumping into him. And then, the first chance he gets in the game, he tangles with Tyrer and Tyrer has completely gone, lost it. He flattens Heppy and gets sent off."

Last One Out...

By February 1978, a Challenge Cup derby was intense enough without an extra layer of bitter, personal vendetta.

***

IT OUGHT TO have been no contest. Rovers were fourth in the league, their drubbing of St Helens in the Floodlit Trophy final having turned lots of heads. "No matter who we played that night, we'd have beaten them," reckons John Millington. "We'd won the Yorkshire Cup a few times but, after winning the Floodlit, that was really the start of our success."

It was Rovers' first major trophy; confidence and belief were growing. It was still Harry's team but Roger Millward had brought Lowe back from Australia and signed Lockwood. And three days later he went after a young back who was breaking records in union at the Hull & East Riding club.

"I played for Rovers as a trialist," says Steve Hubbard. "It was all a bit cloak and dagger. The team bus would pick me up in North Ferriby and, while I was waiting, I would hide in the bushes, hoping nobody saw me. Anyway I played at Headingley and the following week Rovers offered to sign me. Bill Land asked what I wanted but, to be honest, I'd have signed for nothing." With a goalkicking winger signed up, Millward now had every base covered.

As for Hull, their directors ignored 'The Doyle' when he asked for thirty grand to strengthen his team. And they paid the price. They eventually spent £10,000 on Vince Farrar but it was too late and, by Christmas, they were in the bottom four staring relegation in the face. Doyle-Davidson quit, some say he was pushed, and Hull appointed ex-Rovers player and coach, Arthur Bunting. On the same day, world speedway champion Ivan Mauger was also at the Boulevard, signing for Hull Vikings.

Bunting's first match in charge was at home to Widnes, who were eighteen unbeaten. Hull's performance was brave but, with a minute to go, they trailed 8-4, destined for another loss. Then, in the final move of the game, up stepped Keith Boxall, barrelling his way over to score. From in front of the posts, Dave Marshall had the easiest of chances to register a first win since November but hit the post and Hull lost 8-7.

"Chris Davidson went mad at him," remembers Keith Tindall. "At half-time, we were only 5-2 behind and one of the directors came into the dressing room and doubled our winning money." The next week, they lost by the same score and three more narrow defeats followed.

Although results didn't improve, performances did and behind the scenes Bunting was making Hull a much more difficult team to beat. The supporters were prepared to wait but several of the players, still loyal to Doyle-Davidson, weren't happy. "But there wasn't a lot the players could say," reflects Keith Boxall. "You had to be careful in those days. It's not like it is now, with three-year contracts. If you stepped out of line, you might not get picked."

"We'd heard rumours Arthur was coming and when it finally happened team spirit dropped for a while," recalled Graham Bray. "Everyone was fond of Doyle. Arthur had been at Rovers a long time, we didn't know what would happen."

What was going to happen was team-strengthening on a massive scale. The Hull board were about to back Bunting in a way no other Hull coach had been backed before.

The best of those signings was 'Knocker' Norton, but Bunting gradually knocked the club into shape in other ways too, by introducing more varied training methods and better conditioning facilities. He brought his own sauna to the club and had it installed under the Best Stand. He understood the importance of match preparation. "I remember staying up in

Scarborough one night early on," Norton says. "We checked into our rooms and came down for our meal. Most of the lads hadn't stayed in a posh hotel before and when they gave us menus and asked us to order, some didn't know what to do. Arthur went first and ordered prawn cocktail. And steak, medium rare. Most of us didn't know what that meant so, when the waiter went around the table, we all just said: 'We'll have t' same as Arthur'." But there was one man who would never join in. "Alf Macklin would never eat anything Hull FC put in front of him," says Boxall. "He wouldn't entertain it. He'd turn up for away games with a bag full of sandwiches made by his mam, which made him very popular. Everyone wanted to sit next to him on the bus."

For years, Hull and Rovers treated away trips in much the same way. Meet at the ground early for a cramped bus ride heading west. Stop at the Mayhill café, near Boothferry Bridge, for a cup of tea and a sandwich. A game of cards and arrive an hour before kick-off. For a semi-final they might, just might, stay over at a cheap motel, two to a room.

Bunting and Millward did things differently, taking the players away as often as possible, treating them right. But it wasn't easy to persuade the directors to shell out the dough. "Mike Page was my biggest ally as he was a sportsman," says Bunting. "He always agreed with me because he understood why I wanted to do it." Hull stayed at Mottram Hall, rubbing shoulders with Manchester United, Liverpool, Nottingham Forest. The rugby players loved it and started to believe.

By then, they had a new captain, Brian Hancock having given way to Vince Farrar. "When we signed Keith Hepworth he said: 'Look, Brian. I've been playing ten years longer than thee, so shut up.' There was no way I was going to be able to captain the likes of Vince or 'Knocker'."

***

JANUARY SAW THE worst storms in Hull since 1953. Much of the old town was flooded, particularly tragic with the new tidal barrier being built just a few hundred yards away. It summed up the mood in the city. Most of Hull's trawlers were laid up. In March, Ernie Suddaby, ex-skipper of the *Gaul* trawler and then landlord of The Wassand Arms, declared an exclusion zone around his pub. Signs went up: "Icelanders not welcome – 200-mile limit."

By spring, eleven per cent of Hull was unemployed. Even the white-gloved traffic warden controlling traffic over North Bridge was replaced by traffic lights. At the pictures, it was titillation all the way. *Cruel Passion* and *The Pornbrokers* at ABC; *Goodbye Emmanuelle* and *Come Play with Me* at Tower. Equally designed to give the city a lift was the Challenge Cup first round when, for the second year running and fourth time in seven years, Hull and Rovers were drawn together.

Norton, Lockwood and Hubbard had all signed before the transfer deadline and, with Hull's form improving, there was great interest, tickets flew out the door. But, on the Friday before, the weather turned again. The following morning, the Boulevard was a foot deep in snow and ice, there was no way the game could go ahead. In fact, of the sixteen ties, only Leeds' escaped the white-out at Headingley.

The next week, Hull and Rovers tried again but the wintry conditions were no better. Anticipation grew, but fans had to wait and with no rugby available, attentions turned to boxing. It was Valentine's Day, the night before Spinks beat Ali in Vegas, and in a municipal swimming baths on Madeley Street, Joey Wainwright and Jackie Turner were matched for the local ABA Bantamweight title, 'Humberside's Fight of the Decade'. It proved to be stormy. Wainwright was warned for butting in the opening minute before being disqualified for biting in a fight that lasted just 61 seconds. Bottles and glasses rained into the ring. And when Hull and Rovers did finally manage to get it on at the end of February, it was bedlam at the Boulevard as well. Shortly after two o'clock, supporters came pouring out of Raynors, Halfway, Eagle, Parkers. By 2:30pm, long queues had formed at the turnstiles. The crowd was finally recorded as 16,001, the biggest of the season by far and, shortly before kick-off, the Threepenny Stand became dangerously overcrowded. As the teams came out, there was a surge from top to bottom, breaking the perimeter fence and spilling supporters onto the speedway track. Police tried to force them back in, exactly a year to the day since an almost identical incident in the Challenge Cup derby at Craven Park. Seven were arrested, seventeen ejected and horses there to calm the situation were pelted with objects on an ignoble day for rugby league in the city.

Once the match got underway, Rovers scored first, through Sullivan. Tyrer converted and added a penalty goal before, with 27 minutes gone, came his rush of blood. "Tyrer always said he was going to get his own back," remembers Brian Lockwood. "It lost us that match, him getting sent off." But with twelve men Rovers still led until, deep in the second half, an already highly-charged encounter exploded again.

"Throughout the game, I'd been given some pretty rough treatment," says Phil Lowe, "particularly from Chris Davidson and Tony Duke. They must have smacked me three or four times and nobody seemed to be doing anything about it so, after one high tackle too many, I just stood up and belted Davidson. He got taken off. I think I broke his cheekbone, but the referee, Ronnie Campbell, never did anything about that either. Later in the game, I made a break out wide and Alf Macklin jumped on my back. I shrugged him off and he went down like he'd been shot. Campbell blew his whistle, called me over and sent me off. I said: 'I never touched him, Ron'. 'I know you never' he said, 'but I should have sent you off when you hit the other fella, so I'm sending you off now'."

John Sexton, in the *Hull Daily Mail*, was outraged. "Alf Macklin turned on a performance that would not have been out of place in the National Theatre," he wrote. And it was Macklin who provided the killer blow. Deep into injury-time, he scored the try that levelled the scores. Boxall, cool as ice, slotted the conversion and Hull were in the second round.

***

A FORTNIGHT LATER, 14,000 were back at the Boulevard for the next round against Widnes. But Hull were never really in it and five goals from Paul Woods steered the visitors to a comfortable win. In the league, they were seven points from safety with nine games left and the drop seemed a formality.

The first of those was at Dewsbury, where a last-minute Boxall penalty secured an 8-7 success, Bunting's first league victory. Then it was another derby.

On Good Friday, in front of another raucous, five-figure Boulevard crowd, Hull dominated throughout to collect a three-nil clean sweep in derby fixtures that season. Rovers' performance was slammed. Sexton called it 'pathetic' and revealed 'all is not well at Craven Park'. Millward called the squad in for extra Sunday morning training. The players saw a new side to their coach as he went ballistic. Lowe, Hartley and Dunn were all dropped for the Easter Monday game with Leeds. Into the side came Hubbard, on debut.

For Millward, 30, yet another season was passing him by. Having failed in his fourteenth attempt to reach Wembley, and then suffering another defeat to the more-than-likely-relegated Hull FC, it was tough to take. To compound Rovers problems, Len Casey publicly criticised some teammates, blaming them for playing without passion. He asked for a transfer and was listed for £20,000.

Over at the Boulevard, things were looking up. Rockets were fired off the roof of Best Stand as Ivan Mauger debuted for the Vikings and another Hull FC win over Warrington narrowed the gap to just three points with five games to go. But the optimism was short-lived and defeat at Wakefield effectively ended hopes of survival. There were impressive wins against Leeds and Salford still to come, but the run of form had arrived too late and relegation was confirmed when Hull lost at Bramley; a game notable for yet another poor goalkicking display. Hull were relegated by just two points.

Nevertheless, the upturn in fortunes was enough to convince Bunting and the board that they had a good thing going and both parties agreed to extend the 'trial period' with a three-year contract. His immediate future secured, Bunting sought to strengthen his squad and, again, looked to West Yorkshire, approaching Featherstone for Charlie Stone and goalkicker Steve Quinn. Both bids were turned down.

It was a ruthless approach that did not always sit well with players who had been at the club for years., but Bunting was adamant. "Everything had to change, didn't it?"

***

DESPITE THE MID-SEASON injury crisis, signing Lockwood kept Rovers on course and a big win at Castleford in the penultimate game of the season secured fourth place, the second top-four finish in a row leaving no doubt that Rovers were now one of the game's biggest clubs. All that remained was to convert that promise into something more tangible.

One area in need of strengthening was the goalkicking department. For three years, the duties had been shared around between Fox, Tyrer, Millward and Hall, but there was a new kid on the block. Having tasted first team action over Easter, Steve Hubbard was back in the 'A' team scoring points for fun, six tries and fourteen goals in his next two games. So it was no surprise when he was brought back into the first team for the play-off with Widnes, kicking five from five. "I struggled to break into the side," he admits. "It was cliquish and I had a lot to prove. But, after a time, the team realised I could make a contribution and I was accepted a bit more."

In May, Rovers and Millward agreed a two-year deal for him to stay on in the player-coach role. Even though he was 30, he still had a few years left in him as well as a burning desire to fulfil that one last ambition; playing at Wembley. The new contract would take him to May 1980 after which his playing days would be over and he could coach full-time. If he hadn't made it to Wembley by then, well, *que sera, sera*.

While Hull and Rovers were fighting battles at opposite ends of the league, in the round-ball game Hull City were also embroiled in a season-long battle against the drop in Division Two, going through three managers, John Kaye, Bobby Collins and Ken Houghton, before relegation after a 2-1 loss at Orient. With the season over though, thousands of rugby fans still had much to anticipate. Thirty coaches and eight special trains carried some 6,000 supporters to Wembley for that year's Challenge Cup Final, Leeds versus Saints.

It was a busy week beneath the old Twin Towers. Seven days earlier, Ipswich had beaten Arsenal to win the FA Cup and, on the Wednesday, Kenny Dalglish scored for Liverpool as they beat Bruges to retain the European Cup. On Friday night, at the Empire Pool, Hull's Jackie Turner, in front of a packed and boisterous crowd including hundreds from Hull, won a points victory and his second ABA Championship. The next day, Leeds beat St Helens and Hull and Rovers supporters dreamed of a day when they might support their own team there.

It had, after all, been a season with many highlights. Hull's average attendance had risen to nearly 5,500 and the team had star quality. Most importantly, it seemed to be going places. True, they were going into the Second Division, with trips to places like Huyton, Hunslet, Batley and Bramley, but there was no doubt in anyone's mind, especially the players', that they would bounce straight back, a force to be reckoned with. The only downside was the lack of impact made by younger, local players. Terry Lynn, Peter Hall, Ian Wilson, Mick Sutton and Colin Lazenby all had a go but it was only when Farrar and Norton arrived that the team picked up.

John Sexton also reflected on progress made in the east of the city: "For the past few years, Kingston Rovers have stood on the threshold of a real breakthrough. Each season has started with promise and ended on a note of what might have been. While 1977/78 has followed that pattern to some extent, there are signs that the goal is in sight."

1978/79: Champions

7

IT WAS A World Cup summer. Ticker tape and Mario Kempes; Archie Gemmill and Rod Stewart; Abba, Boney M and the Boomtown Rats. It was the summer of Ian Botham and Buster Mottram, Salford's Keith Fielding won the BBC show *Superstars* and everyone wanted a skateboard.

But it was also a turbulent and fractious time. The Yorkshire Ripper was at large and the Labour Government battled with the unions over wages while Thatcher's Tories watched and waited. Hull's fish dock was all but silent and Ross closed its factory on West Dock Street, as another three hundred lost their jobs. In August, hospital supply workers went on strike and so did the dockers. The teachers waited until the kids went back to school and then they walked out too. Work on the Humber Bridge almost ground to a halt; the bosses blamed the workers, the workers blamed the bosses and everybody blamed the weather. The project looked as if it might shudder to a halt, a pair of half-finished towers sticking two fingers up at the world.

There was a similar mood of defiance at the Boulevard
and Craven Park. Hull struck seven off their playing roster,
Rovers went further and axed seventeen. Both sides returned
to training earlier than ever and Hull found the Boulevard
had been given a make-over. Bunting told the *Hull Daily Mail*:
"It is our aim to get back into Division One at the first
attempt." Season tickets had sold well and ten new clubs had
joined the Hull amateur competition. Hull, they were saying,
was now the capital of rugby league. There was optimism in
the air and then the Airlie Birds signed Sammy Lloyd.

***

AFTER BUNTING ARRIVED in January, Hull lost nine more
games. Of these, five were lost by two points or less. Hull were
relegated for the want of a goalkicker. While David Marshall
had pinged over just fifty-four goals, Castleford's Geoff
'Sammy' Lloyd passed the century for the fifth year running,
with a strike rate even David Watkins couldn't match.

At the time of his signing, Lloyd told the *Hull Daily Mail*
he had fallen out of love with the game: "All my enthusiasm
disappeared. I just seemed to be going through the motions."
That the spark was re-lit was all down to one man, he said.

"I'd known 'Knocker' since we were kids at Cas and
even after he went to Hull we kept in touch. He had this glint
in his eye and was besotted with how he was treated by the
Hull fans. He didn't give a monkey's that Hull were going to
be relegated, he was having the time of his life." But even
when he heard Hull were contemplating a bid, Lloyd still
needed convincing. "I'd done nearly ten years at Cas and was
contemplating retirement." Arthur Bunting and chairman
Charlie Watson persuaded him otherwise, selling him on
their ambition. "I told them I only had one more season left

in me. The Hull fans were barmy. They were getting about 7,000 but that kept on going up and up. The support was unbelievable, home and away. At Cas, we always enjoyed our trips to Hull because of the craic. We'd go out for a few beers afterwards because the Hull fans were a great laugh."

Lloyd's first game for Hull was at McLaren Field, Bramley, in the first round of the Yorkshire Cup, August 1978. The place was full – with visiting fans. "There were only 3,000 or so, but three-quarters were from Hull. It was amazing."

A few weeks later came Lloyd's home debut against Oldham when, on entering the pitch, the players were treated to a ticker tape reception. For weeks, inspired by Argentina in the World Cup, people spent Saturday evenings shredding copies of the *Hull Daily Mail* and stuffing them in Grandways carrier bags to release into the air come kick-off on Sunday. For Lloyd, the game was remarkable for another reason.

Come the final whistle, Lloyd had taken fourteen kicks at goal from all over the pitch and landed every one, a post-war record unequalled for a quarter of a century. Hull won 61-10, red-hot favourites to go straight back up and Lloyd was on his way to being the new FC poster boy though, truth be told, there weren't too many of those around in rugby league in 1978, and fewer still in Division Two.

"The second division was tough," recalls Steve Norton. "You came up against old-timers, not good enough anymore for the top level but trying to bushwhack you, hit you from the back, elbow you, knock your teeth out, break your nose; anything dirty, devious. You found out where you stood. But getting relegated was the best thing to happen to us. It gave Arthur time to get us organised. We destroyed every team."

Four years after having to get Hull Kingston Rovers out of Division Two, Arthur Bunting was in the same position again. But Bunting knew he had to take a different approach with Hull FC. He didn't have a Ged Dunn or a Clive Sullivan. He couldn't play the same expansive style, smashing records, hammering teams. The secret of Hull's success, according to Norton, was unrelenting defence. "We'd kick the ball to them, say 'come on then', tackle them to death. We bored them, tackled them out of it. They were so frustrated we'd make them cry. Eventually they would give penalties away, Sammy would kick us into the lead and then they'd make mistakes. We might even score a few tries by the end."

Nobody benefited more from that than Charlie Stone. Like Bray and Farrar, Stone turned out for Featherstone in the 1973 and '74 Cup finals, his signing a great piece of business. And Hull were determined to get their man. During July, and once the Featherstone directors had returned from holiday, Hull repeatedly submitted bids but were turned down flat. Featherstone's board insisted that none of their players were for sale and were prepared to take action against any club making an illegal approach. That meant Hull FC.

Three days later, though, Stone signed for Hull and Featherstone got fifteen grand. The Boulevard pitch in the late '70s most often resembled a quagmire, conditions which suited Stone perfectly. For eighty minutes, forty-five times a season, he would stick the ball up his muddy jumper and grind, knee-deep, up the middle of the pitch. In defence, no one would get past him, efforts that earned him the Second Division Player of the Month Award in February and a place on the Lions Tour to Australia in the summer.

Hull's other piece of close-season business was the acquisition of a mystery trialist from Wales. The player came highly recommended but all anyone knew of him was that he was a 26-year-old scrum-half who could also play fullback or stand-off. He arrived in Hull on Friday, went straight into training and then played in the Eva Hardaker Trophy game on the Sunday, incognito in case it didn't work out. With the Hull clubs in different leagues, it would be the only derby of the season, so nearly 5,500 turned up to see a keenly fought game. Keith Tindall says it was an eye-opener for Vince Farrar – his first derby friendly. "He came off at half-time and said: 'What's thee all doing taking bumps and lumps out of each other? Thee's only getting a fiver!' So I said: 'You should think yourself lucky. Last year, we got a tea-set.'"

Hull won 28-24 and the trialist had a fine game; linking well in attack, kicking five goals from seven attempts and pulling off several eye-catching tackles, including one on a rampaging Phil Lowe. In the later editions on Monday, the *Hull Daily Mail* reported that Hull had offered him a deal and the player had returned to Wales to discuss it with his wife. By the weekend, the player was revealed as Paul Prendiville. In spite of the prospect of playing for Llanelli alongside Phil Bennett and JJ Williams, he admitted that he had been made an 'offer he could not refuse'.

With three international forwards and a future Welsh international winger, Bunting's recruitment for the Second Division campaign, for the moment, was complete.

***

BY CONTRAST, ROGER Millward's summer was miserable. After ending the 1978 season with an elbow infection, his pre-season was then blighted by a calf strain and broken toe. But that was nothing to how the Rovers player-coach must have felt once the new season began.

In the opening Yorkshire Cup game, Wakefield were beaten, but the price was high. Millward was carried off with yet more injuries, a groin strain and a dead leg, while Paul Rose was sent off. Worse was to follow the following week at

Bradford. "Inept and pathetic," John Sexton called it. "It is early days to be harshly critical, but if heads do not roll for this defeat, Rovers can forget about winning anything at all this season." In the changing room, players were falling out. Chairman Bill Land had to deny rumours that several players had handed in transfer requests at the end of the match.

Amid the turmoil, Millward stayed calm, his response measured. Furious with the performance, he refused to panic and named the same side for the visit of Warrington. He was rewarded with victory and, in the coming weeks, Rovers' form improved dramatically. As Millward returned to fitness, the players began enjoying their rugby and an unbeaten run of eight league games put them top by the end of October.

For Rovers, it was victory at Headingley at the end of September, their first since 1966, that led John Sexton to this conclusion: "Although it is early to be thinking about the championship, player-coach Roger Millward allowed himself a quiet smile of confidence after seeing his side maintain their 100 per cent record by completely overwhelming Leeds."

***

IN MID-SEPTEMBER, an era came to an end when the Tower and Regent cinemas, which had faced each other across Anlaby Road since 1914, both closed on the same night. In the *Hull Daily Mail*, a visitor from Australia, back after thirty years, felt compelled to write: "I returned expecting to find a vast improvement. My train journey took me past Selby Street, whose bombed-out buildings stood just as I saw them in the 1940s. I then strolled around the city centre, where fish and chip papers blew from the markets and I saw the city docks, which looked more like cess pools. My thoughts were left cold at the lack of progress."

Rugby league, though, was on the up. At the beginning of October, the biggest attendance anywhere that day, 6,106, saw Hull hammer Batley. Prendiville, on debut, went sixty yards to score after four minutes. The next weekend, Hull gave a start to another new signing, veteran John Newlove, signed from Featherstone, who notched one of eight tries in the next emphatic win. Played five, won five and then came Leeds in the Floodlit Trophy. Hull were underdogs but when did that matter with Hull and Leeds? A spirited performance was capped with a late try from Alf Macklin and, yet again, Headingley echoed to a triumphant rendition of Old Faithful.

With both Hull and Rovers topping their respective divisions and remaining unbeaten, confidence had seldom been higher. The *Hull Daily Mail* was equally bouyant, it's correspondent John Sexton suggesting that the city's rugby league fans ought to savour these heady days because they would not come along very often.

On the same weekend, the 1978 Kangaroo Tour got underway with a club game in Blackpool. Four days later the Aussies were in Hull, facing the Great Britain U24s at Craven Park and then back again later in the month, to play Hull FC. Bunting, getting carried away with his side's unbeaten run, claimed to be confident of an upset but Australia scored twice in the first few minutes and won 34-2, Hull's only hammering of the season. Rovers, top of Division One, did not get a game against the tourists and were probably glad of it.

In the Tests, the outcome was to become all-too familiar. The Aussies caught the Brits cold in the First Test. Coach Peter Fox turned to his 'Dad's Army' in the second and squared the series before the host nation was blown away in the decider. Millward, Rose and Norton played in all three games and there were also appearances for Lockwood, Lowe, Farrar and Casey as Fox made numerous changes.

Last One Out...

***

IN MID-NOVEMBER, Hull won 16-0 at Halifax and Rovers beat Bradford 10-6 to record identical records – eight from eight – while retaining their respective places at the summit.

In the *Sports Mail*, Dick Tingle reported that the terrific start was not limited to first teams. In thirty-seven games played by the first thirteen, Hull's 'A' team and Colts had lost just five while collectively amassing over 1,000 points. It was a remarkable record for a squad whose core was relatively unchanged from the dire days of the mid '70s but who now had a sprinkling of quality in Newlove, Hepworth, Norton, Stone and Lloyd. At Boothferry Park, Hull City added to the optimism with their own impressive start, the goals of Keith Edwards, signed from Sheffield United, helping them to the top of Division Three.

But over at Craven Park, success hadn't made everyone happy. Roy Holdstock demanded a transfer after struggling to gain a first team place, despite being a regular in the GB U24s with 120 club appearances under his belt. "As a young kid, playing for your home team, you want to be in every week," he said, "but, when Rovers signed Lockwood – there was no doubting that he was a good player – I didn't get much of a look in after that."

But then, with both teams otherwise sitting pretty, there was a blackout, as regional sports journalists went on strike. For eight weeks, Hull and Rovers supporters learned nothing about their teams from the *Hull Daily Mail* as the back pages, using national sources, told instead of England's cricketers trying to regain the Ashes in Australia and the feud between Yorkshire CC and sacked captain Geoff Boycott. It wasn't long before TV was affected too. Approaching Christmas,

Yorkshire Television went off and didn't return until January. Hull's Rediffusion service subscribers were able to turn the dials to receive the Tyne Tees signal, but there wasn't much rugby league interest up there.

Amid the silence, both clubs nevertheless ended 1978 active in the transfer market. Castleford scrum-half Clive Pickerill, fed up of playing understudy to Gary Stephens, asked for a move. Hull KR, thinking of the future, offered £15,000, double the record £8,000 paid for John Cunningham in 1975. "I went over to Brian Lockwood's pub in Wakefield to meet him and Roger," Pickerill recalls. "They talked to me about signing and I said I would go away and think about it. But then Kenny Foulkes rang and asked me to go to the Boulevard. It happened to be training night and there were a couple of hundred supporters there watching them. I'd never seen anything like it. The supporters were coming up to me, knew my name and were amazing. That's what persuaded me. That night I went home and told my wife, Jean, that I'd signed for Hull. I just couldn't get over the spectators."

Despite missing out on Pickerill, Rovers stayed in the hunt for Phil Hogan, one of the brightest prospects in the game but a signing that looked set to make Len Casey surplus to requirements. It didn't sit well with many senior players who made their feelings known, but their views fell on deaf ears and Rovers pressed ahead, paying Barrow £32,000 to smash the world record fee Hull had paid for Steve Norton. Sure enough, the following week, Casey was on his way to Bradford for an estimated £25,000 which included scrum-half Paul Harkin moving in the opposite direction. It wouldn't be long before Rovers came to regret it.

In the wider world, the new year arrived with a shiver. Blizzards hit the north, the temperature falling to -17 near York. For 2,000 lorry drivers across North Humberside, there was no return to work as they went on strike in a dispute over pay. Suddenly, everyone was at it. A strike by one hundred milkmen led to the setting up of special selling points around Hull and neighbouring villages. North Sea Ferries, with barely any lorry traffic, suspended their Zeebrugge crossing. The *Sports Mail* was not published on 7th January due to a shortage of paper, as well as a shortage of sport; Rovers hadn't played since December 30th, Hull since Boxing Day.

As the country ground to a halt and Prime Minister Jim Callaghan returned from a Caribbean summit saying "Crisis? What crisis?" debates in Parliament referred to Hull as the focal point for some of the worst flashpoints of the dispute and stores across the city had begun to ration stock. By the middle of January, the *Hull Daily Mail* reported the "...progressive shutdown of industry..." as newspaper headlines screamed: "End the Anarchy on Humberside."

When the Boulevard did finally stage its first game of the year, Hull only just scraped home 8-5 against Bramley to extend their unbeaten league record to fourteen. Bunting blamed the weather and his team's enforced inactivity for a poor display. In response, he stepped up training, asking his players to train daily. Ten West Yorkshire based players began to train at Pontefract racecourse, led by Kenny Foulkes.

Then came more snow and icy roads made dangerous by a shortage of grit and salt. Nevertheless, when Rovers staged their first game in three weeks, they showed no loss of appetite for the league title, beating Leigh 38-3 at home.

The combination of six knock-out competitions, a fierce winter and ill-equipped stadiums combined to turn fixture lists inside out. Hull's game at Batley, originally scheduled for New Year's Eve, became a nightmare to reschedule. With no floodlights, the 'Gallant Youths' found it impossible to stage the game at Mount Pleasant and so accepted Hull's offer to switch the match to the Boulevard. But it remained an ongoing issue, postponed six times before finally going ahead on 20th February. Hull won comfortably, 20-0, in front of an unusually low crowd of just over 4,000. But, then again, it *was* an away game. By then, there was a backlog of forty professional fixtures. RL secretary David Oxley accepted it was a headache but refused to extend the season as Hull managed to play their first game in nearly three weeks, winning at Swinton to make it fifteen on the trot and extend their lead at the top to eleven points. Rovers defeat at Warrington, meanwhile, saw them drop to third.

The weather lifted sufficiently for the Challenge Cup to start on time. Hull, yet again, turned Leeds over in the televised fixture. Next day, Rovers despatched New Hunslet and both clubs went into round two. The draw was made on Monday night. Postponements meant there were twenty-five teams in it but the balls were kind to Hull, sending them to Keighley. Not so Rovers, who faced a trip to Bradford.

***

THE NIGHT OF February 14th was the worst of the entire winter by far. 'Snow-Siege City' declared the *Hull Daily Mail* with hundreds stranded in the centre. Trains were cancelled, roads blocked, cars abandoned. City centre hotels were forced to put extra beds in function rooms. Schools were closed and any shops open shut early.

Further disruption to rugby league fixtures prompted discussions about playing games on midweek afternoons or extending the season into June, by which point some Hull and Rovers players would be on tour in Australia. Many uncompleted Challenge Cup first round fixtures were moved to the weekend designated for the second round.

Last One Out...

One of the few games to take place on the middle weekend of February was Rovers' clash with Castleford. An army of volunteers arrived at Craven Park with their own spades and shovels from 8.30am and got the pitch playable. The work paid off. Rovers won 19-13 and, with fifteen games gone, were back on top of the First Division. Millward was still on the sidelines with a hamstring injury and left little doubt what he was saving himself for. "Although we want both points, we have a lot of important games coming up and if I played on Sunday, I'd risk more serious damage."

On the final weekend of the month, Hull demolished Keighley, thanks to a hat-trick from Prendiville and 16 points from Lloyd, but Rovers' cup tie was postponed. They kept themselves busy, re-scheduling a game at Workington and managed to record their first ever victory at Derwent Park. After sixteen league games, both sides were top. Hull were unbeaten, Rovers had lost just two.

Faced with ever mounting backlogs of games though, the Challenge Cup added yet another level of complexity. A club might be hoping to play a league fixture only to find that the side they were due to face had, in the middle of the week, progressed in a rearranged game and the cup took priority. Often at short notice, clubs might go without a fixture. Which is what happened to Hull FC at the start of March. Huyton, after their opponents won a rearranged second round game in midweek, were also game-less. So on Friday morning, hoping to schedule a game postponed earlier in the season, Hull put a call through to Alt Park: "Fancy a game Sunday?" Huyton were up for it but local police could not sanction the match at such short notice. "Come to our place instead,' Hull suggested, bringing yet another away game to the Boulevard. It produced a crushing seventeenth straight victory.

But the confusion led to the inevitable mix-ups. In mid-

February, Bradford set off for Workington. Fortunately, en route, they stopped to phone ahead and discovered that the Workington team had set off in the opposite direction for a game they believed they were playing at Castleford. It came as no surprise when, at the next RL Council meeting, Bradford proposed a switch to summer rugby.

In the late '70, there were few tougher places to win than Odsal, but that's what Rovers needed to do to progress any further towards Wembley. In March, on a heavy pitch and with a bitter wind blowing around the vast bowl, it was a daunting proposition. But Rovers were top of the league, weren't they, no mugs. And in Millward and Lockwood they had all the experience and smarts needed. But Millward, now in his fifteenth season without a Wembley appearance, had decisions to make. Allan Agar, his first choice scrum-half, had missed the previous game and his replacement, Paul Harkin, had impressed in his place. Millward opted for Harkin to face his former club. He also chose Paul Rose, despite the forward struggling with a shoulder injury. A final key decision came when winning the toss. Millward decided to start with the wind at their backs, a decision with which several players took issue, disagreement vindicated when an invigorated Bradford held Rovers in check, negating any advantage that the wind might have given the visitors in the first half. In the second, Rose's injury diminished his tackling and Harkin faded. Millward himself had one of his worst games of the season and Rovers crashed out as Bradford won 14-7.

There was no hiding the disappointment in the Rovers dressing room. It was arguably the strongest side the club had put together in many years, but the home side had done their homework. Worst of all, they were beaten by an old mate. "Casey won it for them," said Lockwood. "We should never have let him go." The next day, Bradford drew Hull FC.

***

IN MARCH, DURING a brief respite from the arctic weather, Hull and Bradford played out two epic games within four days in front of over 36,000 supporters.

First up, an estimated 8,000 Hull followers travelled to Odsal to see a gripping 8-8 draw. Keith Tindall, hospitalised just two weeks earlier, scored both Hull tries. Tickets for Wednesday's replay went on sale at 10am on Tuesday. Hours before booths opened simultaneously at the Boulevard and Ewbanks store in the city centre, long queues had formed. Some supporters bought as many as they could for mates at work and Ewbanks soon got rid of their 5,000 allocation. Bradford sold their initial 2,000 in no time at all and were sent another 1,500 mid-afternoon. Anticipation reached fever pitch for a game with a prize of a semi-final date with Widnes.

Hull's players managed to get Wednesday off work and began with a light training session followed by a trip to the cinema. After lunch, they had their final team meeting during which Bunting checked on injuries and named the team.

The replay was every bit as tight and ferocious as the first game, played in an unbearably tense atmosphere. Some 17,000 baying Hull FC supporters on a cold evening – there was nothing like it. Two towering penalty kicks from Sammy Lloyd from just inside his own half were all that separated the sides at half-time. But, in a devastating eleven-minute spell after half time, Bradford scored two unconverted tries and kicked two drop-goals for an 8-4 lead. Although the lead was narrow, that knocked the confidence out of Hull and the final twenty-five minutes did not bring another score.

The very next day, winter returned with a vengeance. Three-foot snow drifts cut off many Wolds villages and brought yet more chaos to the roads. By the weekend, the weather had also postponed Hull's home game with second-placed New Hunslet. The season was duly extended and Hull took advantage, re-scheduling it for May 18th, three weeks after the Division Two campaign was supposed to end.

Yet by the end of March, the weather eased and Hull were able to make the trip to Whitehaven. They set off the day before, travelling via Warrington to watch Keith Tindall make his England debut against France. The squad, including Tindall, then travelled up to Cumbria. A refreshed and happy Hull team won easily – their eighteenth successive win – as they closed in on Bradford's Division Two record of nineteen.

Rovers weren't doing badly either. With Lockwood and Hogan on international duty, Millward was supreme as Rovers beat St Helens at a canter. Rovers were level with Warrington, two games in hand. For the first time, they were beginning to look like genuine favourites for the league title.

Back in December, Rovers had also qualified for the semi-final of the John Player Special Trophy, a game that had been due to take place at the start of January. Fat chance. The competition was put on hold until spring, the final delayed to mid-April. Rovers finally lost to Warrington on April 1st but bounced straight back in the league, hammering Widnes to give themselves a two-point lead at the top. All that could stop them from a first ever title was total collapse in the ten league games left to play. Only three were scheduled for Sunday afternoons with the remaining games on Monday, Wednesday, Thursday and Friday nights.

The fixture backlog meant a ludicrous workload. "We just trained and played," said Dave Hall, "no time for any rest. We seemed to be playing every couple of days and, if we weren't, we'd still be training twice a week. And don't forget that we worked for a living. I'll always remember Millo. He used to work on the roads, on the diggers. We'd start training at half-six and Millo would turn up at Craven Park covered in muck and shit. He'd get changed, train, get home about ten and then be up on the road first thing next morning."

Millington hasn't forgotten it.

"When we came home from games, Roger would get off the bus near Castleford and the last thing he said was 'ten mile run Tuesday night, Millo, don't forget.' And he meant it. But I was a builder and I'd have been lugging tons of concrete all day. I was knackered by the time I even got to training. It was alright for Roger. He was an electrician, so the most he did was change a fuse. John Moore would have been the same, he worked in an office so never did 'owt all day. And Ged Dunn was a schoolteacher; the hardest thing he had to do was give an assembly!"

At Hull, the final few weeks of the season were all about breaking records. They equalled Bradford by crushing Keighley, 45-5, then went past it when they beat Dewsbury. With six games to go, the target now was to win them all and become the first team to record the 'perfect season'.

***

FOR ROVERS THERE was no collapse, but they did wobble. Injuries and illness hit the squad. Those who could play went to Barrow on a freezing wet Sunday afternoon. They lost, unsurprisingly since some were dragged from bed, which made injuries and illness even worse. Two days later, due to play Featherstone, Rovers had twenty-three sick notes and cancelled the game, a decision that landed them a £2,000 fine.

To prove their point, Rovers printed a blank teamsheet in the programme on Good Friday, but it was a strong enough team that took the field. It put Huddersfield to the sword,

Steve Hartley scoring five tries, Hubbard 27 points and Sully his 100th for Rovers (a penalty try – he didn't touch it down) as Rovers won 57-3 and moved back on top by two points.

The tries took Hartley past thirty for the season, a remarkable turnaround for a man who had not been allowed to settle, moved from centre to stand-off to accommodate his player-coach. "Stand-off was my preference," he said. "You get more freedom than centre, where you're restricted to an area. At halfback, you've got the freedom of the field but it was effective either way." Two more wins followed and with six games left, Rovers had one hand on the trophy.

The next home game with Workington looked like a banker, but it didn't work out that way. They fell to a surprise defeat and Brian Lockwood blamed the official who after the match admitted he'd had a "shocking game". Lockwood was in no mood to be sympathetic, replying: "You haven't half. You've lost us the championship." The rugged Cumbrians put in a series of high shots that saw Hogan and Millward carried off with concussion. Both incidents went unpunished.

Straight afterwards, Rovers jumped on their coach for the short journey up the coast road to Bridlington, where they stayed for three days, a mini-break designed to recover from injuries, reconnect as a group and target the final run-in.

They trained each morning, often on the beach, then relaxed in the afternoon. 'The perfect tonic', said Millward and it worked. The following Friday, Rovers scored a comfortable win at Castleford. And the Wednesday after, hours before Polling Stations opened on the last day of the Labour Government, they saw off Featherstone.

Three games to go, just two points needed, and a first chance to wrap it all up on Bank Holiday Monday, two days after the Challenge Cup final. But they couldn't take it and St Helens turned them over. Rovers would have to wait yet another week to secure the title, unless, that is, Warrington were defeated that night at Cas.

And so Millward, Lockwood, Hogan, Sullivan, Watson, Agar and several hundred Hull KR supporters headed to West Yorkshire, where the red and white contingent cheered on Castleford with more noise and passion than their own. And when the hooter sounded on an 11-2 home win, they got an even greater ovation – finally, Rovers were Champions.

Naturally, that meant celebrations in the Cas clubhouse, but for ex-player Brian Lockwood that led to an unpleasant experience. "They wouldn't let me in!" he recalled, thirty-six years later, still bristling at how his former club had treated him. "The steward said I had to go to the main office to get an ex-players pass, while all the other Rovers players were let straight in. I told 'em to stick it and went home."

***

On the same Bank Holiday Monday, while Rovers fans were jumping for joy, Hull faced Oldham in their penultimate league game of the season – number twenty-five. In recent weeks, they had chalked off one milestone after another.

Over Easter, Hull fans made up the majority of a 9,000 crowd at York but almost witnessed the first loss. Down 13-9 with fifteen minutes to go, it was only when John Newlove stepped up a gear that Hull cruised home 24-13. Whitehaven were then fed to the slaughter before a trip to Blackpool where around 2,500 made the journey over to see a twenty-third straight win. Halifax fell in midweek, then Oldham.

There was just one game left. One hurdle between them and a hundred per cent league record, something never before achieved in rugby league and hardly ever in any other major professional sport. They faced second-placed New

Hunslet, probably the only team capable of ending a perfect run, but that had to wait because Hull were going on a jolly.

In mid-season, the directors organised an end-of-season tour/holiday to France, to celebrate promotion. They were due to depart on Friday May 11th, fly back the following Monday and then prepare for New Hunslet.

A big squad set off from Heathrow airport, spent a day exploring Bordeaux and then headed to Tonneins on the Saturday for their only fixture. The first shock was on the opposition teamsheet – it didn't resemble the usual Tonneins team. The hosts had drafted in a number of 'guests' from the surrounding area and Hull ended up facing six international players. So Hull pulled in a few ringers themselves. Stone and Norton, off to Australia the following week, were only along for the ride but they ended up playing.

"Okay lads, it's an exhibition game," said Vince Farrar, as the players took the field. "Let's chuck it around and put on a bit of a show." A brutal ten minutes later, Farrar had a cut eye, Stone a busted nose and Farrar had changed his tune: "Right, let's get stuck into the bastards." Hull trailed twice, but a try by assistant coach Ken Foulkes proved decisive.

***

WITH THE TITLE secured, the rest of the season was an anti-climax for Rovers. Millward chose to rest some of his senior players ahead of the Premiership competition and the last two league games were lost. And when on Tuesday May 15th Rovers were presented with the Division One Trophy for the first time in sixty-seven years before playing Bradford in the Premiership first round at Craven Park, they lost again.

A champagne reception was laid on but the evening fell flat. One supporter was heard to say: "I've supported Rovers fifty years and on the night they get the Championship, they do that to me."

The Rovers board held an inquest into how the season had fallen apart so badly. In the papers, John Sexton thought tourists Millward, Lockwood, Watkinson, Smith and Hogan were distracted. Brian Lockwood, meanwhile, was playing a waiting game. With Hull KR keen to hold onto him and Salford interested, he said: "I shall decide what I am going to do in Australia. It may be that I shall call it a day. But I have told the board that if I decide to play next season it will most probably be with Rovers."

At the Boulevard, Hull versus Hunslet drew the first ever five-figure attendance for a Division Two game. A crowd of 12,424 was recorded, most hoping to witness a little piece of history. But under coach Bill Ramsey, Hunslet themselves were unbeaten in seventeen. It wasn't going to be easy.

Reporter Dick Tingle saw a battle royale. "The sides pounded away at each other like ferocious gladiators," he wrote. "The commitment was total, the determination intense and the tackling thunderous."

Norton dropped a goal in the first half. Tony Dean equalised for Hunslet and that's how it remained until the 70th minute. Sammy Lloyd had a rare off-day with the boot and had already missed three penalty kicks. He was finally successful ten minutes from time. At 3-1, it was still in the balance until Stone ploughed over for a rare try with five minutes to go and Hull won the game, 6-1.

Everyone stayed behind to watch the presentations. I was in the Best Stand and, by the end, my cousin Steve and I managed to work our way along the Well, so that we were pressed against the metal cage that guarded the players as they came on and off the pitch. When they returned to the field to thunderous cheers, we were able to pat them on the back. Better still, a man in a suit then emerged, carrying the Division Two trophy. Cheekily, we asked if we could touch it and he just handed it over to us. So there we were, clutching the silver bowl, just a few minutes before it was handed over to Vince Farrar.

Truly, we felt a part of history.

***

FOR BOTH HULL clubs, the season had surpassed their wildest expectations. Despite Widnes's domination of the cup competitions, week-in-week-out success in the league and the winning runs dominated the season.

Victory for Hull and Rovers became as regular a Sunday feature as *Songs of Praise* and *Last of the Summer Wine*. Crowds were back and profits recorded the like of which had never seen before. Hull made £16,458, not including the £20,000 earned from the speedway franchise or income from the Vice Presidents Association. Rovers, despite a wage bill in excess of £120,000, raked in £17,194 having also instaled floodlights and a new clubhouse.

It meant that in the coming months and years no-one could compete with Hull and Rovers when it came to signing players. There were seven Hull-based representatives on the 1979 GB tour and five more tourists would play in the city within a year or two. As spring turned to summer, Hull's Steve Norton and Charlie Stone joined Rovers' Phil Hogan, Brian Lockwood, Roger Millward, Mike Smith and David Watkinson on the trip down under.

There the good news ended. Not only were they among the first Lions team to lose an Ashes series 3-0, the trip was a shambles, especially for the Hull contingent. Millward tore knee ligaments, which delayed his start to the new season.

Last One Out...

Watkinson tore a shoulder muscle, out until the following spring. Hogan (knee), Lockwood (broken finger, ankle), Smith (ankle) and Norton (calf and suspension) were added to the injury list and all missed some part of the trip.

The tour though went on and on ... and on. Having begun in May – two days before the 1979 Premiership Trophy final – it finally ground to a halt twenty-seven games and eleven-and-a-half weeks later in Auckland on August 11th, by which time Hull and Rovers had already played the pre-season Eva Hardaker friendly and were preparing for their first round Yorkshire Cup ties.

PART 2

The Curtain-Raiser –
Floodlit Trophy Final, 1979

8

THEY BEGAN TO arrive long before kick-off. By 6.30pm, they were pouring out of clubs on Subway Street, Dee Street and further afield. Pubs quietly opened early and even with all tickets sold days before, several hundred hoped to get in or just soak up the atmosphere. It was the only place to be.

Hull's secretary reckoned they could have sold another 10,000. In the event, the police were persuaded to allow five hundred 'ringside' seats on the speedway track at the Airlie Street end. All told, they were expecting 18,500, the biggest crowd ever seen at a Floodlit Trophy game by a mile.

There was nothing like a night game at the Boulevard. Squeezed tightly between rows of narrow terraced houses, the ground had ramshackle charm. When night fell and the lights flickered and popped into life you could barely see from one side to the other. "Put 50p in the meter," someone would shout from the Threepenny Stand.

What an atmosphere though. The smell of cigarette smoke, Bovril, hot dogs, beer, sweat and piss. The sound of cursing, moaning, groaning, chanting and singing ... *Oh, my lads, you should have seen their faces ... The famous Kingston Rovers went to Rome to see the Pope ... Cooooooooooome on you 'Ull ... Old Faithful, we'll roam the range...* Frequently, a red and white scarf would be tied to a wooden roof stanchion and then be set alight. As the scarf burned and crowd cheered, chunks would fall, burning, onto supporters stood below. No-one seemed to mind.

A flare was thrown from the Threepenny Stand which landed near the touchline and fizzed for a while, sending plumes of red across the pitch before a constable put it out. The loudspeaker crackled a warning, coaxing some fans down from scaffolding that held the television crews.

In the Rovers changing room, Lockwood tried to calm his teammates' nerves. "What's up with all you cod 'eds?" he is supposed to have said, receiving a volley of abuse for it.

Hull though were relishing the waiting reception. "We used to sing 'Three Steps to Heaven'," reveals Steve Norton. "You came out of the dressing room, went through a tunnel and then there were these three steps that led up to the pitch. The noise just hit you. Me and Paul Prendiville would sing the song as we went up."

Once outside, the teams lined up, facing each other for a few moments, shouting abuse, threats and intimidation at their opposite numbers, though barely heard. The noise was deafening. On a cold December evening, the 1979 Floodlit Trophy final was a chance to gain local bragging rights on a big stage for the first time since the Yorkshire Cup final of 1967 and so the biggest derby in over a decade.

But though nobody knew it yet, the match was also a dry run for an occasion whose impact would be far longer-lasting. An encounter that no-one in Hull would ever forget.

***

THE SUMMER OF 1979 was one of rapid change in Hull. A marina was planned for Humber Dock; a luxury hotel chain had its eyes on a site overlooking Queens Gardens; Princes Dock was tipped to become a shopping centre, the old ferry moored alongside as a floating café bar.

Roger Millward came home early from Australia to find his Championship squad decimated. Smith, Watkinson and Lockwood were still down under, while Lowe, Rose and Sully had been injured during pre-season. Arthur Bunting, meanwhile, was in a slightly better position. Stone and Norton were also still on tour, but his squad was healthy.

August 5th saw the first derby, only 5,000 interested in what would be the last Eva Hardaker Trophy fixture. Lots of substitutes were used, players were on and off and there was no fluency to it. Referee Lindop stopped the game at one point, counted that Hull had fifteen players and awarded a penalty. Hull won a low-key affair, 27-20.

Bunting had tried desperately to strengthen but with players and directors on holiday or on tour, had no success. Ray Gravell, the Welsh union centre, was the main target but couldn't be persuaded north. Once the season began, though, the coach got down to business. Ron Wileman, a 25-year-old miner at Grimethorpe Colliery, was first to sign from York. Alan Maskill went the other way in a £25,000 deal.

He was signed too late for the season opener at home to Featherstone in the Yorkshire Cup, a game that turned out to be a disaster. Stone was sent off, Lloyd broke his arm and Hull lost. At the same time, Bunting learned that Norton's groin injury, suffered on tour, would keep him out and was fuming. Why drag him around Australia for six weeks when he could have been home seeing a specialist? Mike Smith

77

came back with a similar complaint having been forced to train while injured.

With three forwards out, Bunting moved fast to sign Charlie Birdsall from Rochdale. Birdsall had started out at Castleford, but found chances slim in a pack that included Norton, Reilly and Lockwood. He moved on to Keighley for a while before landing up at Hornets, his journeyman career seemingly at its end. A stint in Australia whetted his appetite to return down under until Norton put a good word in. For £4,000 Bunting got an honest, grafting back row forward who could also kick a goal or two. There was no guarantee of first team rugby and 'no play' meant 'no pay', but Birdsall still chose to join up with some old mates. He didn't regret it and nor did Bunting, who still reckons it among his best deals.

Birdsall and Wileman made their debuts in the first league game at home to Castleford, which ended in another defeat. It was a bad day all round. In the second half, a Hull fan jumped over the fence and assaulted the referee, Gerry Kershaw. It wasn't the first time that had happened. Vince Moss had been assaulted at another Hull game at the end of the previous season. On the same day, in Workington, Rovers supporters were in trouble. As crowds grew, an undesirable element had begun to creep in, small but worrying.

Hull managed just one victory in the first five games and by mid-September were already out of the Yorkshire Cup and John Player Trophy. In the backs, only Prendiville offered any threat. In quick succession, Bunting landed three more.

On a recommendation from Charlie Birdsall – "I told Arthur he was a lunatic, but one you wanted on your side" – Hull signed the famously pugnacious Welsh halfback Paul Woods from Rochdale. On the bus home from Blackpool after Woods's debut, Hull agreed to trial former Welsh Guard and amateur boxer Graham Walters, who then turned out for the

'A' team against Featherstone, appearing in the programme as AN Other. He was signed up within the hour, making his first team debut two days later and scoring two tries as Hull beat Huddersfield in round two of the Floodlit Trophy.

The Featherstone 'A' team game also saw the earlier than expected return of Lloyd and Norton from injury, but things didn't go to plan. The former finished the night with his arm back in pot, facing several more weeks out. Norton was sent off, later to be banned for two games. Survival in Division One already looked a tall order but, despite the results, Bunting was satisfied with recruitment until another opportunity came up and he took a punt on Tim Wilby.

Wilby, as a teenager, was a member of Leeds's 1977 Challenge Cup final squad. A useful, hard-running centre or back-rower, he possessed a rare determination to maximise his talents and so, in the summer of '79, decided on a whim to head to Australia to watch Great Britain, taking teammate Roy Dickinson with him.

"We knew most of the lads in the squad," he said, "so jumped on a plane to Sydney and tagged along with them. After a few weeks, I organised to play for a team in one of the Sydney leagues." As there was an international transfer ban at the time, Wilby played under a false name for a club called Campbell Town Collegians. "They hadn't won all year and my first game was against league leaders Bowral, who happened to be coached by the ex-GB prop Mervyn Hicks. It was a very low grade amateur game and I helped my team to win quite easily. But it didn't take long for Mervyn to discover I played for Leeds and there was an uproar. It hit all the front pages in Australia and Kevin Humphreys, the ARL chairman, gave me an immediate ban. The fuddy-duddies at Leeds weren't impressed and, when I got back, I found that they had sold me to Hull."

Last One Out...

After a slow start, Wilby battled his way into the starting line-up and became an integral part of Hull's Cup-chasing team. Yet despite all the new signings, by mid-November, Hull had won just six of their first fifteen. Sitting in tenth, the season looked like being a battle to stay up.

***

There were no new signings at all when Rovers returned for training in early July. Something they might have regretted, given the injury concerns awaiting Millward on his return. A few weeks later, Watkinson was also home early, crocked. His injured shoulder showed no sign of improvement and, in early November, he went under the knife. He faced a much longer spell on the sidelines. It would be spring before Watky pulled on his boots again.

Three defeats in the first five games was not the form of champions. Did doubts emerge? Were they past their best? It wasn't a young side. Lockwood, Lowe, Watson and Agar were all over thirty. Sullivan was 36. The player-coach, at 32, was still younger than most but had every reason to feel a decade older.

Until becoming Rovers' full-time player-coach, Roger Millward's routine had been exhausting in the extreme. In his autobiography, *Roger*, written with Mike Sterriker, he told how he'd managed to combine his work commitments with rugby league training:

> "I'd been up at five o'clock in the morning, done a full shift down the pit, crawled about the face, 220 yards long, with a toolbox around my neck. Then I'd get out, get changed, go home, get a quick bite, pick my gear up and then walk the best part of a mile to the meeting

point – before I even started the trip to Hull. I'd then do an hour and a half's training and invariably it would be about midnight when I got home. And then I was up at five again the next morning. I was traveling over five or six times a week along that motorway. There was a stage when I could tell you exactly when the road surface was going to change – and that when I went off the concrete road and onto the tarmac – was exactly 29.4 miles away from Kippax."

By the end of the 1970s, Millward had been making the same journey for nearly fourteen years. Four hundred and fifty times he had pulled on his Rovers shirt and gone into battle. At five foot four, Rovers' play-maker, goal-kicker, captain and player-coach had taken some punishment. Taken out of the game so often he lost count. But that was only half the story. Millward had also toured Australia on six occasions and spent a summer playing club rugby there. That amounts to an awful lot of rugby league, an immeasurable number of hard knocks and it was beginning to take its toll.

With Millward absent from the side, Watson, Hall and Smith were all tried alongside Agar, to little effect. Three defeats in the first four games was not the start of champions and by the end of September Millward was finally back in the first team, steering Rovers to a win over Warrington.

Then it was the derby. But no ordinary derby because this meant a changing of the guard.

***

IN HULL, THE 1980s began on October 7th, 1979.

Throughout the 1970s, Hull derbies had been contested by more or less the same group of blokes; Devonshire and Davidson; Flanagan, Casey, Crane; Millward, Rose, Lowe;

Hall, Hartley and Millo; Hancock, Harrison and Wardell. Two, three or four times a season, they slugged and fought it out. Hull FC had, down the years, been the more successful but, by the end of the decade, there was no doubt that Rovers were now top dogs. Champions, full of internationals, fast and exciting. But, at the Boulevard, the crowds were flocking back and there was something in the air.

In midweek, Bunting and Millward named their squads. Nine would make their derby debuts; Hogan and Hubbard, Walters, Prendiville, Newlove, Pickerill, Wileman, Stone and Birdsall. In addition, Hull had Norton back from injury, Rovers had Millward, Hartley and Lockwood. And the supporters were ready for it. On the Monday before, Hull reported 11,000 tickets sold. By Thursday it was 14,000.

It was Hull Fair week and the city was tense. The Yorkshire Ripper had struck again and the *Hull Daily Mail* joined a national publicity blitz to try and flush out the killer. It warned that 'even ordinary women' were now at risk, the latest victim a student. With the buses on strike, women were warned not to walk home alone.

Before the game, Hull's directors were anxious. Earlier in the week, a group of Hull FC fans had been in court for incidents at the Wakefield game. One man had been arrested for rolling naked on the floor outside a pub, 'debagged'. And, on Tuesday, the club was due to explain the referee assaults to the Rugby Football League.

Hull deployed one hundred police officers and waited nervously as the crowd streamed towards the Boulevard. By kick-off, there were 16,745 inside, smashing the Division One attendance record. In the event, the game passed off without incident, in many ways a sign of things to come. Played in great spirit, it was tough but clean and the players laid on a feast of entertainment, scoring eight tries in a blistering, high octane encounter that ended in a see-saw 20-20 draw. But there was more frustration for Millward. He bust his knee and would be out for another few months.

Unable to find our usual spot in the Threepenny Stand, my dad and I watched from the bridge that ran over the speedway tunnel in front of the Sportsman's Club. The place was packed; we could barely move. After the game, we tried to leave through the main gate into the Airlie Street car park. And so, it seemed, did everyone else. As we inched along, packed together, at times my feet were off the ground.

It was exhilarating.

***

HULL'S SEASON STUTTERED along after the derby draw. Win one, lose one, win one, lose one, with hiccups along the way. Farrar picked up his morning paper to read that he had been dropped for the game at Bradford. Furious, he asked for a transfer. It was a communication problem, Bunting said, and Farrar accepted the apology, a distraction they didn't need.

The injuries continued to mount. Walters, after just four games, broke his knee cap; Prendiville broke an unspecified bone in his leg; Wilby pulled a hamstring and then broke two ribs in a car crash; Lloyd's broken arm refused to heal; Norton was troubled with his groin injury for most of the first half of the season, while injuries also beset squad players Chris Harrison, Mick Sutton and Colin Lazenby. And then, at the end of November, came the visit of St Helens.

At half-time, trailing 8-0, totally outplayed, it seemed like situation normal, Hull slipping to another defeat. But powered by second-row pair Boxall and Birdsall, they were inspired in the second half, storming back to draw the game 8-8, thanks to Birdsall's late, towering drop-goal. Even Lloyd managed to make an appearance as a late substitute. And two days later, Hull beat Leeds (unbeaten in eight) in the second round of the Floodlit Trophy and never looked back. It was the first of a nineteen-win streak in twenty-one games. But first there were back to back matches with Leigh. Away on Sunday in the league and at home on Tuesday in the Floodlit.

Hull had never won at Hilton Park, Leigh were strong, with stars like Des Drummond and John Woods. Yet cheered on by a huge away contingent, Hull won, 10-5. Paul Woods was sent off near the end and Lloyd broke his arm yet again but it was a significant victory. Hull crept into the top eight.

Hull went into the Floodlit Trophy tie much weakened. Norton pulled out late, while Prendiville, Walters and Lloyd were also missing. Bunting had tried to persuade Hancock out of retirement but the veteran said no. The key man for Leigh, as always, was going to be John Woods. But Bunting had a plan. Having seen Paul Woods sent off for several high tackles at Hilton Park on Sunday, he moved the utility-back to off-half, directly opposite his namesake. The plan was to keep him quiet and intimidated and it worked. John Woods was subdued and 11,500 witnessed Hull's new-found ability to grind out narrow wins, in this case 9-6. It was now four games unbeaten and Hull were in their first final since 1976.

As autumn turned to winter and pitches grew wetter, Hull prospered on surfaces that nullified the pace of their opponents. "We are better suited for the heavy winter grounds than many teams in the league," said coach Bunting.

***

AFTER THE DERBY, Rovers' form was slightly better – win two, lose one. There was also a change in philosophy, a more pragmatic approach. "Usually we come here, throw the ball around and lose," said Millward, after watching his side win at Bradford. "Today, I decided against open rugby, told the players to hold the ball, drive forward and let Bradford make the mistakes. Everything went as planned and I was never worried. I only smoked two cigs in the whole game. Usually, I get through a full packet." A third successive away win; not bad for a side only supposed to be able to play at home.

The team found their best form when Allan Agar was paired with David Hall but, despite this, as soon as he was fit, Millward picked himself at off-half for the Floodlit semi-final against St Helens. Rovers were trailing 2-0 when, in the seventeenth minute, Millward was hit with a late tackle, off the ball, by a St Helens prop. It hurt like hell but he played on and his side battled their way back into the game, at half-time leading 10-7. In the changing room, Millward decided he couldn't continue and was replaced by Hartley.

The second half was scoreless, so Rovers went through to a final that, the semi-final draw had already determined, would be played at the Boulevard.

After the Saints game, Millward went to Hull Royal Infirmary where an X-ray on his jaw proved inconclusive. It had not been displaced so didn't need to be pinned, but it looked quite likely that there was a crack in it. Millward went home, but couldn't sleep. The next day, he couldn't eat and a second X-ray found that the jaw had definitely been broken, putting him out for another six weeks.

Both sides played on the Sunday before the final. Hull bettered Wakefield and Rovers beat Blackpool, having won seven in eight now, Hull seven in nine. It was a remarkable turnaround that put Bunting in reflective mood. "I said it would take three years to get the club established in Division One and we look like being ahead of schedule," he said, before giving an insight into the momentum building at the club. "We used to find it difficult to persuade players to sign for Hull, but once word spread about our support and positive thinking, the situation altered. I do not know of one player who wouldn't come to the Boulevard now."

There had been a clamour for tickets and enquiries had been made about using Boothferry Park, where struggling Hull City, playing to dwindling crowds of a little more than 3,000, had sacked manager Ken Houghton and his assistant Wilf McGuinness, but the FA had banned rugby league from any professional football ground. The Tigers allowed rugby supporters to park their cars there instead.

***

IT WAS THE 159th competitive Hull derby, but only the fourth time the clubs had met in a cup final. The first, the Yorkshire Cup final at Headingley in 1920, saw Rovers win 2-0. At the end of the same season, they were back in Leeds for the Championship final, which Hull won 16-14.

Headingley was the venue again in 1967, when Rovers won 8-7 in the Yorkshire Cup. Rovers, Hull, Rovers. Was it to be Hull's turn in 1979? Despite their league form – Rovers were fourth, Hull eighth – there was no doubt that Hull believed they could win. They always did at the Boulevard.

"If you couldn't respond to our fans," said Norton, "you must be a lump of wood."

Millward knew what to expect. "Derby matches are tough anywhere, but in Hull they seem to be extra special. The supporters are fanatical. It gets through to the players, even though many of us still live in the West Riding."

On Monday afternoon, the Hull players assembled at the Boulevard then boarded a coach taking them to their country hotel hide away. It was pouring down, the pitch was likely to be heavy, suiting the Hull forwards, slowing down Rovers' pacemen. But Bunting played it down. "Contrary to popular opinion, I'm hoping for a strong wind to dry the pitch," he said. "We intend taking the game to Hull KR."

A nagging doubt was Hull's lack of a goalkicker. While Lloyd nursed his broken arm, Bunting had tried Dennison, Birdsall, Lazenby, Peacham, Prendiville, Woods ... in a tight game, Hull no longer had their game-breaker.

The black and whites took the early initiative. And as ever, it was built on defence. Desperate to find a way past or around, Agar threw a wild pass behind Rovers' line and Dennison was on it in a flash, bursting through, kicking on and regathering to score before adding the extras.

Rovers with no lack of possession, struggled to settle. Although they lost the scrums, 11-14, they won eight scrum penalties due to Hepworth's attempted cunning feed. But Hull's defence stayed determined and resolute and, after 42 minutes, they extended their lead, Hepworth and Newlove combining to send Woods on a jinking run to the line before Evans crossed between the posts, Dennison converting. In those days, not many teams came back from 10-0 down.

But Hubbard didn't give up. Chasing a shrewd Agar kick to the corner at the Gordon Street end, he just managed to touch the ball down and then, just as impressively, side-stepped a blue disabled car, parked just beyond the touchline.

Charlie Birdsall's try shortly afterwards proved to be the last ever in the competition and Hull held on comfortably to win 13-3. On the final hooter, the pitch was invaded, Ray Fletcher of the *Yorkshire Post* writing of 'black and white hordes'. A platform was erected, upon which Vince Farrar lifted the club's first trophy in a decade. Flashbulbs popped, supporters cheered and the derby final sequence continued. Rovers, Hull, Rovers, Hull...

Arthur Bunting did not hide his joy at a side advancing far more quickly than he could have dared hope. "Winning this is a bonus. Our priority has always been establishing our place in the league. The simple things always pay off. We just did the basic things right with total commitment."

Defeat did not sit well east of the river. Letters were sent to the *Hull Daily Mail* questioning Millward's coaching credentials. "As good a player as he undoubtedly was..." they typically began. Rovers correspondent John Sexton appealed for calm, reminding them that Watkinson, Cunningham, Rose and Millward had all been forced to watch from the stands. "Please let there be no over-reaction on the basis of one game. On a different night, a different ground and with a different referee, I've little doubt that there would have been a different result." But years later, the game still hurt Roger Millward.

"We never turned up for that game," he wrote in *Roger*. "It was a big disappointment. I was still out with a broken jaw, but it was matches like that one that worried me. We had the ability to get to the final but then produced a flat display when we should have been buzzing. It was impossible to explain. We never really competed and I started to think how we could change things to make sure it didn't become a habit. It was something that became an obsession with me. To find different ways of training and to introduce new methods that would keep the players focused."

Gentlemen, Please, the Draw...

9

"I NEVER REALLY wanted to leave in the first place. It just seemed the right thing to do at the time. The best thing about it is that, now, everyone wants me back."

There was little wonder Rovers wanted Len Casey back. Sure, they had won the league without him and still boasted one of the most formidable forward packs in the game but, halfway through the following season, it wasn't going well. Starting with the Floodlit Trophy final, the Robins lost six in seven. By the end of January, Roger Millward was admitting: "We need four more points to be certain of staying up."

It was not the season Rovers expected as champions. Supporters' patience had worn thin, with repeated calls for new signings or young players to be given a chance. Sullivan, Watson, Agar, Lockwood ... all past it, the letters said.

And then came the cup draw. Monday night, live on *Nationwide* on BBC1. Hull got the amateurs Millom at home, Rovers drew Wigan away. In 1980, Wigan were in the bottom four – the fallen giants. Only the talents of George Fairbairn gave hope of avoiding relegation, but on their day they were still capable of beating anybody.

The first round would take place on February 9th, before then a cup deadline and some wheeling and dealing to be done. Hull transfer-listed Robinson and Duke; Rovers listed Dunn, Watson and Clarkson. And Rovers had an old friend in their sights. A year earlier, Rovers had liked the look of Phil Hogan and broken the world record for him. Casey, often unsettled, went to Bradford to clear the way. A year later, Rovers were struggling and Hogan, it turned out, was no Len Casey. And word was, Casey didn't fancy the drive.

Casey asked to move, Rovers made an offer. Backwards and forwards they went for a few days until, an hour before Bradford played Rovers at Odsal, Bill Land handed over a cheque for £38k plus VAT, rebuffing a suggestion that Rovers screwed up and should never have let him go: "Our fortunes are at a low ebb, he could be the man to give us a lift." Casey watched from the stand as Rovers lost 10-9.

Low ebb or not, Rovers now had a stellar pack, studded with internationals. But when Phil Lowe then asked to leave, it still shocked most Rovers fans. If York had come some way closer to meeting Rovers' £30,000 asking price, Lowe's career might have ended very differently.

***

AT THE BOULEVARD, the momentum seemed unstoppable and nobody benefitted more than Keith Boxall. On the last Tuesday of January, Eddie Waring's rugby league roadshow came to town during Boxall's testimonial season. Hull were marching up the league with attendances rising week on week, no better time in which to be holding a benefit year.

Tiffany's was rammed, well before chucking-out time

unusually. Box's teammates were there, as were Sully, Rose, Roger, Casey, Neil Fox, Raich Carter and Waggy. Hull's star boxers Rickie Beaumont and Joey Wainwright too. It was said to have raised more money – over £2,000 – than any other night in thirty-four years of Waring's popular shows.

Days later, Hull carried the momentum into their home game with Leeds, who were top of the table, unbeaten in six. But Hull were unbeaten in ten and the Loiners hadn't won at the Boulevard in seven years. "My aim was mid-table," confessed Bunting, "but now I expect us to win every time we play. That's how far we have progressed." In continuous freezing rain, it was Hull's forwards who revelled in the mud and the muck. Boxall, newly minted, was outstanding. Hull won and moved up to fifth, above Rovers for the first time. "But for a poor start to the season," Bunting reckoned, "we would be serious contenders for the title."

***

AT THE START of 1974, David Oxley, old-Hymerian, public school headmaster and Rovers fan, became the first general secretary of the Rugby Football League. Six months later, he was joined at Chapeltown Road by fellow Rovers fan and *Hull Daily Mail* journo, David Howes.

They could not have joined at a worse time, the game was on its knees. Slowly, though, they dragged the sport into the modern era and, by 1980, things were improving. Crowds were up, the profile was higher and the more open approach of the clubs was attracting business interest. Compared to the mid '70s, sponsorship was flooding in. "When we began, there was about £20,000 of sponsorship in the game," Howes said. "By 1980, it was £200,000 and, for the first time, we had a sponsor for the Challenge Cup." But it hadn't gone down well with everyone. "We faced a lot of criticism," continued Howes. "But we had to do it – we're not a rich sport. State Express were very sympathetic to the traditions and came up with lots of appropriate ways to promote themselves and the competition. Prize money throughout and so on."

The 1980 State Express Challenge Cup campaign was the seventeenth time Roger Millward had set off on the road to Wembley. He was in the last season of a two-year deal as player-coach. Injuries were taking their toll and appearances increasingly rare, so it was quite possible this could be his final season as a player. One more, if he was lucky.

No surprise, then, that he left nothing to chance in the build-up to the first round tie at Wigan. His team trained three times that week and, come Friday afternoon, they were together again, travelling over to Bolton, where they stayed in a motel prior to the televised game the following day.

Millward had always expected to play but he was nowhere near match fit. It was a gamble against a team who had won at Craven Park just a few weeks earlier, but Rovers never had Len Casey in their team that day.

"We wouldn't have won the Cup in 1980 without Casey," reckoned Rovers fan Roger Pugh, author of *The Robins*. "He was undoubtedly a better player when he came back and a leader of men. He used to write the match bonus on a bandage on his arm and point to it behind the posts. 'That's what we're playing for today', he would say. He was the man of the match in that game ... brilliant."

Before the game, Millward had left his pack in no doubt about what was expected of them. "Our record at Wigan wasn't brilliant," he said. "I remember saying to our pack, 'Either you're going to have a go, or I'm going'. And it just changed. We beat Wigan at Wigan and kept going."

Rovers, despite scoring four tries to one, only squeezed

through narrowly, 18-13. It was a significant win though and gave the club a huge boost, enough to persuade Phil Lowe to withdraw his transfer request. "Playing alongside Len Casey has made me think again," he said. But the good news didn't last long. The following Wednesday, Rovers were at home to Widnes. Another loss, their sixth in seven league games, was made worse in the dying minutes when Millward succumbed to a jaw injury, a specialist confirming a crack in the same spot. As Rovers' cup run got under way, the player-coach faced yet another spell on the sidelines.

***

MILLOM HAD QUALIFIED for the Challenge Cup as winners of BARLA's Cumbria and Lancashire Cup. They arrived at the Boulevard, having spent the night in a local hotel, to meet a side undefeated in ten games, soaring up Division 1. Hull treated their opponents with respect, naming a full-strength team. Just over 9,000 were there to watch the slaughter ... which didn't occur. After twenty minutes, it was the amateurs that led 5-0 and, by half-time, it was still only 10-5 to Hull. The professionals pulled away in the second half, 33-10, but it was the men from Cumbria who got the biggest cheers from the crowd as they did a lap of honour.

If further evidence were needed of the resurgence of rugby league in Hull, it could be seen at Craven Park on the same afternoon. No, not Hull KR – they'd already played at Wigan. It was the second amateur team in the Challenge Cup that year, Ace Amateurs, facing cup holders Widnes.

After BARLA's inauguration in 1973, the amateur game boomed and nowhere more so than in Hull. Within a few years, there were teams all over the city, from works teams to pubs and social clubs; Beecroft, Mysons, Telephones, Reckitts,

Last One Out...

Savoy, Clarence, Dee Street, Sizers, Ideal, Priestmans, Fenners, Kingfisher, Pheonix, Shiphams, Zetland, Telstar, Lockwood, Crooked Billet and Grapes. In addition, Dockers, Ace and Mysons ran two open age teams, West Hull ran three. Ace and West Hull contested the Yorkshire Cup Final in December, the second year running that it had been an all-Hull affair and the twenty-first successive year that a Hull team had been in the final. It made for an exceptionally healthy pool of games for fans to choose from each weekend and the groundswell of support led to two professional internationals being staged in Hull during 1979-80. Great Britain took on Papua New Guinea at the Boulevard in December, and then faced France at Craven Park in April.

It was victory over West Hull that earned Ace their place in the cup. The Boulevard being unavailable, the game was played in the east of the city and drew 4,286 – the round's fifth highest. They lost 22-5 and were cheered from the pitch.

"I was a great fan of the traditions of the cup," says David Howes. "There were only 32 teams in it. Thirty pro clubs plus two amateur teams and then it was all down to the draw. Games would be played every fortnight up to the semi-final, which meant you really had a cup run. And we always did the draw on the Monday night, which meant that if you'd had a bit of a giant-killing you had the chance to enjoy it before the draw for the next round. Nowadays, you might have a good win but then the draw is straight after the game and you might draw Wigan in the next round before you've even had chance to celebrate. Sometimes, the draw can even take place before some teams have played."

Having dispatched Millom, Hull got lucky again, home to York. Newly promoted, the men from the Minster city had struggled and looked likely to go straight back down. It was a cushy draw and Hull's eighth home tie in nine cup games that season. York's coach David Doyle-Davidson had never been short of an opinion: "It might be a cracking draw for Hull but, for us, we could not have picked a worse one. Who in their right minds would pick a trip to the Boulevard?" But Hull made hard work of it again. York led 8-6 at half-time and it was only thanks to the goal-kicking of Sammy Lloyd with six from six that they went through to the next round, while the Doyle received a tremendous welcome from the fans as he walked along the track to his seat in the Best Stand dugout.

"It was great to know you had not been forgotten and the warmth from the fans will not be forgotten," he told the *Hull Daily Mail*, before paying the supporters a back-handed compliment. "It also shows that the Hull supporters are nowhere near as bad as some people like to paint them."

Rovers second round tie – at home to Castleford – was, on paper a much harder game but, once again, Millward took no chances. The players were back in for training on the Wednesday and, on Saturday night, they stayed overnight in a hotel, this time the Crest Hotel, on the outskirts of Hull.

Even by 1980, it was still something of a novelty for Rovers' players to stay in a hotel, especially for a home game, and it usually led to laughs. "I ordered Frog's legs," recalls Steve Hubbard. "As you can imagine, most of the other lads turned their noses up at them. But when my food arrived, they all wanted to know what they looked like and what they tasted of. Next time, half of them ordered Frogs legs!"

Come Sunday morning, the players were refreshed and relaxed as they boarded the team bus for the eight-mile trip to Craven Park. Once again, preparation paid off. Castleford were no match for Rovers who romped home, 28-3. With Casey in the team and Lowe settled, Rovers were capable, should they need it, of deploying an eight-man steamroller.

Both second round games kicked off at 3pm, Sunday

afternoon. Both games were all pay. Nevertheless, Hull's crowd of 12,618 and Rovers' gate of 9,137 were by some distance the biggest two crowds of the round.

There were now only eight teams left in the Cup and two of those were from Hull. They had already been drawn together in four Challenge Cup competitions since the start of the 1970s; surely it couldn't happen again, could it?

It didn't, and the competition suddenly got tougher. Rovers were drawn at home to mid-table in-form Warrington, while Hull were away to Bradford Northern, who'd knocked them out of all three competitions the previous season, were the only team to have beaten them in the last fifteen games and who would win the First Division. "It was only to be expected," said Bunting. "After all our home ties, the law of averages says we would get an away draw but, by the same token, the law of averages is on our side to beat Bradford."

***

THE CUP GAMES came thick and fast, just a fortnight apart. Between rounds, there was a league fixture and, on the same weekend, the European Championship began, starting with England versus Wales at Craven Park. Six Hull-based players were selected. For England, Eric Ashton picked Rovers trio Smith, Holdstock and Casey, while Kel Coslett chose Hull's Walters, Prendiville and Woods for Wales.

It was not ideal for either coach, but Bunting must have despaired at the antics of Paul Woods. As England closed out a comfortable win, Holdstock scoring a key try and Casey named man of the match, Woods saw the red mist in the closing minutes. With ten minutes to go, in the act of scoring the clinching try, England fullback George Fairbairn was stamped upon, for which Woods got a yellow card. And then, in the final minute, he flattened the England stand-off Steve Evans and was sent off. It was a bizarre end to the game that left him certain to be suspended for the season's final weeks.

Two days later, Hull faced a tough trip to Warrington, the first of ten league games in seven weeks, a programme that was sure to test the depth of Bunting's squad. Enter Brian Hancock. Again.

After twelve mostly unsuccessful years at the club, Hancock had chosen the perfect time to retire – at the end of Hull's unbeaten 1978-79 season. Hull moved on, Newlove was the new number six and Hancock had no problem with that. "John was a very classy player. He'd throw a dummy and everyone fell for it. When I did it, I got smacked. I could never understand why everyone took his dummies but not mine. It was a mystery to me. But he was a good player and I had been happy to move on." Although Hancock had officially retired, he continued to train occasionally with the club and also returned to Beverley RUFC, playing the odd game there. By March, the Boulevard needed him again.

Hancock's unexpected return against Warrington saw him line up alongside the 37-year-old Keith Hepworth and the 39-year-old Terry Clawson, on a short-term contract with his ninth club. It was a brutal afternoon. Hull fans battled with Warrington's throughout and defences dominated the game. Hull's only points came from Dennison's 75th-minute penalty, but that was enough to clinch a 2-2 draw.

With Hancock back in the fold, Bunting continued to rotate halfbacks, shuffling his hand. Newlove and Pickerill; Hancock and Hepworth; Dennison, Woods. No shortage of options, too many really. Momentum was lost and fluency suffered. But all thoughts were now on the Cup. On Friday, two days before the quarter-final, Bunting took his players to their West Riding hideaway. Still unsure of his starting line-up, a twenty-man squad was needed. Friday night was spent watching video tapes of Bradford's recent performances, but rumours began to emerge of a dispute between players and club over the size of win bonuses. The club had apparently offered each player £300 to win, the players wanted £400, but Bunting was keen to downplay it. "The lads have one thing on their minds – it is not pay – it's just beating Bradford."

Hancock recalls that this kind of dispute was common in those days. "Every time we'd play a big cup game, there'd be some kind of argument over what the blokes were getting. The club would offer one figure and the lads would ask for another hundred or another fifty. It was a lot of money at the time, but there were never any serious disputes. The club knew that the players were going to settle but it amazed me that we'd still be arguing about it the day before a game. I'm sure it could have all been settled much earlier."

The bookies had Widnes as 11/4 favourites to win the Cup. Bradford were 3/1, Hull KR 7/2 and Hull FC 13/2. Temptingly, Rossy Bros were offering 20/1 on an all-Hull final. On Saturday, the *Hull Daily Mail* reported on each side's key concern. Lloyd, for Hull, was troubled by a hamstring; for the Robins, Agar was struggling with a leg injury.

***

SUNDAY MORNING, JUST outside of Harrogate and, after a light breakfast, the Hull players had a gentle training session. Afterwards, Bunting named his team. Lloyd was fit and returned along with Stone, Woods (as yet unsuspended), Newlove, Pickerill and Farrar, in seven changes to the team that had drawn at Warrington the week before.

Odsal was packed to the rafters with nearly 22,000 supporters, around half of them from Hull. Few had come expecting to see an open, free-scoring game and Bradford's pack made their intentions clear from the outset. After 12 minutes, an attacking move from Hull was halted when Wilby was taken out by a late tackle. Before the ref could stop play, another big hit laid Wileman out. As both men received treatment, Hull were awarded a penalty and Lloyd began to line up a kick at goal.

The pitch at Odsal that day, in the words of Steve Norton, "was like running on a thick mattress". Somehow, though, Lloyd managed to lift his kick out of the quagmire and aim it between the posts – 2-0 to Hull. The rest of the first half was just as relentless. There were no more scores and the players took their half-time break at the side of the pitch.

The second half played out in an atmosphere so tense that the watching crowd of 22,000 could barely draw breath. Defences stayed on top, chances rare and any opportunities were snuffed out by a fearsome cover tackle or last-ditch clearance. But as time wore on, Northern's pack – Thompson, Bridges, Van Bellen, Grayshon – was ground down by Hull's six. With five minutes left, Hull built a strong position and fed the ball to Pickerill who smartly dropped a goal – 3-0.

As the hooter went, there was an outpouring of relief from the visitors, devastation from the home support. Hull's black and white hordes poured onto the pitch, trudged through the mud and muck and mobbed the players, many lifted high on supporters' shoulders. I was among them. We had watched the game from high in the main stand opposite the dressing rooms and a huge surge moved down the steep terraces sweeping aside all in its path. Over the perimeter fences we went, on a tide of celebration.

Victory at Bradford had been seen as one step too far; this was the team that knocked Hull out of three competitions the season before. And now, nilled on their own muck. By the time me and my dad found our way back to the coach, we were already making plans for the semi-finals, speculating whether it would be in Leeds or further afield.

Hull's dressing room looked like a battlefield. Newlove had been supreme. In spite of the ferocious hits flying in all around, he had seemed to be strolling it until exhaustion got the better of him at the end and he sat staring at the wall, spent. Wilby, still concussed, was reported to be babbling on about Premiership play-offs. "Jeff Grayshon took me out," he recounted thirty-odd years later. "I watched it on TV afterwards and I got up like a boxer who'd been knocked down. My legs were wobbling and everything. I managed to carry on but between waving to my parents from the team bus on the way into Odsal and waking up the next morning, I didn't remember a single thing."

A shame really, since most people believed it was one of Wilby's best games for the club.

***

MILLWARD'S RECOVERY FROM his broken jaw had been aggravated by a wisdom tooth. Although the stitches were removed just before the quarter-final, he was still weeks away from playing, his season appearances limited to just five. Yet again, he stuck to his pre-match routine and so, on Saturday afternoon, Rovers prepared at the Crest Hotel for a game that now assumed huge significance in a legendary career.

Rovers took the lead with an early converted try from Hubbard but Warrington hit back, leading 9-5 just before the break. Casey had been involved in some forward battles in his time but none bigger than with Warrington's. The game between Bradford and Warrington the year before had been one of the most appalling, ugly games anyone had seen, with

Casey in the middle of it. Such was the mutual antipathy he had been left out of Rovers' most recent league game at Wilderspool but, come the cup tie, there was never any doubt that he would play. And, once again, he was immense. It was his fine solo try before half-time that gave Rovers a slender lead they never surrendered, turning the game. Further tries from Lowe and Hubbard earned a comfortable 23-11 win and most of the 11,961 fans were celebrating long before the end.

For the first time, both Hull sides were in the semi-finals of the Challenge Cup. Widnes and Halifax the others.

As usual, the draw was held on Monday evening, at the end of *Nationwide*, just before *Question of Sport*. If the Hull teams were kept apart, there was chance of a Wembley derby. If they were drawn together, the city would have a team at Wembley for the first time since 1964, but that would mean a semi-final too intense to bear. Both sets of supporters just wanted to draw Halifax. As did the coaches. Each began their interviews with the line: "No disrespect to Halifax, but..."

Prior to the live broadcast, there were two rehearsals. Why it was necessary to practice the removal of four small, wooden spheres from a velvet bag is anybody's guess, but it had long been an intriguing part of the drama. When the show went live, viewers were unaware that the first rehearsal had seen Rovers drawn against Halifax and Hull drawn with Widnes. The second rehearsal went Rovers v Widnes, Hull v Halifax. Surely, it was now inevitable that Rovers and Hull would draw each other. Halifax were number 10, Hull FC 12; Hull KR 13 and 27 was Widnes.

"I was watching it at home," said David Hall, "and the phone rang straight away. It was Steve Hartley screaming, 'Yes, we're there, we're going to Wembley' and we all felt that way. We really didn't think Halifax could beat us. We met up and went out for a drink, just to celebrate the draw!"

Last One Out...

"I suppose Rovers are glad to have drawn us," said their coach Maurice Bamford, "but so were Featherstone, Barrow and Wakefield ... and we are in the semi-finals." Brave words but the bookies too saw it otherwise and Rovers were 6/4 favourites to win the Cup. Hull, though, weren't expected to get past Widnes, who were 7/4, Hull 3/1 and Halifax, the outsiders, 10/1. The all-Hull final was now only a 2/1 bet.

***

SOME SAID THE draw was rigged. There were, after all, plenty of motives to keep the Hull teams apart. The prospect of more than 20,000 rival fans descending on Headingley would have troubled the RL. As attendances grew, crowd trouble crept in, particularly in derbies.

Then there were the financials. An all-Hull semi-final was a guaranteed sell-out and a massive earner for the RL. Kept apart, both semi-finals would attract huge gates and the prospect of an all-Hull final would see a full house and huge publicity. Throughout the 1970s, the full house signs had only gone up a handful of times at Wembley.

David Oxley, RL general secretary at the time, admitted later that rigging it would have been easy: "There were only four balls in the bag," he said, as we chatted over lunch in the summer of 2015. Oxley, 78, was still ebullient and slightly mischievous and I wondered if he was kidding. Over a glass of wine, a salmon salad and a nostalgic chat about the good old days and HM the Queen Mother, had I lulled him into a revelation about warming the balls and thereby engineering the perfect final to catapult the game's profile into the 1980s?

"But we didn't do that," he continued. "It would have been totally against the integrity of the game." And with that, and a twinkle in his eye, he forked another piece of salmon.

Semi-Conscious

10

IT'S HARD TO imagine now, but in March 1980 the only person who seemed capable of, or willing to, save Hull's fishing industry was Margaret Thatcher.

Although the industry had collapsed on Labour's watch and the Tories had done bugger all while in power to help any other industry, there was still hope they might help the fishermen, if only to repair their own declining popularity. James Johnson, Labour MP for West Hull, went so far as to call Thatcher the 'Fairy Godmother' of Hull's trawlermen, so her first visit to the city on 14th March 1980 was eagerly anticipated, the first visit to Hull by a serving Conservative Prime Minister since Churchill came in 1941 to see if the bombing really had been as bad as it said in *The Times*.

The trip itself, a routine visit, had been organised months earlier. But, in March, the Tories delivered one of the most savage and vindictive budgets in recent times, causing further misery to Northern cities. Any journey north was sure to be hostile but, in Hull, the political atmosphere was deadly.

Last One Out...

In late February, an internal memo to the PM said: "The situation in Hull has deteriorated further ... In effect, the final collapse of its deep sea fishing industry has taken place this week. If you go to Hull ... you cannot ignore the overriding impact of these developments.There is time available to add to your programme a meeting of representatives from both sides of the industry. But feelings are clearly running high in the area ... The three Labour MPs for the area are in an angry mood." The private letter, only released in 2010, ended with the blunt question: "Are you prepared to go to Hull in the face of the tremendous problems of the area?"

In 1973, there were 111 trawlers operating out of St Andrews Dock employing 2,307 fishermen. They had made 1133 landings a year – more than three per day. This level of activity was responsible for the indirect employment of 11,000 men in associated industries and firms. By 1976, only 73 trawlers remained employing 1,850 men responsible for 850 landings and by 1982, when the EEC's Fisheries Policy was finally agreed with slightly better terms for UK fishermen, there was little left. Just 18 active trawlers (and even then only occasionally) employed 619 men (rarely and intermittently). There were 114 landings (two per week on average), of which most were foreign vessels. The merchandising and processing sectors had been resilient, finding other sources of fish, but employment was still reduced to around 2,500.

If that sounds like a lot of numbers, consider the men. A fisherman who might have earned a hundred pounds a day at sea, got nothing when on shore. Instead, he found himself queuing to pick up his £25-per-week dole. After giving most of it to his wife to pay the rent and the bills, he might have a few quid left, and time on his hands, to drift down to Raynors or Wassie Arms or Stricky to find out when there might be a ship going out. So much for the 'Three Day Millionaires.'

A way of life changed dramatically, but, aside from the protests and representations from any industry in decline, there was no wailing for pity. By and large, the men and women took jobs in the business and retail parks that sprang up. And, increasingly, they turned their thoughts to rugby league and the teams that were now the best in the country.

The week after Margaret Thatcher came to town, Hull FC were at home to Leigh. It was a Friday night and, amongst the crowd of 9,500, were a number of men who should have been working on the Humber Bridge. Instead, they got their mates to cover for them, bunked off their shift and headed for the Boulevard. It probably wasn't the first time that had happened and, normally, they'd have got away with it. But, around eight o'clock – midway through the first half – a 30-ton gantry strung between the bridge's two towers, slipped out of position and crashed onto the road decks below. Two of those decks – each weighing 145 tonnes – broke free and were left dangling precariously at a 45-degree angle above a row of Riverside cottages on the North bank; a major incident was declared. Only four men were injured but, when a roll call was conducted, many more were found to be missing. It didn't take long to figure where they might be. "Get back to work," said the tannoy announcer at the Boulevard.

***

THE BEST THING about being an eleven-year old in 1980 was Saturday telly. It began in the morning with *Multi-Coloured Swap Shop*, whose guests were always a bit weird for children's TV – David Soul, *Starsky & Hutch* actor turned pop singer, and Scottish songstress Barbara Dickson in March.

From lunchtime it was sport, starting with 'On The Ball' on ITV or 'Football Focus' on the BBC. Then the Five Nations,

105

Bill Beaumont's England winning the Grand Slam. On the other wide was wrestling, featuring Big Daddy, 'Cry Baby' Jim Breaks and Giant Haystacks. Then later: 'Final Score', *Wonder Woman* and *Jim'll Fix It*, before the likes of Little and Large, Match of the Day and Michael Parkinson took care of Saturday night. That month, however, the day's viewing was all about *Grandstand* and, for two successive Saturdays at a quarter-to-four, live second half coverage of the Challenge Cup semi-finals. Eddie Waring and Alex Murphy were the commentators.

In the fevered atmosphere of Hull, there was no doubt which team had the best draw; not only had Rovers landed Second Division Halifax, they only had to go to Leeds. Their supporters would be back in East Yorkshire well before opening time. The black and whites, on the other hand, were to meet the holders, Widnes, who in six seasons chalked up seventeeen cup final appearances, as well as winning the First Division Championship. In 1978/79, they'd won all four knock-out cups. Not for nothing were they called 'The Cup Kings'. And if that wasn't tough enough, Hull had to play the Chemics in Swinton, their own back yard. Secretary Peter Darley was furious and complained to the RFL. A short hop down the road for Widnes was more like two hours for Hull supporters. But the RFL refused to budge. David Oxley says: "It had always been a tradition that we had one game in Yorkshire, one in Lancashire, and usually at Headingley and Station Road. I always made sure we announced dates and venues straight away, more business-like, you see."

Confidence at the Boulevard neverthless remained high, with local bookies offering no more than evens on a Hull win. On Tuesday, East Yorkshire Motor Services announced their coach fares: £2.10 to Headingley, £3.60 for the longer trip to Swinton. And then there were the trips from pubs and clubs.

Whoever was organising, seats were in high demand, leading coach companies to hire extra buses from out of town. Tony Roberts remembers the trip from his Humber Sportsmans club: "We ran a bus trip to every away game but, by the time we got to the semi-final, we ran three and could have organised more. The demand just went through the roof."

Rovers were way off the pace in the league and so their game against Leigh the week before had nothing on it, except to avoid injuries. Lowe, Rose, Casey, Millington, Holdstock and Smith sat out a meaningless match for everyone except David Watkinson. This was his first game since he'd bust his shoulder on tour, eight months ago. Selection as a tourist was a dream-turned-nightmare for a player who signed from York in 1976. In Sydney, he made his international debut, but the injury came in the very next game and he was forced to come home early, the problem worse than first thought.

"I tried to play for the 'A' team early in the season but my shoulder just wasn't right. I went to a specialist in Leeds which led to an operation and I was out for months. In those days, you didn't get paid if you didn't play and I couldn't work either, so was living off sick pay most of the winter. It was a very difficult time but all I really wanted was to get fit so I could play rugby again."

At half-time, Millward withdrew Ray Price and threw on Watkinson who was brilliant in the second half and Rovers won easily. Millward had a tough decision to make about who would wear the number nine shirt in the semi-final, but at least it took his mind off whether he should play himself.

***

ROVERS HAD A busy week, training Tuesday, Wednesday and Thursday and then an overnight stay on Friday. Nor were Hull putting their feet up. They had three games to play and the sequence offers a remarkable contrast to the modern game.

Newlove couldn't make the trip to Saints on Tuesday night because he couldn't get the time off work. Fortunately, Hancock was available so stepped into a side that recorded its first win at Knowsley Road since 1961. Hancock, however, was going on holiday to Majorca the next day, so Newlove was back in the team for the game with Leigh on Friday. Hull won that one 25-14, but the star was Leigh's young stand-off, John Woods. So impressed were the Hull FC directors that they besieged the Leigh directors after the game, determined to sign him. The bidding, at one point, reached £40,000 – a world record. But it was still turned down.

The week ended with the visit of Workington. Having picked up back-to-back wins in midweek, Bunting gave several of his first-choice players the day off and into the team came Robinson, Dennison, Hepworth, Crowther, Lazenby and Boxall. Hull still won easily to pick up six points in six days and in the papers Dick Tingle reflected on a season that had "surpassed their wildest dreams." It was still technically possible for Hull to become champions, though top four was most likely; a remarkable achievement for a newly-promoted team, especially one that had looked destined for a relegation battle in October, winning just two of their first seven games. Yet the fixture backlog was taking its toll and, as Bunting counted the cost of a busy week, he had to deal with injuries to Woods, Lloyd and Wileman.

Woods's knee ligament injury was the most serious, making him a major doubt for the semi-final. It was decided that he would spend the following week in Hull receiving regular treatment rather than face the regular journey over from his home in Rochdale. With a reputation as a diabolical house guest, his teammates shared the responsibility, leaving Woods to move house every few days.

***

BY FRIDAY AFTERNOON, as Rovers boarded the team bus at Craven Park, there was still no indication as to the likely line up at Headingley. For one thing, the West Yorkshire-based players were meeting up with the squad in Harrogate. Keeping his options open, Millward had named eighteen men including ten forwards. He would go with the plan that had got them this far; two forward substitutes.

But he still hadn't announced if he would play himself. The last injury prognosis suggested a six week lay-off, which just happened to end on March 22nd – the date of Rovers' semi–final. Even if fit, would Millward really bring himself back into the team for such an important game? At 32 and obviously not match-fit, it was clearly a risk, especially in those times when only two subs were permitted and with the Hartley-Agar combination knocking along nicely. The players were told the team on Friday night. Everyone else would find out at Headingley the next afternoon.

Meanwhile, in the Halifax camp, Maurice Bamford took his team off to a Turkish Bath on the Thursday and revealed their pre-match ritual would involve a light training session on Saturday morning at Thrum Hall, followed by a pub lunch and a game of bowls before going to Headingley. He had a simple game plan too. "If we can score every time we get into the Rovers' 25-yard area, we can win it. We'll take a shot at a drop-goal every time. If we get twenty chances, we'll take them. Twenty points is more than enough to win a semi-final."

Despite his comments, Bamford was taken seriously.

He had worked wonders at Halifax. It had only been two years since, languishing near the bottom of Division Two, they had been knocked out of the John Player Trophy by the Hull works team, Cawoods. Soon after, Bamford became coach and his mercurial talents were employed to brilliant effect as he guided them up the league. With just a few weeks to go until the end of the season, 'Fax were certainties to be promoted back to Division One.

Over the next few years, Headingley became a second home for Hull and Rovers. So often did they return there, parking their buses on Victoria Road, supping in the Original Oak and Skyrack, queuing out of the door at St Michael's Lane chippy, that they, eventually, dared even take over the South Stand. In March 1980, Rovers fans vastly outnumbered supporters from Halifax and the streets around Headingley were a sea of red and white long before kick-off with 'Red Red Robin' and 'We're on the march, we're Roger's army' drifting down the narrow terraces. It was a celebration. Few fans anticipated an upset and most expected a fairly routine win for the Robins. But just after lunch, news began to trickle out that Roger Millward would be playing.

Halifax took an early 4-0 lead (two penalties, no drop-goals) but then Brian Lockwood took hold of the game. At times it looked as if the maestro was playing an entirely different game to the other twenty-five men on the pitch. He was ably supported by Agar and Millward and Halifax had no answer. Sullivan swept in for a great try, converted by Hubbard. Soon after, he was over again in exactly the same position following another move involving Lockwood.

In the second half, Agar finished them off with a try of his own and Millward dropped a goal. Halifax put up a brave fight but the result was never in doubt as Rovers cruised home, 20-7. Long before the end, celebrations began among

the Rovers supporters and – with a few minutes still to play
– hundreds of younger fans climbed over the barriers and
lined up along the touchline ready to invade. Once the hooter
sounded, on they went. Millward, in the centre of the scrum,
was shouldered off the pitch. Could anyone imagine how he
felt? After sixteen unsuccessful attempts and quite possibly
in his last season, back from injury, not match fit, he'd won
the man of the match award and was off to Wembley.

Clive Sullivan had waited even longer. Sure, he'd
captained Great Britain when they played Australia in 1973.
But there'd been less than 10,000 there then, it didn't count.
"Wembley meant so much to him," his widow Ros said. "I
remember years earlier when he was playing for Hull against
Barrow in a quarter-final. They only just lost and when he got
back in the house he cried. Every year, Clive used to say: 'This
will be the year'. That was his dream, to play at Wembley. We
wouldn't go to the cup final because he always said the first
time he wanted to go was as a player. But as he got older –
and he hadn't got there - we did. Afterwards he said that he
was really glad of that because you couldn't imagine the
atmosphere until you had actually been there."

"After the game I was sat in the dressing room and I'll
never forget the sight of Roger and Clive hugging each other,"
said Brian Lockwood. "And they were crying. That was one
of the best sensations I've ever had anywhere – seeing those
two embracing like that." But elsewhere, the overwhelming
emotion was relief. Being favourites had put pressure on the
Rovers players and many were just pleased not to have lost.

"In those days, it was the ambition of every player to
play at Wembley and each year you got one bite at it," said
David Watkinson. "You were worried it might pass you by."

In some respects, the game itself was an anti-climax and
did not generate the excitement seen at Swinton the following

week. Rovers had had everything to lose, red-hot favourites. A party was planned back at Craven Park and the players were keen to get changed, get through the formalities and be back on the coach back to Hull, but for Brian Lockwood it wasn't so straightforward. "I told Bill Land I wouldn't be able to go," he said. "We had a pub to run in Wakefield, Saturday nights were our busiest and I couldn't afford not to be there. Well, Bill was a bit taken aback by this. He asked how much it would cost to get extra staff on and I told him about forty quid, so he gave me that and I went to Hull for the party."

Over the weekend, Roger Millward shared his views on the supporter invasion at the end of the game. "I know the fans meant well, but it was frightening," he said. "So many people crowded around me I thought I was going to go down and be trampled on." And there were other incidents more worrying. Twenty-seven Rovers supporters were arrested during the afternoon, leaving a black cloud on the day. Following crowd trouble at the derby at the Boulevard back in October, little wonder that some people were worried at the prospect of an all-Hull final.

At Wembley, fencing had gone up a few years earlier after repeated pitch invasions by Scottish football fans but they had not – to date – been in place for rugby league finals. The authorities had thought about it when Widnes fans got on the pitch in celebration in 1979 and, after similar invasions by the Rovers fans at Headingley, they thought hard about it again, deciding that fences would indeed be necessary. David Oxley explains: "I suppose there was some apprehension that there might be trouble at the game, but we had certainly not asked for them to be put up."

It wasn't enough for another RL official, quoted in the *Hull Daily Mail*: "If Hull and Hull KR meet in the final, we shall need fences in the trains never mind at Wembley."

But Hull FC weren't there yet and, the following week, it was all about tickets. On Tuesday, Hull announced they had sold their semi-final allocation, all 11,000. Rovers topped that the next day, telling their fans how they could get their hands on ones for Wembley; two tickets each for season pass holders mischievously on sale on the morning of Hull's semi. There was then a spat when Rovers refused to give Hull tickets for the upcoming Good Friday derby. After protests from the Airlie Birds and even an attempt to buy 3,000 direct from Hull KR for resale, Rovers relented, making 2,000 tickets available. It was a storm in a tea-cup but raised tensions a further notch.

***

THERE WAS NO *Hull Daily Mail* on Thursday 28th March due to a strike, which meant no coverage of Rovers' win over Castleford the night before. That was a shame, as it saw Millward's first try of the season and – in the final minute of the game – Clive Sullivan's 400th career try.

Hull, preparing for their first Challenge Cup semi-final since 1961, went into camp on Thursday. Arriving at Mottram Hall mid-afternoon, they were relaxed and confident. Why shouldn't they be? One defeat in twenty-one games brought back memories of the previous year. They must have felt unbeatable. But the weekend got off to a disastrous start.

Paul Woods had been in Leeds for the afternoon, up in front of the beak for his sending off for Wales the previous month, and received nine matches. It was heart-breaking, there were only seven first and 'A' team games left. If Hull made it to Wembley, Woods wouldn't be able to play. Hull immediately lodged an appeal while he contemplated his future. "I am so disillusioned I cannot see the point in continuing because it just seems I am being victimised."

In truth, Woods had form. He'd been banned for four matches in December and his reputation as one of the game's most brutal competitors was well-deserved. But the length of this ban was particularly severe, especially in an era when attempted murder was not necessarily a red-card offence.

Ironically, Woods would still be available for the semi-final due to a change in the rule that allowed anyone banned between two semi-finals to be treated on the same basis as someone playing in the first. It meant Woods's ban wouldn't actually begin until five weeks after he committed the offence, during which time Hull had played seven games – none of which were eligible to count towards his suspension.

It got worse. Paul Prendiville pulled up injured during Friday's training session and then, on Saturday morning when they had a run out at Station Road, came another blow. John Newlove, only jogging along the pitch a few minutes, bent over to pick a ball up and his hamstring went.

"Arthur Bunting was standing with his head in his hands," remembers Charlie Birdsall. "It couldn't have been a worse start to the weekend." Dennison came in for Prendiville, fairly straightforward. But to replace Newlove, Bunting had to shuffle. He decided to promote Paul Woods to stand-off and so there was a sudden call up for veteran full back George Robinson. Who was at home in Hull.

"I was sat watching *The Muppets* with the kids," said a man who'd been a ballboy in Hull's last Wembley appearance in 1960, and who expected to head for Halifax to play for the 'A' team that Saturday lunchtime. "After that, we planned to go to Swinton to watch the first team. Then the phone rang. Peter Darley came around and told me I had two hours to get to Mottram Hall because I was playing." A fast car was sent to despatch Robinson to Cheshire.

***

BETWEEN 1946 AND 1970, Station Road hosted twenty Challenge Cup semi-finals as well as twelve Great Britain Test matches. Opened in 1929, it was one of the sport's newer grounds and its position next to Swinton's train station made it one of the sport's premier venues.

By the 1970s, however, it had failed to keep pace with other stadiums and was used less frequently for showpiece fixtures. By 1980, it was already quite dilapidated and some terracing was out of use, strengthening Hull's argument that the game should have been played at Bradford or Leeds. Not that Hull's contingent of 11,000 didn't seem to mind. They massed in the long, low edifice opposite the main stand.

Throughout the game, cameras picked out many home-made banners. A bed-sheet and black marker pen was all that was needed. Occasionally they showed great wit and, at other times, didn't. "Sammy Lloyd strikes more often than Hull Dockers", read one, "Hissing Sid is innocent – So is Paul Woods" another. The singing started early and didn't stop; 'Old Faithful', obviously, but also 'You'll Never Walk Alone', a huge, noisy mob of passion and an intimidating sight for opposing players. "When we got to a big game, you couldn't avoid the supporters," said Steve Norton. "They'd take over the place, making such a lot of noise and so you got this feeling in your bones that 'we can do something here'."

To begin with it was all Hull, dominating territory and possession with Widnes barely able to escape their own quarter. So it was against the run of play when Les Gorley scored a converted try and Widnes held onto the lead until half-time. After the break, Hull were again on top but this time got their reward, Graham Bray scoring in the corner.

Hull, back in it at 5-3 and with an increasingly strong

wind behind them, continued to dominate territory; at one stage it took Widnes seventeen consecutive tackles before they could clear their 20-yard line. On 62 minutes though, Reg Bowden finally found a chink in Hull's defence and darted through. As the tacklers closed in, he found Brian Hogan in support who rounded fullback George Robinson and raced into space, twenty-five yards out, with a clear run to the line, certain to score. A try then would break Hull's hearts and – at 10-3 – it could be the killer blow. But Ronnie Wileman had not given up and chased back. If he couldn't bring Hogan down, he might just force a knock-on or an error in grounding. Just feet from the line, Wileman launched himself at the ball carrier, bringing him crashing to earth. But the hit came too late and Hogan was still able to stagger over and touch down. Wileman's effort seemed to be in vain.

Hull needed divine intervention and it duly appeared. Referee Fred Lindop was in no doubt that Hogan had made a double movement, disallowed the score and gave a penalty to Hull, who had to thank the determination of a man who, like Wileman, also chased back and was in perfect position to make the decision.

"I lost a kidney playing for Eastmoor and had to stop playing rugby," Lindop explained later. "I was only 18, so decided to become a referee. But when I looked at my peers, I realised that they didn't take fitness very seriously. Quite a few had pot bellies which I thought insulted the players. So I started to train. At first, I trained with the Wakefield players and then my local club, Oulton. I used to run five miles there and five miles back. You never get every decision right but I believed you gave yourself a chance if you could get there."

It was a big call. Had the try stood, there could have been no real argument from the Hull players. Had the try stood, it would have given Widnes a seven-point lead. Had the try stood, there may have been no all-Hull final. Widnes, the Cup Kings, would have been firm favourites to retain the silverware. No fairy-tale for Millward. Or Sullivan. But with the no-try call the momentum switched back to Hull, who launched attack after attack towards the Widnes line.

As the clock ticked down, on *Grandstand* Eddie Waring and Alex Murphy did their best to convey the excitement to the viewing public, using words and phrases the meaning of which only they understood. And they had lots to describe. The final six minutes contained more incident than the rest of the game and the semi-final the week before combined.

On 74 minutes, Woods launched an 'up and under' and set off after his own kick. Immediately, he was obstructed by Hogan and Lindop awarded a penalty, 25 yards out, 12 yards in from touch. Two points in arrears, Lloyd did not hesitate to go for goal. As the BBC cameras closed in, Hull fans could be seen behind Lloyd, hands clasped in prayer, some with their backs turned on a kick which – if successful – would tie the game, 5-5. When he kicked it they went into raptures.

On the restart, Hull received the ball deep in their own half and immediately mounted an attack. Bray cut inside and the ball moved quickly through the hands of Walters and Wilby to Dennison, on the left flank. Dennison raced up the touchline but ran out of space and opted to kick over the top instead. A desperate Widnes defender blocked his chase and it was another penalty to Hull. Lloyd again had no hesitation in going for goal, this time just two feet inside the left-hand touchline. Kick this and Hull were off to Wembley.

***

WHEN WE MET in 2014, Lloyd's first thought about the semi-final was that he shouldn't have been there.

"My year had been riddled with injuries. I broke my arm early on against Featherstone and was out for six weeks. Then I broke it again in the same place and was out for another eight weeks. I missed the Floodlit final and most of the season. I had to strap a soccer player's armguard to my right arm and it made me look like bloody Popeye!" But Lloyd was fit and well for the Challenge Cup campaign and found himself in a position to take the team to London.

"The wind was fierce, straight down the middle of the pitch. I mean, real gale-force. And I will always remember the two goals I kicked near the end, two of the best I ever kicked. When it came to the second, I knew that the only chance it had of going through the sticks was if I aimed almost for the corner flag and really give it some lift. That was the gamble. Straight away I felt the wind getting hold of it and knew it was going to be close."

Close enough to soar between the posts in fact and the banks of Hull fans watching from behind his kicking position began cheering long before the touch judges raised their flags. A few dozen spilled onto the pitch and the noise levels went even higher. Hull now led 7-5 with just a few minutes left and just needed to retain possession. But from the kick-off, it got better. Hull attacked again, this time down the right. Birdsall offloaded superbly to Bray who broke through. Every yard and every second meant less chance for Widnes to get their hands on the ball, but Bray wasn't thinking about them. Finding Wileman alongside him, he offloaded to the hooker who scampered over for the clinching try.

In the space of three frenetic minutes, Hull had scored three times and turned the game on its head. Hundreds of fans rushed on, swamping the players and bringing the game to a chaotic climax. There was little effort to remove them so Lloyd had plenty of time to prepare his conversion. Having kicked two stunning penalties, he scuffed this one badly though, pulling it some way to the left of the posts. Hull led 10-5 with a minute to go, their fans already jumping up and down with only a handful of uniformed bobbies between them and the playing surface.

But the drama still wasn't over. Widnes re-started and Hull, rather than close it out, again went on the attack. They moved it left, Walters in space but flattened by Alan Reardon. Lindop gave a penalty and was sworn at by Hogan. As Lindop moved to send the culprit off, a scuffle broke out behind him. Hull physio George Kendall ran on after Walters jumped up and hit Eric Hughes. Hundreds of Hull fans, preparing to invade the pitch had no idea what was going on. Lindop sent Walters off. Nobody noticed.

A scrum was awarded and, three play-the-balls later the hooter sounded as the stand previously occupied by Hull FC fans emptied onto the pitch. "Well I've never seen scenes like this for many years and it's good for rugby league," Alex Murphy told 'Uncle Eddie' and the BBC's watching millions. Hull fans certainly agreed.

Tony Daddy was one such invader: "I'd been a Hull FC fan since I was a kid and had been to one or two big games, but I'd never experienced anything like that semi-final. The atmosphere was beyond belief, everyone in it together. I swear thousands of Hull fans must have blown that ball between the posts when Sammy kicked it. And when the hooter went! When I watch back the DVD, I'm sure I can see myself running. I had my hair permed like Sammy Lloyd so I stood out a bit!"

Hull had done it. They would be at Wembley on May 3rd. And how they enjoyed the moment. "We went back to the Black Swan in Normanton," remembers Charlie Birdsall. "We often used that pub when heading back from Lancashire.

Anyway, a load of fans must have followed the bus because, when we got there, the place was soon packed with black and white. It was a long night."

***

AS THE FINAL dramatic six minutes unfolded, spare a thought for *Hull Daily Mail* FC reporter, Dick Tingle, who faced the tightest of deadlines in order to get the match report into that night's *Sports Mail*.

The 'Green Mail' as it was known in Hull, tended to hit the streets from around 5.30pm each Saturday. The paper couldn't go to print without a report on the big game that afternoon, so it was down to Dick to submit it on time.

"Basically, the game was due to finish at twenty to five and I had to send in my report at twenty to five, if not sooner! But, for Saturday games, I did what was called a runner. Every ten or fifteen minutes, I'd phone in with what had happened during that period to a copywriter who would start writing it up. And we'd do that throughout the match. Then, at the end, I'd send in my two or three paragraph introduction which basically told the reader who had won and how well or badly they'd played. They'd copy that down, send it off to the compositors and off it went to print."

But, with Hull still trailing 5-3 at half past four and looking set to crash out of the Challenge Cup, it made for some hasty rewriting as Hull surged back into the game.

"You can imagine how difficult it was to send in my intro for the semi-final. The editor was screaming for it and I had to keep rewriting it. In the end I got it to them and I think the paper came out on time."

Hull, Featherstone and Castleford

11

BRIAN LOCKWOOD REMEMBERS vividly the meeting in Sully's room the night before the game. And he remembers the response he got when he tried to calm the players down. 'It's not just another game', they told him. 'It's okay for you, you don't have to live in Hull'.

"It's true I could go back to Cas," admitted a man with just four derby games under his belt, but three appearances at Wembley. "I wouldn't have got the stick they'd have got. But they were wound up like a clock and it was no good for them. They needed to calm down."

"But it wasn't just a game to us Hull lads," insists John Millington, 36 years later. "It was a way of life. Locky and them could get back in their cars but we had to face everyone. They didn't even have to read what was written in the paper. We'd go to work or for a pint and everyone would be either patting you on the back or giving you abuse. There was no escaping it. That's why I had a go at him. When we played Hull FC, you could never say that it was just another game."

"We actually placed a lot of emphasis on what it would be like to get beat," revealed Steve Hartley. "We talked about what it would be like going back to Hull and it didn't bear thinking about. That fear was one of our main motivators and I think Locky understood afterwards. No matter where the derby is – Craven Park, Boulevard, Wembley, Headingley, East Park or Pickering Park – you have to win, and that was the derby to end all derbies."

Roger Millward named nine Hull-born players in his fifteen-man squad, plus he and Sullivan were essentially adopted Hull men themselves. There was a small influential contingent of out-of-towners led by Lockwood, with Agar from Featherstone, Watkinson from York and new signing Phil Hogan the only Cumbrian in either set-up.

Not only were most from Hull, they were tightly-knit. Millward, Lowe and Rose made debuts in the '60s. Hartley, Holdstock and Millington signed in 1971. Hall and Smith followed a few years later and, with the addition of Agar and Casey (1976) and Watkinson (1977), the bulk of the side had been together for many years. Collectively, they had over a hundred years of professional rugby league experience and had played in 134 derby games between them. "We were all mates," sums up Roy Holdstock.

But none of those derby games came remotely close to what they were going to experience the following day.

***

ROVERS' LAST PERIOD of success had been in the late 1960s when Colin Hutton had built a strong team around a nucleus of Millward, Frank Foster and Bill Holliday – out-of-towners. Once they left, the club sank into decline very quickly. And when Featherstone-born Arthur Bunting inherited a team of mostly local players from his predecessor John Whiteley, he looked west. Neil Fox and Bernard Watson were soon signed. Later, Harry Poole followed the same path, with the signings of Agar and Watkinson. Then, his successor, Millward, signed Clarkson. But it was 1978 and the signing of Brian Lockwood that signalled Rovers' determination to sign whoever they needed, regardless of where they came from.

Sports historian Tony Collins has written extensively on rugby league and, as a Hull KR supporter, is well qualified to analyse Rovers' progress at the end of the 1970s. "It was an indication of the level of professionalism at Hull KR and Hull FC," he reckons. "Both sides knew who they wanted and went out and got them. Hull picked the eyes out of Featherstone and Castleford, while Roger picked out the players he wanted and the club went and signed them. It was much more planned than it had ever been before."

Lockwood himself was well aware of the qualities he brought: "Without being disrespectful, I'd always said that Hull kids aren't any good once they get out of Hull. It's a mental thing. They just don't know what to do when they're playing in West Yorkshire and they've no idea in Lancashire. Well that didn't bother me."

And so, at various times, Rovers' bunch of eager, local lads was bolstered by a sizeable number of incomers; Watson, Fox, Colin Tyrer, Lockwood, Agar, Graham Brittain, Geoff Clarkson and the like. Allan Agar recalls as many as twelve at a time, in three cars, the lay-bys outside Glasshoughton the picking-up point. "The Hull lads called us 'Wessies', short for West Riding Bastards and take the piss out of the money we made on expenses." But the indignation was genuine.

"We resented it, to be honest," admits Holdstock who broke into the Rovers team in 1972. "When you're young, you want to play. It was frustrating to be in and out of the side."

"You might train all week, but if you didn't play at the weekend you'd done it all for nothing," says John Millington. "Whereas the out-of-town blokes might get a tenner for their travelling expenses and, if it only cost a fiver to come over, they'd be a fiver a week better off, whether they played or not. That added up to quite a bit of money in them days."

"We were definitely second-class citizens," confirmed Mike Smith, signed in 1975. "The out-of-towners didn't come for nothing. They got what they wanted – it might have been a car or more money – while the rest of us didn't have contracts and didn't get paid if we lost our place."

"But there was no tension on the field," insists Dave Hall, who made his debut in 1971. "We were a team, no matter where we came from."

Nevertheless, there was unrest. Even in the promotion season of 1974-75, Hall, Heslop, Hartley, Millington and Holdstock found reason to submit transfer requests. Tellingly, none left and Rovers undoubtedly benefited in the long run. In the opinion of Brian Lockwood: "It was the local lads that gave us the edge in 1980. We had the better side and that was because we had more Hull players." More local lads, yes, but there was no denying the influence of player-coach Roger Millward, Lance Todd Trophy winner Lockwood and the man of the match of everyone else, Allan Agar.

***

AS ROGER KAHN wrote in *The Boys of Summer*, his brilliant account of the Brooklyn Dodgers' efforts to win the World Series in the 1950s: "You glory with the winners, but fall in love with the losers."

If that is the case, then the Hull FC team of the mid '70s was one you could easily fall in love with. Never has a Hull side taken the field with so many local folk-heroes. Alf, Keith, George, Bill, Kenny, Brian. Under the enthusiastic coaching of David Doyle-Davidson and in front of dwindling crowds they repeatedly tried to battle their way out of Division Two. Each year they set out with great ambition but each year the lack of quality was exposed and Hancock, Foulkes, Davidson, Boxall, Robinson, Macklin and Co came up short again.

'Doyle' knew its limitations better than anyone. "Show me the money," he'd tell the directors and, between them, they would find themselves linked with dozens of players. Eddie Cunningham, Alan Hodkinson, Kevin Ashcroft, Eddie Bowman, Harry Beverley, Brian Hogan ... all were rumoured to be joining Hull but nothing materialised. Some suggested the club was stoking the rumours to keep supporters happy. "I think there was truth in that," said Dick Tingle. "Some attempts were genuine, but the club was happy to be linked with players even if there was no chance of signing them."

All that changed when they went after Vince Farrar, whose twelve seasons with hometown Featherstone was the most successful period in their history. Fev won the Cup in '67 and '74 and were runners-up in '73. In 1977, with Farrar as captain, they won the Division One title, five points clear of St Helens and it was then that Hull first came calling, without success. Undeterred, they tried again in August, but that approach was also turned down. Mischievously, Hull tried to sign his teammate Jimmy Thompson, but he opted for Bradford instead. Then came the tipping point.

"We'd just been beaten by Bradford," recalls Farrar. "One of our directors came in and said I shouldn't have been playing, that I wasn't good enough. I wasn't happy at that and rang Mike Page, asking if he still wanted me."

Hull didn't hang around. Next day, the deal was done. Featherstone got ten grand and Hull one of the finest props of his day, admired by his new teammates. "I'd played with Vince for Yorkshire," said Brian Hancock. "He was just so professional in every way. How he prepared and the way he played. He did it properly. That signing got people talking." But Farrar's signing alone wasn't enough and, by December, a return to Division Two was near certain as fellow strugglers New Hunslet came to the Boulevard.

"Utter rubbish," was how Tingle described the 23-3 defeat. It proved too much for Doyle-Davidson, who resigned the next day. It was, he said: "the most gutless and heartless performance I have seen by a Hull team. I no longer feel that I can motivate the side." The Doyle was nothing if not honourable. And honest. "I resigned," he later reflected, "but I'd probably have been sacked if I hadn't. I'd lost the dressing room by then and was smart enough to realise that."

Enter Arthur Bunting, Rovers' ex-coach. Although the next five games were lost, confidence improved and crowds grew, as we've seen. Nor did it do any harm when Bunting won his first two derbies and signed Steve Norton. And then the floodgates opened.

There is an old, somewhat hackneyed, saying that Hull FC stands for Hull, Featherstone and Castleford. In 1978, it appeared to have some truth. Even though relegation could not be avoided, Bunting continued to raid both clubs. Within a few weeks in August, Bunting and his irrepressible ally on the board, Mike Page, had tempted Sammy Lloyd from Cas and Charlie Stone from Featherstone. John Newlove, another ex-Fev captain, was lured away in October and Clive Pickerill left Castleford in December. Within a year, six men had left F/C to join FC. Suddenly, barely half of Hull's starting line-up could remember the bad old days.

Newlove, Stone and Farrar had all played at Wembley and won the Division One Championship. Norton played for

Great Britain. Farrar and Norton had played club rugby in Australia. Bunting was buying quality and experience. Few of the Hull-born players now have a bad word to say about Norton or any of the other West Riding imports. There is acceptance that the team benefited, though some regret that most of the local lads who kept the club going during the mid '70s missed out on the success at the end of the decade. Some make references to a 'Featherstone Mafia', others tell of being marginalised or neglected, afraid to voice concerns for fear of being dropped. Even Norton saw it happening. "Arthur got rid of most of my mates," he says. "When I joined, Boxall, Macklin and Hancock were all in the team. They were good players but one by one were replaced."

"With every new signing, somebody, usually a lad from Hull, dropped out of the team," says Keith Tindall. "I kept waiting for it to happen to me, but it didn't, not really."

Bunting himself had no regrets. "Everything had to change. If players have to go, you can't have any sentiment if you are going to move forward."

There were also historic rivalries between those who hailed from Featherstone and Castleford. "Aye, there was hatred between Cas and Fev," confirms Norton, "but when we joined up together at Hull there were no problems at all. Featherstone lads were different to Cas players though; more professional, focused and less likely to socialise with their teammates, but still great, great players."

There are countless stories of the meanness of the Fev players. How they would argue over whose turn it was to buy orange squash after training. How they'd arrive ahead of the Cas lads, in order to get their hands on the packages of fish that supporters or sponsors took to the Boulevard as a treat for the players. "When the Cas lads arrived", said Sammy Lloyd, "we'd say: 'Is there no fish tonight?' And they'd tell us that there wasn't any, while all the while Vince or Charlie had stuck it in the boot of their car."

***

WEMBLEY 1980. OF the thirty men who took part, eleven were from Hull or Beverley, six from Castleford, four from Featherstone, two from York, one from Doncaster and one from Leeds. Twenty-five in total from Yorkshire. None from Lancashire, but four Welshman and a Cumbrian.

Featherstone/Castleford provided the Challenge Cup final with both coaches, both captains, all four halfbacks, the Lance Todd winner and Allan Agar. The heart of Wembley 1980 was in Hull, but the brains came from Fev and Cas.

Dick Tingle reported on Hull FC for the *Hull Daily Mail* for over thirty years. "Hull had to sign West Riding lads to get them over the Ouse bridge," he said. "Hull players were happy to be big fish in a small pond, whereas West Yorkshire and Lancashire players just wanted to be big fish. Full stop. Arthur and Roger both knew that neither side were going to win anything with teams full of Hull kids. They knew that as soon as they got over Boothferry Bridge, their mentality changed and their heads went down and they couldn't win."

Professor Tony Collins is in agreement. "If you look at how many international players the city has produced, it doesn't compare to the likes of Wigan. There is something to it – too much in their comfort zone. To understand why, you have to look at the history of the rivalry between both clubs. The rivalry still motivates both teams. It's the yardstick by which each club measures its success. Each sees themselves through the prism of the other."

And yet... there is another way of looking at it. Good Friday, 1978. Eleven-and-a-half thousand squeeze and elbow their way into the Boulevard to watch soon-to-be-relegated Hull beat Rovers for the third time that season. Two years later, most of the team, local lads, had gone ... Robinson, Barr, Macklin, Lynn, Duke, Young, Boxall, Wilson, Davidson. Hull's tries scored by Macklin, Duke and Boxall, stalwarts of the 70s, still turning Rovers over but their days numbered.

Despite a burgeoning colts team, set up by Bunting and which soon began producing bright prospects in the shape of Colin Lazenby, Mick Sutton, Steve Dennison, Carl Sanderson and others, chances for young lads were few. When Bunting needed a new player, he looked elsewhere. "I don't know what happened to Lazenby," wonders Steve Norton. "He was great but totally disappeared. Arthur must have shot him."

Hull were promoted in style, but still Bunting pressed on... Birdsall and Wileman from Rochdale and York and then, having hoovered up most of the available talent from the West Riding, he turned his attention to South Wales and a pair of AN Others signed within a few weeks; Woods and Walters. It meant Hull's Wembley team had a transient look, with a combined experience of just sixty-two derbies, twenty of those from Hancock alone. For Woods, Wilby, Lloyd, Prendiville and Walters the final was only their second derby.

Contrast with the Rovers squad and their 134 derby appearances, six players boasting more than ten. To whom did it matter the most? Who was best prepared? Might Hull's 1978 team of local lads, the team everyone fell in love with, have fared better beneath the old Twin Towers?

On the night before, the Hull players relaxed. Joined by their wives and girlfriends, they followed Arthur's advice and enjoyed themselves. Across London, meanwhile, Rovers' predominantly local team was holed up, anxiously agonising over the reaction on their return to Hull should they lose.

***

ANOTHER LOOK AT the Wembley teams reveals a further insight. Eight had played club rugby down under. Birdsall, Rose and Wilby played at a relatively low level and Farrar's single season at Cronulla was a low-key affair, but the others made a huge impression on the Australian game. Not only did Norton, Lowe and Lockwood all appear in Grand Finals, their impact, along with that of Millward, would have major repercussions for British rugby league in the 1980s.

Says Tony Collins: "The wave of British imports in the 1960s and 1970s ... brought new skills and approaches to the Australian game. Wigan's Dave Bolton went to Balmain and redefined stand-off half play. Malcolm Reilly brought a whole new combination of technical ability and uncompromising ferociousness. His Manly teammate, Phil Lowe, built on Dick Huddart's legacy as a free-running second row forward. If the Australians had suffered in the past because its talents were siphoned by British clubs, the reverse was now true."

Above: Steve Hubbard touches down. 'Oranges' never worked in training but, after nine minutes at Wembley, Lockwood's pass to Hubbard put Rovers ahead.

Above: Clive Sullivan spots his wife, Ros, in the crowd.

Right: "I don't think she heard a word I said but, when you watch it back, it looks as if I've whispered into her ear and touched her arse!"

Y 1654

Above: When Hull came to a halt. Led by their chairmen, the teams walk out.

Right: Roger Millward struggled after the high shot from Wileman.

Below: Hubbard is injured after his try: "Keith Tindall still ribs me that I should have got an Oscar for that!"

Above: Phil Lowe sprung a shoulder two weeks before Wembley, a peripheral figure throughout the game.

Below: Tindall is over but the try was disallowed. "If I'd scored, you never know, I might have won the Lance To..." and his voice trailed off.

Above: "I was very nervous while I was sat on the bench," said John Millington, centre, "but, once I got my first touch and my first tackle, then it was just like another game. Until I looked up into the stands!"

Below: The Hull Kingston Rovers players, enjoying their lap of honour, spot Steve Hubbard hobbling back onto the pitch.

Above: Rovers' team bus travels down Jameson Street.

Left: "It was the biggest disappointment of my life," said Keith Tindall. "Nobody ever lets me forget it. It'll go to the grave with me."

Below: In the shadow of Windsor Castle, the Rovers squad is put through its paces.

Above: "An equerry came to see us," said Sammy Lloyd. "'One does not shake Her Majesty's hand. One merely receives it.' We all looked nervously at Paul Woods, fearing what he might say or do."

Above: Roger Millward, suitably deferential, exchanges pleasantries with the Royal Guest

Above: "We were really well looked after all weekend..." – Ros Sullivan and other wives and girlfriends join in the celebrations

Right: Rovers supporters make themselves heard at Paragon Station

Above: "I was very nervous," said Millward. "I remember I was trying to chew a piece of gum and take big gasps of air at the same time."

Below: Norton, with a head resembling a badly dented watering can, leads his team into battle. "After we signed Knocker, everything changed," revealed Arthur Bunting.

Up for the Cup: Millward in his Cowboy Hat; Millo with his State Express flag

Have You Got
Your Tickets Yet?

12

EARLY IN 1980, long before the competition began, my dad saw an advert on the wall in the Cross Keys on Endike Lane. Two nights in London, four-star hotel, train, match ticket, trip to Portobello market – Cup final weekend for £55 a pop. He and mam booked it with no suggestion that I would go with them. Pub trip, no kids allowed. But, as Hull progressed, I began to wonder ... what will happen if they get there?

When we got home from Swinton, mam and dad went straight out, while I stayed up for *Match of the Day*. On their return, they brought fish and chips and an envelope.

"What's that?" I said, as dad dropped it in front of me.

"You didn't think we'd go without you, did you?"

***

THE SCRAMBLE FOR tickets, travel and accommodation was unprecedented. Each club had an allocation of 22,000, but the demand was far higher and there were few directors at either club with any experience of a Wembley Cup Final. It showed. David Howes, the RFL's PR man, was keenly aware of how clubs could maximise the windfall: "Putting them on sale too soon was a mistake. Some clubs used to ask for their ticket allocations straight after the semi-final and actually leave the ground with them so they could have them on sale straight away, but with five or six weeks to play with, you had time to do it properly. There was a lot of money to be made. You'd want to make sure your season ticket holders got theirs first, to encourage them to renew their passes, but then you had the chance to put some packages together."

The clubs didn't make anything on selling the tickets directly but, with the smart addition of coach travel or a hotel package, a £5 ticket could suddenly be sold for £50, adding to the bottom line. "When I was at St Helens in the mid '90s," Howes says, "we made over £200k from that sort of package." But in 1980, none of that happened and the tickets were flying out of the door within days.

Rovers had a week's start and put theirs on sale before they knew their opponents. Hull supporters, desperate not to miss out, besieged the club as soon as the whistle blew at Station Road, but the Boulevard was deserted, offices were closed, so they called on the only place open – Humber Sportsman's Club at the top of the western terraces. Manager Tony Roberts had barely returned when he was overwhelmed by supporters asking if he was running a trip to Wembley.

Tony organised his first away trip in 1975 and has done so ever since. In the dark days, he struggled to fill a minibus. Sometimes, there might be enough demand for two, maybe three, coaches. But nothing compared to 1980.

"The first people were there before me, with money in their hands, desperate to get on," he says. "Within an hour or so, people were queuing right down the steps and into the car park. By the end of the night, I'd taken enough bookings to fill nine buses. We'd had a birthday party on in the club but I'd spent all night on the door taking money. On Monday morning, I began ringing up to try and find enough buses to take them all to London, then I had to get organised myself. I got receipts printed and wrote a number on each one, which showed which bus they were on. We used a company called Club International."

But that was just the beginning. Tony's wife, Andrea, recalls the chaos that descended upon their home. "We lived on Carrington Street, opposite the ground. People used to go to the club office and ask if they were running any coaches to London, but they would just send them to our house. Total strangers knocked on the door and gave us handfuls of cash. They were queuing down the street. Each ticket we sold was for the match and a seat on the bus, there and back, same day. I kept going to see Cyril Fowler, Hull's club secretary, and asking for more and more and he'd just hand over envelopes full of them. I doubt he had any idea how many he gave us. By the end, we'd managed to fill twenty-six buses. We only stopped because Club International couldn't find any more."

Tony remembers the numbers exactly. "In total, we took 1,421 people to Wembley. I had to go to the bank three or four times a day to get rid of all the money. The final bill to the coach company ended up being £7,600, an astronomical amount back then. We couldn't believe what we'd got involved in. And, on Saturday morning, when 1,400 turned up to catch their bus at the Boulevard, we weren't even there. We'd to go to the final every year anyway, going down on Thursday, so that's what we did. I trusted the bus company to provide us with the vehicles and I put people on each bus to sort things out any problems. I got lucky. We only had one complaint ... and I think that was about Fred Lindop!"

Last One Out...

The recollections of a number of people suggest that both Hull and Rovers were totally out of their depth and struggled to keep track of what they'd sold and hadn't, Steve Hubbard among them. "I asked the office for some tickets for my family and was just given a bunch. Days later, I asked for a few more and was given them as well. At some point I was expecting, and was prepared, to pay but nobody asked me. I might've ended up with twenty but nobody was counting."

Hull KR Supporters Club would be there, of course. They always were. "Our first Wembley weekend was for the 1963 final," explains member Bryan Leason. "I was fortunate to get on the outing in 1964, when Rovers were there and, by the 1970s I was treasurer, so me and my brother collected the money. People used to put their names down at the start of the year and pay us weekly or monthly. We ordered our tickets straight from the RL and had it all organised very early in the year, so it was great when Rovers won through. I'm sure there were lots more people who would like to have come with us but the trip, hotel, tickets etc – they were all booked. We ran nineteen coaches just for the day."

Tickets did go on sale to season pass holders first, but it was only when they went on general sale that the true scale of demand became apparent. "We queued all night," says Pete Smedley who, at 15, went to the Boulevard with his 17-year-old brother. "The tickets were on sale at 9.00am so we got there about six o'clock the night before. There were loads there. It was amazing to be sleeping out all night in the car park on Airlie Street. Really exciting. The club opened up the gates so we could use the toilets, and there was a little bakery that stayed open all night, selling sandwiches and cups of tea. Next morning, we got our tickets and walked past hundreds that were still queuing all the way down Airlie Street."

Less than a fortnight later, Hull announced they had

sold or, more accurately distributed, all of their allocation. "It is difficult to say exactly how many, but it is in the region of 20,000 ground and 2,000 seats," said Peter Darley, vaguely. Rovers, meanwhile, confirmed that they too had nearly sold out – with just a few hundred ground tickets remaining.

Nowhere was there greater pleasure at the demand than Chapeltown Road, Leeds, where Hull Kingston Rovers supporters David Howes and David Oxley were rubbing their hands at the prospect of a full house. Oxley recalls: "The 1980 final generated huge interest. I think we sold our last few tickets within four days and we were trying to take back tickets allocated to other clubs and organisations to ship them off to Hull."

Of course, in such circumstances, it helped if you knew a player. "I was working on a building site at BP in Saltend," recalls John Millington. "At the time, loads of the Rovers lads were working there – Phil Hogan, Roy Holdstock, Dave Hall, Ian Madley, as well as Mike Smith and Keith Tindall, who worked for BP themselves. Well, one day, I got called into the site manager's office. I thought I'd done something wrong but he said: 'Can you get hold of four hundred tickets for me, John?' Four hundred! Anyway, I told him I'd see what I could do. So I got in touch with Ron Turner [Rovers' secretary] who said he'd sort it out. When I asked what they were for, the manager said: 'We're having loads of trouble with absence and sickness, so I'm going to give tickets away to blokes who put a full week in.' Signs went up all over the site, offering blokes the chance to go into a draw. The atmosphere was incredible. There were about 1,500 blokes on that site and we were all working there. The banter and craic was brilliant."

Twenty-two-year-old Hull fan Tony Daddy already had his tickets. He'd booked them earlier in the year from the RL. Two best seat tickets, alongside the Royal Box. But he didn't want them. "I'd gone the year before with my mate and we had great seats, but when Hull got there I realised I wanted to be stood in the Hull end, so gave them to my mam. But she didn't want them either; she was a season ticket holder and had her own friends to go with. In the end, she did take them and went with my wife, seven months pregnant at the time."

***

FOR THOSE SUPPORTERS who had managed to get their hands on a ticket, the next question was how they would get to London. Each year, up to 6,000 travelled down from Hull no matter who was playing. Those fortunate, now smug, ones had already made plans, booked a hotel and probably paid for their trips in full. For everyone else, it was a frenzy. Spare places on club and pub trips were snapped up and organisers tried desperately to get more tickets, coaches and rooms.

No one knows for sure how many went. Estimates vary widely. Taking account of all forms of transport, including British Rail and National Express scheduled services, it is impossible to accurately measure the number of people from Hull that attended the game or travelled to the capital.

With both clubs allocated around 44,000 between them, it was already likely that the Hull contingent would exceed 50,000 and that's before any enterprising individuals found tickets via other channels. What's more, most weekend trips had plenty of people aboard who weren't going to the game. Wives, sisters, daughters and Hull City supporters mainly. On that basis, over 60,000, a quarter of the city's population, seems reasonable, creating a unique exodus. How would this migration, this evacuation, take place?

Many let the train take the strain. Within days, BR said they would be running an unspecified number of special services. Early on Good Friday, two ticketing offices were set up in Paragon Station, one for each set of supporters. At that stage, BR were not able to state departure times or even the destination station, still in talks with the Metropolitan Police over how best to manage the influx. A week later came news that twelve 'specials' would operate on Saturday morning, four for Hull KR supporters and eight for Hull FC fans. The trains would leave Paragon Station at roughly fifteen-minute intervals between 6.24am and 8.34am. BR had gone to great lengths to ensure fans would not come into contact with each other. Hull fans, oddly, were given blue and white tickets while Rovers' were green and white, £12 each, very much a no frills ride; no refreshments and no transfers – you had to return on the same train that had taken you south. Various stations were used, since Kings Cross would not be able to cope with the extra numbers.

The twelve Saturday specials had capacity for 5,530 seats. There were three further services on Friday, plus eight charter trains – the usual number that operated from Hull to London on Challenge Cup final day – as well as high levels of demand for the normal scheduled services to London any time from Thursday. Over 10,000 probably went by train.

National Express soon got in on the act. The week after Hull's semi-final victory, the state-run coach and short-break company were advertising Wembley Weekend Specials. For £57.50 per person, supporters had a two-day trip, staying bed and breakfast at the Luton Crest hotel, including a £7 match ticket. At the same time, scores of coach operators were offering day-trips from £8.50 per person (ticket not included).

Car ownership was still relatively low and hundreds chose to make their way south in a hired car. Ten transporters brought in extra hire cars to meet the demand.

The supporters weren't the only ones trying to finalise

plans. Bunting and Millward still had a league programme to fulfil, so each wanted to settle their Wembley arrangements as soon as possible.

Hull's choice of hotel wasn't actually their own. Widnes had stayed for years at the Royal Chace Hotel in Enfield, twenty miles north east of Wembley, via the North Circular. Upon reaching the semi-final, they had booked themselves in there again in the event that they should need it. "It's just what clubs did," explained Hull assistant coach Ken Foulkes. "It was portrayed as them being arrogant but it wasn't."

Once Widnes were beaten, they handed the booking over to Hull FC whose players, by 1980, were accustomed to staying in hotels before games so the four-star splendour did not faze them. The location also had the advantage of being a few minutes down the road from Botany Bay Cricket Club, where Hull planned to set up their training base.

In mid-April, with a few days free, Peter Darley and Arthur Bunting took a trip to check on their Wembley HQ and training facilities. "Ideal," proclaimed Bunting. Rovers had also chosen their base. Following in the footsteps of Saints and Wakefield, who'd stayed in 1978 and 1979, Rovers chose the Runnymede Hotel in Egham, Surrey. It hadn't been a lucky choice for the other two clubs, both lost, but Rovers pulled off a coup with their training ground. With the help of Les Horton – a guardsman who lived in Windsor, but hailed originally from Castleford – they secured the use of Windsor RUFC's ground.

***

WITH THE IMPORTANT plans sorted out, both coaches could concentrate on more pressing matters. It was the end of March and the final was five weeks away. Five weeks to prepare for the biggest game that most of the players, coaches and officials would ever be involved in. Five weeks to keep the playing squad fit, fresh, healthy and composed enough to stand a chance of succeeding on May 3rd. Five weeks to complete their respective league campaigns and to make a cursory effort at the Premiership play-off competition.

With the league programme due to finish on Sunday 20th April, that meant each team had just over a fortnight to play their last five league fixtures which were scheduled thus:

Hull FC

Friday 4th April ....Hull KR (A)
Monday 7th April...York (H)
Friday 11th April ....Salford (A)
Tuesday 15th April ....York (A)
Sunday 20th April ....Workington (A)

Hull KR

Friday 4th April ....Hull FC (H)
Wednesday 9th April ....Widnes (A)
Sunday 13th April ....Hunslet (A)
Wednesday 16th ....Wigan (A)
Sunday 20th ....St Helens (H)

Once those games were completed, the top eight Premiership would begin. First against eighth, second v seventh, third v sixth, fourth v fifth, played the weekend before Wembley. At Easter, Hull were fourth, Rovers seventh. Nobody wanted another derby the week before the Challenge Cup final.

Week One

Once the achievement of reaching Wembley sank in, to some it didn't seem like such a good idea after all. Not everyone was delighted that it would be Hull against Rovers.

"We were pleased we'd got to Wembley but when Hull did the same, it took the gloss off a little bit," confessed Carol Millward. "There was a bit of disappointment. We thought there'd be trouble and it would spoil the whole day."

For John Millington, Hull's presence just added to the nerves. "I watched Hull's semi-final on telly. When they won I thought: 'Oh, no.' I was going to be nervous enough as it was, this was going to make it ten times worse. I was terrible before derbies, couldn't sleep all week."

Colin Hutton was in no doubt however: "We wanted Hull to get to the Cup final because Widnes were so good!"

With the tension building, the last thing either side needed was to face each other again but, six days after that Hull semi, the Good Friday derby was scheduled for Craven Park. Memories of recent clashes and apprehension about Wembley meant heightened fears of hooliganism.

Rovers secretary Ron Turner laid it on the line: "There will be no bars open and anyone bringing bottles or cans will be refused admission. Any fans arrested or ejected from the ground by police will be barred from both Craven Park and the Boulevard in future."

Tensions in fact were high across the country. The Tory budget had set entire communities against the Government. As the decade began, it do so on a rising tide of frustration and rage. This was the era of *Boys from the Blackstuff* on the box and 'Ghost Town' and 'One in Ten' on the juke box. Bristol was set ablaze and copycat riots sprung up elsewhere. In Hull, 800 lost their jobs in March alone.

As for the city's latest league derby, the formbook favoured Hull. Rovers hadn't beaten FC for more than three years and Bunting hadn't been beaten in his first six meetings with the old enemy. It got worse for Rovers when Lockwood was hospitalised with stomach pains and Casey suspended.

Hull, though, had been given good news. On Tuesday, Paul Woods saw his nine-match suspension reduced to seven on appeal. He could now play at Wembley. They also found a replacement for the injured Newlove. "I was on holiday in Majorca when I got a telex at the hotel," says Brian Hancock. "It asked when I was due home because they wanted me for the Good Friday derby. Luckily the holiday was nearly over. I got back in the early hours, went to bed for a bit then went to Craven Park."

Later that morning, Paragon station was awash with Hull and Rovers supporters signing up for Wembley special trains. The segregation unravelled before it began as large families turned up wearing both black and white *and* red and white, asking which train they should book for. For the first time, there was a bright atmosphere and optimism that the event may not be the bloodbath some feared.

By mid-afternoon, nearly 15,000 were off to Craven Park, the second largest league attendance of the season, after the reverse derby in October, and the biggest crowd at Craven Park since the 1930s. Despite the hype and excitement, both sides were a shadow of the teams expected to line up in four weeks' time. Rovers lacked Millward, Agar, Lockwood and Casey, while Phil Lowe was benched. Hull were bereft of half their first team with Woods, Walters, Prendiville, Pickerill, Tindall, Birdsall and Lloyd all sitting it out.

Some Hull fans were in the ground early but, with the stadium bars closed, many decided to stay in the pubs until the last possible moment. As the latecomers surged into the Holderness Road end, some spilled over onto the Greyhound track just before the teams came out. There was no chance of police or stewards forcing them back so hundreds took up their positions to watch pitchside, along the hare rail.

Wherever they sat, they witnessed a cracker. An end-to-end thriller that left John Sexton drooling for a Wembley repeat, as that would: "...provide one of the great finals."

In a relentless first half in 70-degree heat, Rovers, in blue jerseys for reasons unknown, raced into a 12-2 lead, thanks to tries from Hartley and Smith. Hull, steered around the field by the veteran Hepworth, hit back just before half-time. Heppy's try, created by a lively Tim Wilby, pulled Hull back into it, 12-9, against a backdrop of increasing tension on and off the pitch. However, it was the introduction of Lowe that swung it Rovers' way. Within a minute, he scored and later in the game helped set up Watson for the decisive try. But the game ended on a worrying note.

As Mick Crane crossed late on for Rovers, a group of home fans ran on in celebration. Several dozen Hull fans followed them, scuffles broke out and the game was halted as police cleared the field. Trouble continued as supporters spilled on to Holderness Road, with missiles thrown and arrests for fighting and urinating in the street. BBC and ITV crews had been inside the ground interviewing supporters all afternoon, though chose not to capitalise on the scenes, so repercussions were limited. The greatest concern seemed to be £1,500-worth of damage to the hare rail, which led to the cancellation of Saturday's greyhound meeting and one of the *Hull Daily Mail*'s greatest ever headlines: "INVASION PUTS DOG MEET OFF".

As for the result, Arthur Bunting thought it no guide to Wembley, though Roger Millward suggested the open game they'd employed had been far more effective than the 'down the middle' approach of the Floodlit Trophy final. Also over the Easter Weekend, the weekly newspaper *Hull Times* hit the streets, its Cup final coverage focussed on the activities of a little-known psychic, Peter Shilling. The man of mystery boasted on its front page that he could predict the winning team, the correct score, the number of tries and man of the match. He would write down all four predictions, seal them in a wine bottle, padlock it inside a box and place it in the safe of Mac Stone, Hull City's secretary, who was "entirely neutral" having no interest in rugby league at all.

Over the coming weeks, readers were reminded of Shilling's bold predictions. But, on April 18th, doubt crept in. Referring to injures to Lockwood and Lowe, he said: "They are both key players and that could cause problems with my prediction. It didn't stop him adding to the list. "It should be a fast open game" he said and claimed there would be controversy: "Perhaps a disallowed try or injury."

***

EVEN BEFORE THE semi-finals, the RL announced that the Wembley guest of honour awould be the Queen Mother. It was a coup for David Oxley, Hull-born ex-public school-master. Each year, with aristocratic rugby league president Edward Stanley, the 18th Earl of Derby, he sought to persuade a member of the Royal Family to attend.

The Stanley family were steeped in sport. In 1780, they established the Epsom Derby and, generations later, another Earl donated a trophy for a Canadian ice hockey competition that became the Stanley Cup. The current Earl resided at Knowsley Park, where he set up a safari park in 1971. The northern roots of the family chimed with rugby league history.

"The Earl was a terrific supporter of the game, a real fan," said Oxley. "He was also rather close to royalty and, in my time at the RL, he helped us to invite Princess Alexandra, Princess Anne and Prince Philip twice. But persuading the Queen Mother to attend was something very special and she charmed everyone."

Last One Out...

Week Two

Easter Monday: Hull v York. It's a celebration, Hull's only home league game between the semi and final. Into the team came Robinson, Hancock, Crowther and Coupland. Nearly 12,000 turning up to watch. York, promoted the previous season, were put to the slaughter, 40-0. Tindall went half the length of the field for a try, then even further for his second. Merchandise was on sale, the place buzzing. 'Dance Yourself Dizzy' was Number One.

Wednesday night and Rovers were at Widnes. With seven wins in eight and scoring points for fun, there was still an outside chance of a top-four place and a home game in the play-offs. Instead, Hall, Hartley, Agar, Holdstock, Lockwood, Rose and Casey were all given the night off and it was all over in the first twenty minutes as Widnes surged to a 13-0 lead. A watching Millward realised his mistake and vowed not to make it again. But Hogan, Crane and particularly Watkinson impressed, the hooker dominant in the scrum opposite Great Britain hooker Keith Elwell. The number nine shirt was his to lose. In Hull's Market Place, it was the end of an era. Bob Carver's outside chippy closed down and moved to an indoor restaurant just yards away in Trinity House Lane.

After the game, the Rovers squad headed back to Yorkshire. But not Roger, or Ron Turner. They stayed in a hotel in Widnes and then, next morning, went to London to check out the facilities at the Runnymede Hotel.

Arthur Bunting was also at Widnes, keeping an eye on Rovers. He drove on to Mottram Hall, doubtless feeling confident. Next day, his players joined him in Cheshire to prepare for Friday night's trip to Salford. A win would clinch third, making a play-off against Rovers all the more likely.

Barring injuries to Newlove and Prendiville and the suspension of Woods, it was as strong a team as Bunting could name and it had to be. Although Salford were past their mid '70s peak, they were tough to beat, especially at home.

The preparations seemed – at first – to have gone well. A rare try from Stone gave Hull a 3-2 lead which they held until the 60th minute. Then Whitfield scored for Salford and Hull collapsed. Losing 15-3 was a hammering in 1980 and the defeat gave Bunting worries. Third place was still unsecured.

***

IT HAD BEEN a busy week. Boulevard and Craven Park bustled every day, around the clock. The players, still training and holding down jobs, tried to get their own plans in order and those of their families. It worked out perfectly for Roy Holdstock though. "I'd booked to go with my parents," he said, "but when we got to the final I gave my tickets to Dave Hall's parents, so they all went together and stayed at the British Legion."

"I'd booked a trip from the Royal on Newbridge Road," remembers John Millington. "I'd gone with Steve Hartley and his dad the year before and we were going to go again. So once we got through, I gave the tickets to my mam and dad, and Steve did the same."

It was every player's dream, but a bit of a problem for Graham Bray and Clive Pickerill. May 3rd was also Bray's sister's wedding day. "At the start of the season, my sister told me she was getting married," he said. "I told her not to pick the first weekend in May because I thought we'd get to Wembley. So what does she do? I remember scoring the try in the semi-final and thinking I wouldn't be able to go." Their parents, meanwhile, missed out on the trip south. Pickerill's problem was worse. May 3rd was *his* wedding day.

For Pickerill and his fiancée, Jean, rescheduling was

needed. "Thankfully, we managed to change the date and we ended up getting married a few months later."

When it came to merchandise, both clubs were quick off the mark. As early as Easter Monday, Hull FC had a new range available. The Portakabin at the Boulevard served Hull well for years, knocking out everything from replica shirts (£7.50 for a 24ins up to £12.50 for 48ins – the largest shirt available), sweatshirts (£7.50) printed with: 'The Airlie Birds', 'Hull FC Are Magic', '26 out of 26'. Cheaper options were satin scarves (£1.10), bobble hats (£1.25), car stickers (20p), key fobs (40p), sweatbands (75p) and player photos (40p each). Taking advantage of the boost in demand, the club also announced it would be extending the opening hours of the souvenir shop beyond matchdays, on Saturdays 10.00am to 12.30pm and every night until 9.30pm in Wembley week.

Runnercare, Allsports, Intersport and Arco were also in on the act. As were the twin sports shops owned by Sammy Lloyd and Clive Sullivan. Lloyd recalls how they cashed in. "Clive and I were one of the first out of the blocks with our version of Wembley jumpers. There was a club version but in those days it was about who could be first to market. We did our research in terms of finding the best quality, price and delivery. The club ones had the official club logo on, that only they could produce, sold from the supporters' shop. We put the Wembley logo on ours and sold a ton." At £11.95 a throw, it was good business.

Other Rovers players took notice. "We got hold of some blue jumpers and put a badge on it," John Millington explains. "They were really nice – we wore them ourselves on our walkabout at Wembley. They sold like hot cakes. We had all sorts of things going on, it was like a testimonial season." And as the two clubs made money hand over fist, the players demanded their fair share.

"We were on £1,000 to win," remembers Agar.

"We were on £1,300, if we won," recalls Casey.

"I think we got £1,450," is how Holdstock remembers it. "£450 of it was taxed, the rest tax free."

"Hull were on the same as us," says Agar. "I'm sure the directors would have got together to discuss it. It wouldn't have been a coincidence."

As well as the win bonuses and sidelines in souvenir jumpers, there were plenty of other money-spinners. David Howes again: "We organised a roadshow, a brochure and plenty of events where you could raise extra money to put into the players' pool. The Rugby League were involved but it was really up to the clubs themselves to maximise profit."

For some, though, the money didn't come into it. Keith Boxall, who played in John Player Trophy and Floodlit Trophy finals for Hull FC, said: "You knew you were on a bonus, but it was the sort of thing you'd remember when you were in the bath after the game, getting drunk. Someone would say: 'Eh, we got five hundred for today'. The money was nice, but none of the lads played for the money."

Dave Watkinson agrees it was the same in the Rovers camp. "Some players thought they were motivated by money, but I don't think many players could have given any more no matter what they earned. Whenever I played for Rovers, I always knew I couldn't have put much more in."

Clubs often found themselves in dispute with players over win bonuses but, it would seem, not so in 1980. "I never wanted to argue about money," insists Steve Norton. "You have to agree it ages before the game. You can't be arguing about money just before you're going to play Rovers."

As the bandwagon rolled into gear, the demands on the players grew and grew. Take the Wembley suits. "That was hilarious," says Steve Hubbard. "I think it was Southwells

the Tailors who came down to Craven Park to measure the
lads up but, as you can imagine, there was a good deal of
mickey-taking so they weren't very accurate measurements
at all. A week later, when we turned up for training, our gear
was hanging up on our pegs. It didn't take long for the lads
to realise that some of the stuff didn't fit them very well, so
those that had got there first started rifling through everyone
else's gear, looking for stuff that would actually fit them. By
the time I got there, I had Allan Agar's trousers and Phil
Lowe's jacket. It was a right laugh sorting it all out."

"Every time we turned up for training, there was some
new gear," said Roy Holdstock. "We loved these fluorescent
green training kits we got from Adidas. And Steve Hartley
was gutted when he had his nicked from his washing line.
One night we turned up for training and there was some
bloke with a cow! It belonged to a sponsor. We all had a photo
taken with it and, the next week, it had been chopped up and
we were given a load of steak! Roger got a leather rug."

Tim Wilby took his clothes seriously and revelled in the
hullabaloo. "There were all sorts of different outfits to try on,
sponsors to meet and lots of fans' events. I'd gone as a squad
member with Leeds in 1977, so had an understanding of what
goes on, but with the whole of Hull at fever pitch it was a
million times more special. Most of the lads didn't live in Hull
and, for five weeks, they hardly spent any time at home with
their families. It was all playing, meetings, travelling and
training. But I would not have traded it for anything."

***

ROVERS WERE BACK in action at Hunslet on Sunday and
Millward, stung by what had happened at Widnes, named
his strongest team for what turned out to be little more than

an extended training exercise. The Robins barely broke sweat as they hammered the hosts, 38-8.

Week Three

Hull won in similar style two nights later at York. With only the suspended Woods missing from his Wembley line-up, it was a satisfying night for Bunting. Hull's new-look three-quarter line up scored five tries between them and Lloyd knocked over seven goals as Hull won 35-14 to guarantee a top-four place. But there was anxiety for Keith Tindall. "I thought I'd broken my thumb. I knew I'd done something bad but daren't get an X-ray in case they said it was broken and put it in a pot. Our physio, John Stimpson, had a feel and then just strapped it up, so I carried on playing."

Wednesday saw Hull's £3.5m tidal barrier opened and confirmation that the Football Association had turned down a request from Hull City, struggling along at the bottom of Division Three and attracting crowds in the low four figures, to rearrange their game on May 3rd with Southend. The next day, Millward's midweek team travelled over to Wigan for the penultimate league game of the campaign. Millward said nothing to the press, but he didn't look too bothered about missing out on sixth and avoiding a play-off at the Boulevard.

In came Leighton, McHugh, Watson, Robinson, Harkin and Price while, even against a soon-to-be-relegated side, Rovers were lacklustre and lost 21-13. It might have been different were it not for the talents of Wigan fullback George Fairbairn. John Sexton wrote it up as a "one-man-show" and within twelve months Rovers smashed the world transfer fee record to sign the Scotsman.

Sexton, tongue in cheek, reflected on Wigan's demise. "Wigan are doomed to spend next season in the Second Division of the rugby league," he wrote, "something that a few years ago would have seemed about as likely as Hull and Rovers meeting in two major finals in the same season."

April 20th was the final weekend of league fixtures and the day began with Hull – away to Workington – third, and Rovers, at home to St Helens, in seventh. A win could push them as high as sixth, while defeat could see them finish as low as ninth. A win for Hull would secure third place; defeat, and a win for Salford over Leigh, would push them to fourth. Whatever the permutation, they both wished to avoid the Premiership first-round game that nobody wanted.

Millward played the tinkerman once again. Hogan was switched to centre, his chance to win a place on the Wembley bench, and had a stormer. Crane and Millington impressed. Perfectly to plan, the game was all over by half-time, but though Millward had hoped to give Phil Lowe the second half off, an injury to Brian Lockwood meant he couldn't. Six minutes from time, Lowe's world came crashing down.

"Eric Chisnall it was," remembers Lowe. "A big, tough bastard. He caught me off the ball and I sprung my shoulder. It just popped out. I knew straight away ... that's dislocated. Out for six weeks, a fortnight before Wembley. I remember Eric saying: 'Sorry, Phil. That's you out.' But that was never going to happen. I would have played at Wembley with no arms." And in the second half, by taking their foot off the gas, Rovers missed the chance to add to their points difference. At the final hooter, they finished on 33, a difference of +94.

Bunting had no interest in fighting for the two points in Cumbria and left most of his Wembley squad behind. In came Robinson, Dennison, Hancock, Hepworth, Clawson, Crowther, Boxall, Lazenby, Peacham and Coupland. Only Prendiville and Newlove were in the likely starting 13 at Wembley. Town won easily and the few hundred disgruntled Hull fans who travelled let the players know about it.

***

HULL AND ROVERS went straight to their dressing rooms to switch on the radio. The first reports were that Leigh had won. That meant Hull finished third: Rovers and Leigh on 33 points in joint-sixth. "What was the score?" everyone shouted. "14-10 to Leigh," which meant a +92 points difference. Rovers on +94 were sixth and would meet Hull after all.

"No, hang on, it's not finished yet," said someone else, "they're still playing." Come on Leigh! And Leigh duly did score again, winning 19-10 to end the season on 33 with a +97 points difference, which pushed Rovers down into seventh by the narrowest of margins. Hull would host Leigh, Rovers were off to Widnes. The waves of relief were palpable from Derwent to Craven Park.

Week Four

With a fortnight to go, the RFL announced that there were no tickets left: 95,000 would be at the game on May 3rd, only the fourth Challenge Cup final to sell-out. And in record time.

The governing body also confirmed that both clubs would play in their traditional kits. In 1959, Hull FC wore a black 'V' when playing Wakefield, the following year they were in black and white hoops against Wigan, but wore black shorts. Four years later, Hull KR made their bow at Wembley in plain red shirts. And so, for the first time, Hull would enter Wembley wearing their famous black and white irregular hoops and white shorts, while Rovers wore their broad red band. Since both sides had lost all of those previous visits it was seen as a lucky omen, although presumably one that kind of cancelled the other club's out.

The Rugby League hadn't yet made up their minds,

though, about whether 'Old Faithful' and 'Red Red Robin' should be part of the community singing, for fear that each would lead to a negative reaction from opposing fans. Quite what else they expected to happen was not made clear.

In Hull, meanwhile, a special Challenge Cup final record was produced. A Hull trio, John Cambridge, Terry Halliwell and Denny McInerny recorded a double A-side single: 'Hull For Me' and 'Oh Rovers'. The disc went on sale across the city; Syd Scarborough's, Bolders Record Bar, Regis, Tempo and Marshalls.The trio hoped to sell 4,000 and already had advanced orders for 90! The final was all anyone in Hull was talking about, a World Cup, Olympics, Royal Wedding and Coronation rolled into one. There was no avoiding it.

One city centre pub, the Sandringham, segregated the bar. Red and white and black and white nooses hung from the ceiling, indicating at which end the supporters should sit.

A restaurant segregated their menu, offering a Red and White Lunch (tomato soup with cream for starters, followed by salami and tomato in a white bread sandwich, finishing with strawberry delight). Or, how about a Black and White Lunch (potato and mushroom soup followed by chicken and cheese sandwich on black bread. And ice cream for dessert)?

For years, Hull FC fan, Ron Goldspink, had driven the number 56 bus from Hull city centre to Longhill estate, deep in the heart of Hull KR territory. One morning, he decided to stick a Hull FC flag to his fare box and began to entertain passengers with verses of 'Old Faithful', prompting a return chorus of 'Red Red Robin'. All good fun until one passenger complained and Ron was told to take down the offending flag and shut up.

On May 3rd, countless supporters were head to toe in their team colours. Some had Herschel Harris to thank for it. "A couple of lads came in off the street and asked if they could have their hair done black and white," explained the hairdresser. Harris saw the potential and began offering hair colouring for a tenner, which included a promise to return it back to its normal shades after the game. But when Robin Red Breast won its debut race at Edinburgh at odds of 11/4, Rovers fan and bookie Len Beecroft took a hit. "I've never taken so much money on a horse without form," he said. "A lot of Rovers fans made their Wembley expenses out of me."

And everywhere, there were stories of supporters going to ever increasing ways to show their devotion. At Wembley, there would be Hull and Rovers supporters flying in from around the world, from Saudi Arabia to Australia.

One man though would not be there. A fortnight before he was due to represent the City of Hull at Wembley, Maurice Rawlings, the 57-year-old Lord Mayor, died suddenly. His deputy, Alex Clarke, would take his place.

***

BOTH SIDES TRAINED on Tuesday night. John Sexton, looking for clues, pressed Millward on the team he planned to take to Widnes for the play-off encounter. It was a fixture the tetchy player-coach didn't want. "It is impossible to even consider naming a team, we have so many injuries," he said, a smokescreen to conceal his only real concern, Phil Lowe.

Bunting, on the other hand, had a full squad to pick from. It was amazing how the injury list had cleared up. As Charlie Birdsall explains: "After training, you'd always have a few lads with sore knees limping off. But in the weeks before Wembley, you'd see lads with a knock jump straight back up like there was nothing wrong with them."

Bunting was probably more concerned with building momentum. His side having played twice a week for the past two months, he had become expert in squad rotation, but three of their last five games had been lost. For the visit of Leigh, Bunting named what most considered his strongest possible team, including Paul Woods in his first appearance since suspension. The only doubt now surrounded Graham Walters. Sent off in the semi, he was up before the disciplinary committee on Thursday, a nervous wait, but he got the news he wanted: 'Sending off sufficient'. Meanwhile, just four days after dislocating his shoulder, Hull KR announced that Phil Lowe had returned to training and the prospects for him appearing at Wembley were said to look much brighter.

Newspaper coverage of the Wembley build-up was sporadic, at best. The printing unions and publishers were in dispute and there were frequent breakdowns at *The Sun* and *Daily Mirror*. It looked like the unrest might spread to regional newspapers next. One week before the big day, though, on Saturday 27th April, the players and coaches of both clubs had more pressing matters to think about.

Rovers began with a 10am appearance at Nationwide Building Society in the Prospect Centre, before moving on to Binns in the afternoon. Steve Hubbard remembers it well. "They set us up behind lots of desks and the fans lined up for photos and autographs. Hundreds turned up and we were signing anything put in front of us ... programmes, shirts, books. We even signed women's knickers, breasts – you name it. Right in the middle of Binns!"

Hull FC started at WH Smith before heading off to Boothferry Park for Hull City's game with Brentford. Hull's players were introduced to the crowd before kick-off, but it was not an especially warm welcome. Bunting had asked FC fans to turn up and support the Tigers but there were few black and white scarves or shirts to be seen, leaving a bitter taste with some City fans

Gary Clark's account of the afternoon in his book *From Boothferry to Wembley* captures the mood:

> It was before the 1980 Challenge Cup final when they chose to humiliate us, in a game against Brentford. Hull were invited as part of a Wembley send-off. I was there and remember a couple of hundred scruffs turning up, all dressed in an assortment of hand-knitted black and white garb. They gathered together in the vast emptiness of the North Stand (still there in those days) and supported the other team. City won 2-1 and the crowd was a little over 3,000.
>
> Of course, several bouts of fisticuffs broke out, mainly from the City fans who objected to this little troop of misfits chanting for a team none of them probably knew anything about. It was an important match for City too because we were in danger of relegation; our eventual saviour being Keith Edwards, who scored in this game and the famous 1-0 win over Southend a week later on 3 May 1980, the day that 'all of Hull' – except the 3,700 who turned up at Boothferry Park – went 'Down that London'.

On the same day, the *Hull Daily Mail* announced the winner of their Best Wembley Caption competition, the prize being two tickets for the final:

> Forget about winning the cup, Rovers;
> Forget the base and the lid;
> You'll have more chance while you're down South,
> Of catching 'Hissing Sid'!

The winner? Hull FC fan and jovial bus driver Ron Goldspink, getting his name in the paper once again.

***

SO WHAT DO you do in the last game before the cup final? Name a full-strength team? Have a go at the Premiership and get some momentum into the side? Or do you rest them all and send in the kids?

Millward, cautious, had no hesitation in sending his 'A' team to Widnes. He even gave a debut to the guest player, Tim Anchors, an American grid-iron player from Kansas City. Considering their opponents finished second, Rovers bunch of young guns and journeymen put up a spirited display in a 20-10 defeat. Several of Rovers' first team also made the trip and Steve Hubbard remembered the match with a tinge of regret. "I was stood on the terraces with Phil Lowe, Paul Rose and Len Casey, thinking we should have been out there."

In contrast, Bunting named a full-strength team to face Leigh. Another huge crowd of over 13,000 turned up to see the final home game of the season and every last one would have been shocked to see Paul Woods, in his first game back, throwing himself into every tackle, destined to either get sent off or carried off. Hull went behind and never recovered, losing 8-0. Hundreds of supporters waited around at the end to see the players leave the ground. For many, it was the last chance to see their heroes before Wembley. Bunting, surprised to see so many as he left the dressing room, was asked if there were any injuries. "I don't think so, no."

I headed home and listened to the charts on Radio 1, Dexys' 'Geno' knocking Blondie's 'Call Me' off number one. The next week, at school, everybody seemed to be going, the excitement almost too much to bear. Even on *Sportsnight*, as I reached out of bed to switch off my little black and white portable, presenter Harry Carpenter warned us not to forget: "...the rugby league cup final on Saturday, between those two marvellous teams from Hull." Who could sleep after that?

Last One Out,
Turn the Lights Off

13

YORKSHIRE WERE PLAYING Lancashire at Old Trafford in the mid-1950s, whereupon a gentleman from the south joined the spectators. When one of the Lancastrian batsmen struck a boundary, the southerner remarked "Well played, sir," and a Yorkshireman turned around. "Mind thee own business," he said. "It's got nowt to do wi' thee."

***

"SOME THOUGHT WE would struggle to sell tickets outside Hull," said David Oxley, "but that wasn't the case at all. Fans from other clubs saw it was going to be a moment in history and wanted to say: 'I was there'. From day one, the demand was phenomenal and it became the fastest selling final ever."

And although a good number of Hull rugby supporters had experienced a Wembley weekend before, most had not. They were going to make the most of it.

On Sunday night, Arthur Bunting and staff confirmed

that the Leigh game had not caused any injuries. The squad was battered and bruised, but fully fit. Roger Millward's only concern, having sent his reserves to Widnes, was Phil Lowe. The shoulder dislocated at St Helens was nowhere near fully recovered and wouldn't be until June. But ... Wembley. "Phil is doing well," said his coach. "We're confident he'll make it."

As Hull prepared to descend on London, London came to Hull. As did dishy Des Lynam from the BBC. Ros Sullivan was at home on Monday morning when the phone rang. "It was someone asking if they could come around our house to do an interview for *Sportsnight*. I didn't know what to do. The day they came, I'd been working, packing cucumbers with Lynn Casey. And I had to rush home, get the kids out of their school uniform and tidy up. I'd hung my washing out in the morning and they said: 'We'll interview you while you're bringing the washing in'! And they wanted Anthony and Lisa in the background, playing rugby. So there's me on national TV bringing my washing in while Lisa's playing rugby in her best dress! I kept thinking how embarrassing it was and what people would think when they saw this on telly. Des Lynam was really, really nice, but we had to give him extra cushions to sit on because he thought he would look too small in his chair. It was all quite surreal."

Lynam then left the Sullivan's in Hessle and went east. "He turned up at BP in Saltend," remembers Mike Smith. "He did an interview with me and Keith Tindall as we worked there together. Everyone thought it was great to have the BBC turn up at work."

Later, he called in on Rovers' training ground, a playing field behind the Alderman Colgan school in East Hull. "He arrived with a couple of young women, one carrying a video camera, the other must have been a producer. He looked real funny, trotting across the playing field in his long mackintosh and little moustache," recalls Dave Hall. "He was pleasant enough, 'How are you, chaps?' that kind of thing, but I think most of our lads were more interested in the lasses."

"Cameras were camped in Hull for weeks," says Steve Hartley. "They seemed to be at every training session, but weren't just here to see the players. They wanted to see what made the people tick, in the pubs and so on." It had captured imaginations outside the city and outside rugby league.

Tuesday was the last day at work for most players and, in the evening, both squads trained for the last time. At the Boulevard, it was a nervy session. A tonsillitis outbreak had struck and seven players were struggling. Worst afflicted was 'Knocker'. "Norton has almost completely lost his voice," said Bunting. "It is better that he stays at home and rests."

At the end of the session, the Hull coach named his Wembley team, with just the one change from Leigh: Stone was fit, so Farrar dropped to the bench, meaning 'Knocker' would lead them out on Saturday, a decision Farrar had no problem with. "I've no moans at all," he told the *Daily Mirror*. "I'm fortunate to be in the fifteen."

"I was never captain material, Vince was our captain," is how Norton saw it, but the choice was made. If all went to plan, Steve Norton would be the first ever Hull FC captain to lift the Challenge Cup at Wembley. Some might call it fitting. Norton was the man.

At scrum-half, Bunting had a choice. Throughout the season his first pick had been Clive Pickerill, but the veteran Keith Hepworth had deputised brilliantly and had his merits, even aged 38. Who would cope best with the pressure, the atmosphere? In the event, Bunting chose Pickerill. "To be honest, I was confident I would play," the player remembers, "but it was nice to hear it confirmed." If Heppy had been selected he wouldn't have minded. "I'd known him all my life. My dad coached him when he was in the Cas under-17s and he used to babysit me when I was a kid." But the decision wasn't entirely clear cut.

"We were all a bit surprised that he didn't pick Heppy," said Charlie Birdsall. "Forget his age, he was naturally fit. He never trained. He never used to train at Cas either. You never knew what he was going to do, off the pitch or on it."

After training, both sets of players headed to Tiffany's nightclub for the *Wembley Special Rugby League Roadshow*. The place was packed with ex-players, rugby league celebs and supporters. And, of course, thirty men who would be playing at Wembley on Saturday. Players and supporters mingled freely although the squads kept a respectable distance. Except Paul Woods.

"Woods came up to me at one point," says Allan Agar. "'How much you on, Allan? Go on, tell me.' I was sure the directors would have got their heads together and that both sets of players would be on the same money. We were on a thousand pounds each to win but I couldn't resist it so I told Woodsy we were on two grand. He went mad, effing and blinding all the way back to the Hull lads to tell them. It was hilarious."

The coaches took to the stage. Howes, as always, asked the questions and Millward said little, playing it down. But Bunting was buoyant. Bombastic. And he upset some of the Rovers players, as Millington didn't forget. "Arthur Bunting picked up the Cup and told the Hull fans that if they didn't bring it home, he would jump off the Humber Bridge. That was a bit over the top and, after the game at Wembley, I bumped into him as we came out of the stadium. Well, I had to remind him of what he'd said, didn't I?"

Wednesday was miserable, grey and damp as the two squads gathered at Craven Park and the Boulevard in the morning. Several hundred fans turned out and the mood was upbeat and slightly surreal. Cases were loaded, jokes were cracked and the supporters, unsure what to do now they had turned up to watch some people get on a bus and drive away, responded with 'Old Faithful' and 'Red Red Robin'.

Hull Daily Mail reporters Dick Tingle and John Sexton were each on board the respective buses as they pulled out at 9.30am, both apprehensive. A strike by compositors meant the paper hadn't been published all week and there wasn't a lot of point them going to Wembley if nobody read about it.

"John and I were on good terms with the compositors," said Tingle. "We knew there was going to be a strike and we were worried that the editor would tell us to stay in Hull until Saturday. But we wanted to be in London with the teams. We weren't going to miss that for the world, so I turned up at the Boulevard, bags packed, dreading that the *Mail* would ring and tell us to wait. I told Cyril Fowler, the Hull FC Secretary, that if anybody rang he should say the bus had already set off. That way, I would be out of contact for about five hours and – once I was in London – there'd be no point coming back. I don't know if they rang Cyril or not but there was no way that I was going to miss out on the trip of a lifetime!"

Despite the enormity of the occasion, Tingle and Sexton were the only *Hull Daily Mail* reporters there, but that had nothing to do with strikes. "There wasn't as much coverage of sport in those days," says Tingle. "A couple of photographers went down on Friday and that was it. Jack Fluk, the sports editor, would never have allowed the newsdesk to interfere. Besides, it wasn't like the *Mail* needed to chase more readers. The paper was at its peak. They sold over 100,000 copies every day, plus another 30-40,000 *Sports Mails* on a Saturday."

***

THE RUNNYMEDE-ON-THAMES HOTEL and spa is one of
Surrey's most upmarket destinations. Sunday lunch: £18.95.
You get the idea.

Back in 1980, plain old Runnymede Hotel was a little
more homely. It didn't call itself "iconic" and fewer jets flew
overhead, but it was still lavish enough to turn the heads of
the many league teams that made it their Wembley base.

While club officials checked in, the players drifted
around the lobby or wandered onto the terrace overlooking
the river, before heading to their rooms to drop off their cases.
The room-share went: Hall with Holdstock, Hubbard with
Ian Robinson. Along the corridor, Millo with Hartley, Sully
with Casey, Locky with Watky, Agar with Watson, Harkin
with Price, Smith with Leighton, Lowe with Rose and Hogan
with Crane. Roger and assistant John Moore roomed alone.

"The club paid for the rooms and all our food, but if we
wanted anything extra we'd to sign for it ourselves," said Roy
Holdstock. "Some lads had never heard of that arrangement
so there was fun and games at the end of the weekend."

The Royal Chace may not have the same eye-catching
location as the Runnymede, but it didn't lack for splendour
or character. By 2pm, the Hull FC players were also exploring
their capital surroundings. Tim Wilby shared with Graham
Walters. "We were centre partners, but mainly it was because
he was as particular about his hygiene as me," said Wilby.

"I always roomed with 'Knocker'," said Sammy Lloyd.
"Foolishly, Arthur thought I had some sort of influence on
him and that I'd make sure we'd be where we should be, on
time and sober. I didn't always fulfil my duties, I'll tell you."

Elsewhere, Farrar and Pickerill shared, as did Stone and
Newlove. "The 'Featherstones' roomed together when they
could," Lloyd goes on. "to guard each other's wallet." Then
it was Tindall with Boxall, Bray with Evans, Woods with

Prendiville, Wileman with Birdsall. At least that's how Tim Wilby remembers it. "No," says Birdsall. "I shared with Woodsy. I knew him from Rochdale, but basically nobody else was brave enough. It was a long time ago, memories fade." "I recall that we all had our own room," says Clive Pickerill.

Back on the bus, Rovers headed up the road to Windsor RUFC. Despite its impressive location, in the shadow of Windsor Castle and across the river from Eton, it is little more than a public park. Nevertheless, it was hallowed rugby union turf and so permission had to be obtained from the RFU. It might have helped that the club chairman at the time was a down-to-earth Yorkshireman called Arthur Holding, who recounted how the move gained Royal approval. "I spoke to Prince Philip and told him we had to get permission from the RFU for the rugby league players. Philip said: 'I hope they granted it.' He was very pleased that they did."

But training did not start well for Rovers, recalls Allan Agar: "On that first afternoon, Roger flogged us and I told him that was a mistake. He hadn't played much so he might have needed it but we didn't; we were already fit. I had a word and he calmed down a bit after that."

Mike Smith put it down to Millward's nerves. "I think he felt that the more we trained, the better prepared we would be, but sometimes he would kill us in training, Roger."

"As soon as we got there, we trained," adds Dave Hall. "Then twice on Thursday, again on Friday before we went to Wembley," said Dave Hall. "There was no need."

For Phil Lowe, every session was agony. After the first, he was seen walking sullenly away, saying 'My shoulder is no good' and bemoaning his bad luck. Questioned by the media, he explained the pain was no more than a reaction to the long journey down, but no-one was fooled.

After their evening meal, the Rovers players went out

to a pub. In the corner of the bar, the TV news was reporting a siege at the Iranian embassy, but the players were waiting for *Sportsnight*; Alex Higgins in the snooker and Des Lynam's piece from Hull, with Ros Sullivan taking in her washing. The locals did a double-take when they saw Clive Sullivan on the box and stood alongside them at the bar.

***

AS THURSDAY DAWNED, the exodus from Hull began.

"Paragon station was like a refugee clearing centre," says Pete Allen, one of seventy-six patrons of the Halfway House on Hessle Road. "By eight o'clock, it was packed with fans, red and white, black and white, mostly mixed parties. Even the Halfway trip had fifteen Rovers supporters on it. There was plenty of banter and a great friendly atmosphere. A city on the move, history in the making."

British Rail had pulled in rolling stock from all over the country, some of it very old. "There were long trains of twelve and fourteen coaches at every platform. Our train was signed 'WEMBLEY Number 5' – nobody knew which station they were going to be arriving at. We left from the old excursion platform adjacent to Anlaby Road, which ironically had long ago been the point of departure for thousands of Eastern Europeans heading to Liverpool and then America."

And Allen was soon struck by what became a feature of the weekend; the homemade outfits, hats and banners-made-out-of-bedsheets. "All handmade, all original, people dressed head to toe in black and white or red and white, pushing British Rail porters' barrows piled high with crates of beer. On our way down Hessle Road, we even passed a couple of groups of supporters pushing supermarket trolleys towards the station."

Allen's group took up a couple of carriages. "The aisles were full of luggage, some had brought posh mock-crocodile-skin cases, others a pair of pyjamas, toothbrush and bottle of whisky in a plastic bag. In minutes, tables were swimming with beer and there was nothing left of the two trays of Hydes meat pies we'd brought. Everyone started card schools and by the time we got to Doncaster the toilets were out of order."

***

WITH SUPPORTERS ON their way, players began to surface for their first full day in the capital. The challenge for Bunting was to keep them occupied, so a programme of activities was scheduled, players and staff walking the short distance along the A1005 to Botany Bay CC in Enfield.

In stark contrast with Runnymede, Bunting and his squad were relaxed, going about their business with smiles on their faces. The coach told reporters he wanted his players to stay relaxed and enjoy the experience. It worked, for now.

In the afternoon, they travelled to Brent Sports Centre. There weren't many golfers in the Hull FC squad, but Tim Wilby managed to rustle up a couple of foursomes, getting his excuses in early, complaining about his clubs. The rest had a kickabout in the gym. Midway through a five-a-side game, Graham Evans received a pass, slipped, and knew it was bad. Medical help was summoned. He'd torn a muscle in his leg and had it put in plaster, his Wembley dream over. It soured the mood, but there was a wider responsibility to keep spirits up, so everyone got on with their work.

One of Bunting's training innovations had been to split his squad into smaller teams, playing on the competitiveness of his men. Each trained harder, no one wanted to let their team down. Wilby thought it added something extra. "It was mainly forwards versus the backs. Anyone who plays rugby is competitive, but mix some incentive in and West Riding humour and it was game on." Sessions could also give vent to built-up animosities and tensions though. "Many dressing room grudges were settled then. We had so many committed individuals it got dangerous; cuts, bruises, fisticuffs, players having to be prised apart. But by three o'clock on game day, you know the guys next to you would go through a brick wall rather than let the team or themselves down. What we did on the training ground was the best bonding ever."

Bunting might give a small prize to the winning team. On Thursday, Walters and Woods were peerless in training so Bunting, as a treat, promised them a bottle of wine with dinner. Immensely proud of themselves, they made their entrance ... a few minutes later than the allotted time ... only to find no wine. Woods, convinced someone had hidden it, didn't see the funny side. When Bunting revealed it had been withdrawn for arriving late, tempers did not improve. Nevertheless, they weren't late for dinner again.

***

ROVERS DELAYED NAMING their team, waiting on the fitness of Phil Lowe. Thursday morning was the moment of reckoning. If Lowe could get through another tough training session, he would be able to play.

"I could barely lift my arm up," he admitted, years later. "So I told Stuart Lunt, our doctor, to inject my shoulder with novocaine so I could get through it. At the end, I was stood talking to Roger when Stuart came up behind me and cracked me hard on the shoulder. It hurt but, because it was numb, I didn't flinch, so he said: 'You'll be okay'. That was my fitness test. I was relieved. I was 30 years old and there was no way I was going to miss the final. I'd have played with no arms if I had to. But we never told anyone how bad the injury was, we tried to keep it a secret."

The *Hull Daily Mail* reported that Lowe had passed a medical examination and was fit to play. Millward went even further: "Thankfully, Phil Lowe has fully recovered from his shoulder injury. He won't even need a pain-killing jab before the game," he told the *Daily Mirror*. But now he faced another dilemma: "There were times I found it harder to pick the subs than the team, because I had to think of every eventuality," he admitted later. "I'd sit at home and quietly write the team down but then think 'yes, but what if so and so gets injured, how would I cover that?' I'd pick the team in five minutes and then take another few hours deciding on the bench."

Millward stuck with the plan that had got them to Wembley and picked two forwards, Hogan and Millington.

Rovers spent most of Thursday on the training ground, taking a packed lunch. Late-afternoon, they took a trip to Windsor Castle before heading back to their digs. Some took to the pitch and putt course, others tried to beat Cliff Wallis at squash. After dinner, they watched videos of their opponents and counted the hours until game day.

***

HULL AND ROVERS supporters began to arrive in London. "The journey took almost five hours because the train was constantly being driven into sidings while the Scotland to London expresses thundered by," says Pete Allen. "We spent fifteen minutes at Hatfield because someone desperate for the toilet pulled the communications cord. But no-one seemed to care. Everyone was in party mood. I wore a white bib-and-brace boilersuit, a home-made cardboard, irregular-hooped, stove-pipe hat and topped it all off with black and white rosettes, badges and ribbons. Down the length of the train were scarves hung out of windows and posters sellotaped up with messages like 'Bank on Lloyd' and 'Woodsy's Goona Get Yeh!' It was easy to imagine a few mothers a bed sheet or two short. The atmosphere was amazing." Having got there it was time to check in and the Halfway House posse chose to stay at the five-star Kensington Hilton.

"We always stayed in a top hotel," Allen explains, "but never the same one twice, which was pretty wise when you saw what we got up to. The rooms were sumptuous and most of us liked the idea of a bidet. You didn't get many of them on Hessle Road and they were handy for keeping beer in."

Because it was a pub trip and because I had managed to sneak onto the trip late, I was the only kid travelling with the Cross Keys party that met up at Paragon Station on Friday morning, a mixed group in every respect. Male and female, Hull and Rovers, forty or fifty strong. I remember being transfixed by Pete Larney, a giant of a man and deaf as a post, watching him communicate through hand signals, lip reading and stunted words. He found a way to communicate with my dad better than anybody else and they became good friends. Pete was a Rovers fan and scary to me at the time.

Mostly the group were regular working class people who liked their rugby and beer, though Dave Whelan stood out. He spoke a bit differently and it was only later that I realised he must be the first middle-class person I'd met. Dave supported Hull, a regular drinker along Beverley Road.

As the only youngster, I needed a bit of entertainment and recall that someone had brought along a *Connect 4* game. An odd thing to take but I was delighted and, once I started playing, nobody could beat me. As the alcohol took effect on the adults, I came into my own and when we began playing for money I built up my own little fund for a weekend based at a very nice hotel somewhere in Mayfair (Dave Whelan's influence), from where the rest of Friday was spent seeing the sights of central London. Wherever we went, we came across rugby league fans and the group I was with seemed to know everyone. It all seemed like a very small world.

Bryan Leason and his fellow Rovers Supporters Club members also departed on Friday morning. "We went every year and would always set off early from Craven Park. In the early days, it was a long, long drive down to London and we would stop at Bawtry for something to eat. We had a rule that you couldn't open bottles or glasses until we'd got past there. Then, after we stopped calling in, the rule changed and you weren't allowed to drink until we got over North Bridge!"

Another Friday group was the Rovers team's wives and girlfriends. "We agreed to wear red and white," remembers Ros Sullivan. "Somebody had got hold of red jumpers with 'Hull KR' on and we all decided to wear white trousers to go with them. Except Kath Hartley who said: 'I'm not wearing trousers!' and wore a skirt. We had a laugh on the way down and, when we got to London, went straight to Wembley to meet the lads. It was amazing. We walked on the pitch and even went into the dressing room. I couldn't believe where I was and especially how big the bath was."

Television footage shows the Rovers players relaxed, wandering around Wembley and taking it all in. Three of the squad had experienced a cup final walkabout before: Watson, Lockwood and Crane. Sullivan and Lowe had played there for Great Britain. But for most it was brand new. Watkinson was collared by an American TV crew, while Sully tried to get his own instamatic camera to work.

The Wembley groundsman was there, keeping an eye on them, making sure they didn't train on it and telling them,

"don't walk on the lines, I haven't got any more paint left."
But not everyone was impressed. Rovers groundsman, Simon
Hillaby, was on his hands and knees, blades of grass between
his fingers. "There's clover in places and different types of
grass have been used. I prefer Headingley," he said.

Everything else went like clockwork and when the
squad was instructed to get back on their bus, they did as
they were told, with the rest of the afternoon off.

***

HULL FC HAD already been to the stadium, visiting in mid-
morning. The individual members of that squad had much
greater cup final experience but many were overwhelmed by
the experience.

"I just remember thinking 'Oh my God, I'm in the
Wembley dressing room,'" said Sammy Lloyd. "You think
about all of the great players from rugby and soccer that have
been there. It was such a pleasure. Although we had been told
that Rovers were supposed to have been allocated the lucky
one, it didn't bother us. That was bullshit. You make your
own luck."

Access was limited. Members of the squad could walk
on the pitch, were allowed to climb the steps to the Royal Box
if they wished and could see their own changing room. And
that was that. They couldn't wear studs and they definitely
couldn't train or take a ball on. "I didn't know that," insisted
Bunting when asked about it the following day. "When I saw
some of the lads running around with a ball, I tried to call
them back but they couldn't hear me."

"We smuggled a ball on," admitted Lloyd. "We weren't
supposed to but just wanted to have a ball in our hands and
get the feel for it, that was all. I might have kicked it a couple

of times but couldn't take any proper shots at goal because I was wearing trousers and shoes. I wasn't going to give it any welly for fear of getting injured or splitting my cords."

Though they played it down, the tonsillitis outbreak had spread further through the Hull camp. It wasn't ideal but nothing compared to Graham Evans's misfortune. Since joining Hull the previous summer, Evans had made the centre position his own. It was only in the last few weeks of the season that Wilby had taken the shirt from him, but he'd been named as back substitute and would likely get a run. Now he was just a spectator and devastated. But that created an opportunity for Brian Hancock, out of retirement in March to help the team through a fixture backlog. "I never, for one minute, thought I would play at Wembley," he said. "even when I was asked to go down with the squad. I thought I was just going down to train with them, as a reward for helping them out. It was a very nice thing to happen."

***

SUPPORTERS WHO TRAVELLED on Thursday had a day to kill on Friday. Trips to London weren't as frequent as they are now and, for many, it was a rare, if not their first, trip to the capital. Wide-eyed tourists from Hull were everywhere.

The Halfway party spent most of it in the pub but, as Pete Allen recollects, licensing hours meant they needed an extra plan. "Just as we were getting a thirst on, the pub would shut at 3.00pm. Most of the women went to Harrods for a sausage roll, so they could get a carrier bag. The rest of us went to Madame Tussauds, but weren't there long. Someone wrapped a black and white scarf around Winston Churchill and, just as we were about to have our pictures taken with him, we were dragged off by security guards."

Meanwhile, back in Hull, 41-year-old haulier Fred Lewis knocked off work early and went to the fruit market area, from where he and his 18-year-old son Dean, friends Charlie Grantham and Fred Donohue and their children were to head south in Fred's Volkswagen motorhome. Before departure, Charlie picked up an empty cardboard flower box, grabbed a marker pen and wrote perhaps the most famous piece of graffiti in rugby league history.

"We thought it would be a laugh," says Fred, now 77. "As we neared the Humber Bridge, I pulled over, jumped out and found a signpost, to which I fastened our sign before driving off. Never thought anything else about it. It was only a few days later, when we saw it on the news, that we realised how popular it had been."

It read: "LAST ONE OUT – TURN THE LIGHTS OFF."

***

AFTER THEIR WALKABOUT, the Hull FC squad went back to Botany Bay. A light training session ended with a game of touch and pass between the players and directors, keenly contested given that there were five bottles of wine at stake.

Back at their respective hotels, both squads were visited by the Metropolitan Police, who would be their outriders as the team buses made their way to the stadium. Rovers found they had a lucky omen in PC Robert Cooper, who had been doing the job since 1976 and his teams had never lost.

At the Runnymede, dinner was served at 8.00pm. "We'd started to call the place Fawlty Towers," recalls Brian Lockwood. "The place looked good but service was dreadful. We had this head-waiter called Bruno who never came to terms with the fact that some of our lads might want seconds. And Cliff Wallis struggled to get a steak well done. In the end it was burned to a crisp and the waiter was so upset and nervous he ended up pouring gravy down Cliff's neck."

Millward, meanwhile, took no chances with his troops. As Rovers tucked into their evening meal, he acted as waiter, taking breakfast orders, steak and eggs for most, then took them out for a stroll. "We walked into Windsor," explained Len Casey. "And, of course, soon found a pub. So Roger said: 'Okay, if you want a couple of pints so be it – but two, no more.' That's all we had; a couple of lads struggled to force them down. Phil Lowe and Clive Sullivan suffered badly from nerves and hardly touched theirs. I shared a room with Clive and it's a wonder I slept. He snored the entire night."

***

BY EARLY EVENING, Fred Lewis's motorhome had almost reached the end of the A1 and he pulled off in search of somewhere to park up for the night. "We found a nice big pub in Biggleswade. At first the landlord said 'no', so we decided to just have a quick drink and move on. It seemed to be full of Hull FC fans, so I told Dean, a Rovers fan, to leave his scarf in the van. Anyway, the pub was absolutely packed with Hull and Rovers fans, half and half, with no hint of any trouble. So I told Dean to go back and put his scarf on."

Fifty miles from Wembley, the place had been taken over by Hull folk. "It was amazing," remembers Fred, "the banter was good natured, they were taking each other on at pool, darts, dominoes, Hull against Rovers. And every now and again, someone would start singing 'Old Faithful' and then it would be 'Red, Red Robin'. Just brilliant."

By the end of the night, the landlord was persuaded to let Fred park his van after all but warned of dogs patrolling the yard. "We went to bed terrified," says Fred, "but when I woke up, desperate for a pee, I had no choice but to go out. I took a handful of biscuits, carefully opened the door and whistled. Two cocker spaniels and a Labrador ambled up."

Behind them, Hull city centre appeared to have taken his sign to heart, surreally quiet for a Friday night. Those off to London at dawn took an early night or stayed local. The Bali Hai threw a Wembley widows weekend: two nights of disco, games and cheap drinks, but there weren't many there.

In West London, the Rovers' wives and girlfriends went to watch Tony Christie in concert. "We had a smashing night, we were really well looked after," says Ros Sullivan. "All the directors bought us drinks. Kath Hartley and Lynn Casey looked to the manor born, sitting at the cocktail bar with their cigarette holders and Harvey Wallbangers. We got talking to a woman who told us she was a White Witch. 'I don't know anything about your team,' she told us, 'and I can see that it's going to be very close, but your side is going to win'."

In Enfield, the Hull FC wives joined their husbands for dinner. Again, Bunting was determined his players should be relaxed, but the women were on their way shortly after nine o'clock, which still left them plenty of time to make a night of it. So the driver was pressed into taking them into Central London. Chairman Charlie Watson called them 'Charlie's Angels' and chaperoned them around Soho and the West End. "Charlie paid for everything," remembers Vanessa Bray.

Bryan Leason and pals went to the London Palladium. "We always saw a show. We stayed out at Colnbrook, near Heathrow, and our bus driver would take us in. In 1980, we went to see Paul Daniels and he got a Hull supporter up on stage and had great fun with him. Afterwards, we'd arranged to meet our coach on Whitehall, because it was quiet at night. When we got there, the Hull FC wives' bus was parked up, so we covered it in Paul Rose testimonial stickers."

And in Mayfair, the Cross Keys party had taken over the hotel bar. Upstairs, I watched telly in bed; snooker and the ABA boxing finals from the Empire Pool. Someone called Bruno won the Heavyweight belt. Lights out, I tried to drift off to sleep but, out in the corridor, someone heading for bed was singing as he went past our room.

"Wake up, wake up, you sleepy head. Get up, get up, get out of bed. Live, love, laugh and be happy..."

PART
3

May the Third

14

LONG BEFORE DAWN, alarm clocks were going off all over Hull. "I was up at three," recalls Pete Smedley, 15 at the time. "It was so exciting. Shower, sort the packing, flask, scarves, hats and so on. My dad had hired a car and him, me and my brother and his girlfriend went together. We set off at four and there were already loads of cars on the road."

It was still only five o'clock when the first strains of 'Red, Red Robin' floated over Hull city centre. The sun was up and since the first two specials leaving Paragon station were for Hull Kingston Rovers supporters, the majority of those arriving first were in red and white. "We're on the march, we're Roger's Army," they sang. "We're all off to Wembley ... and we'll really shake 'em up when we win the Challenge Cup, 'cos Rovers are the greatest rugby team."

The BBC sent Richard Duckenfield. Surrounded by a gaggle of Robins fans, a woman with dyed hair and a rosette the size of a small pizza called it the biggest day in the city's history and said Rovers were going to win. A moment later, a middle-aged Hull FC fan said: "I came home from the oil rigs just so I could see the game. And there's going to be lots more people going to lose a lot of wages to be at the match."

As he watched wave after wave of supporters boarding their trains, the reporter summed it up poetically. "This great mass of humanity heading south. There'll be an estimated 50,000 from Hull," he said. "The capital of the rugby league world heads for the capital of the country. Whatever the result, the City of Hull just can't lose."

Two hundred miles away, fans were already amassing outside Wembley Stadium. Having been driven through the night, several dozen cars were parked under the Twin Towers, their occupants now stretching their legs, making breakfast and having a kick-about on the tarmac.

***

WEMBLEY STAGED ITS first Challenge Cup final in 1929, in the face of great northern opposition to begin with. But as the years and decades progressed, the annual trip south became not only an accepted part of the rugby league calendar but an eagerly awaited one too, in the words of historian Tony Collins: "...the quintessential Northern English cultural experience."

In 1980, the event's popularity was undiminished. "The Cup final was the game's big pay day," says David Howes, "and everyone paid proper money in those days. There were no discounted tickets – no Groupon – and most spectators bought their tickets months before they knew who was going to be playing, as early as a fortnight after the previous year's game. We had one lady in the office at Chapeltown Road who handled it all. She'd write to all the pubs and clubs asking if they wanted to renew their tickets and almost all of them did, so she'd be taking money all year. Wembley would print the tickets, always the same, without names, and then she'd send them out once they were paid for. She'd keep enough back for the eventual finalists and that was it. By the time the semi-finals came around, they were usually the only tickets left."

The tickets in question were beautiful, old fashioned and archaic in their way, referencing the 'Empire Stadium' and its 'Cup Final Tie'. They had a small map on the reverse and terms and conditions so small they couldn't be read. The best bit: "You are advised to take up your position by 2.30pm." *Take up your position.* It was like going to war.

Just after seven at Runnymede, Allan Agar, who had barely slept, was on the golf course with Cliff Wallis. Several others had woken frequently during the night, laying awake staring at the ceiling. "I never got much sleep," recalls John Millington. "Me and Steve Hartley were up all night telling each other jokes." After breakfast, he went back to bed.

But by nine everyone was up and about and each had their own way of dealing with pre-match nerves. "Some lads tucked into a full English," said Steve Hubbard. "Lowey and Rosey did. I couldn't manage more than a bit of egg on toast."

Millward, who normally enjoyed a lie-in on match day, was up too. "I had a cup of tea and a bit of toast which wasn't like me either. I never used to eat anything before a game."

Time dragged. Some players went to pitch and putt for an hour. Some poked fun at Bill Land's white shoes. Three o'clock seemed a long way away.

***

AT FIVE PAST ten, more than four hours after setting off from Paragon station, the first of the day's rugby specials pulled into London, though precisely where was often mysterious.

"Somewhere near Wembley," recalls Tony Daddy. "I had no idea. We just got off and followed everyone else."

Most passengers were on day trips, so the first priority was to find somewhere for breakfast and then, on the stroke of eleven, the pubs opened their doors, invariably with Hull and Rovers fans waiting outside. Tradition dictated that those Wembley groups staying longer, adopted a place for the three or four days spent in the capital. "Ours was the Prince of Wales in Drury Lane," recalls Pete Allen. "Right in the heart of theatre land, with an upright piano in the bar and a blind pianist called Vernon. When we walked through the door on Saturday morning, he launched into 'Old Faithful' although, by the end of the weekend, he was absolutely fed up of it."

"Usually, we'd go to an Italian restaurant on Vigo Lane," says Bryan Leason. But not this year. "We just didn't feel like eating, we were that nervous." Meanwhile, at the stadium, hundreds of fans were already on Wembley Way, mingling with hopeful ticket touts and the traders who were setting up burger vans, hot-dog stalls and souvenir stands.

Challenge Cup finals are traditionally a celebration of togetherness. Fans of competing clubs mingle happily with each other and neutrals, displaying a shared set of values and respect for the sport and its communities. But, in 1980, there was something else. A shared respect for a city. "Everyone at that final wanted their team to win," says Howes, "but they also wanted to show off their sport and their city in the best possible light. The 1980 Challenge Cup final was a success because of how the supporters responded and behaved."

And along with a sea of well-behaved people, a sea of banners and flags. 'In the beginning, there was Knocker'. 'Hull bank on Lloyd'. 'I'd sooner watch *Crossroads* than Hull KR'. 'Paul Woods cuts out more balls than Dr Herriott'. 'Steve Norton stops more people than Humberside Police'. 'Sammy

Lloyd strikes more than Hull Dockers'. For some reason, most were in support of Hull FC. They kept a closer eye on their bedsheets east of the river.

It was a day too that VIPs did not want to miss, access to the pre-match banquet a hot ticket. RL Council members and professional club secretaries were assured of a seat at the table, as were BARLA representatives. Hull Council took up their full allocation and, as cocktails were served at 12.15pm, Sir Leo Schultz, Pat Doyle, Louis Pearlman and Basil Wood mingled with the great and the good.

Every year, the RFL sent out invitations to hundreds of politicians, diplomats and celebrities. And each year, roughly the same crowd showed up, often with northern connections: Bernard Manning, Bernie Clifton, Jimmy Saville, Cyril Smith, Colin Welland, Kenneth Wolstenholme, Bill Tidy, Dave Allen, Richard Harris, Peter O'Toole, Bill Maynard, Cliff Morgan, Brian Glover, Ed Stewart, Alan Plater, Emlyn Hughes, Jean Rook, Michael Parkinson... the turnout was particularly good in 1980 as they all wanted to see the Queen Mum.

"In my experience," said David Oxley, "members of the Royal Family ask two things when they meet anyone: 'What do you doo?' and 'Have you come faar?' The Queen Mother went much further. She was asking me questions all day."

David Howes was more circumspect in his analysis: "The Royals rarely stretch themselves. We would always send them a briefing note with information about the clubs and some players. She had read what we had given her, but just enough to be able to have a few conversations and not get caught out. They are very professional."

Organising the event wasn't easy. "The only way to run Wembley is off a timetable," Howes continues, one of only five RL staff on duty that day. "Nothing can be left to chance. A week before, we sent out a programme of arrangements to every participant and their guests, saying precisely what they needed to do and when." The Queen Mother's Bentley pulled up at precisely 12.30pm, parking proudly in the mouth of the Royal Tunnel. Her entourage was small, just a driver, a lady-in-waiting and an equerry, and they went immediately to the Royal Retiring Room. Shortly afterwards, she took her seat at the head of the table for the pre-match banquet.

By which time, *Grandstand* was already live and on air. On the greyhound track, in front of deserted terraces, Frank Bough and Eddie Waring riffed about being foreigners and how the game had caught the imagination of the viewing public. Mildly patronising stuff, but it set the tone for what was to follow. Bough told viewers: "A third of the population of the city will be inside Wembley this afternoon."

Oh no, they wouldn't – 266,000 people lived in Hull.

After 'Football Focus' and Higgins versus Stevens in a snooker semi, the BBC then showed a ten-minute preview, filmed over the previous days, in which no stereotype was overlooked ... deserted docksides, rusting trawlers, two men filleting fish in black and white and red and white scarves, trains chugging out of Paragon station and edging past row upon row of terraced houses, coaches in convoy past the unfinished Humber Bridge, blue and white corporation buses heading along Ferensway (past Binns and down the as-yet-unpedestrianised Paragon Street), slum clearance at the back of the Threepenny Stand, a female fan on the Craven Park terraces vowing to kick her husband out of bed if he were ever to support FC, a Hull FC-supporting police constable; Deputy Lord Mayor Alex Clarke refusing to declare his allegiances, Arthur Bunting in his painting and decorating overalls in front of a ladder, Rovers director Percy Johnson chatting about the divided loyalties of the patrons of his Corn Exchange pub ... Richard Duckenfield summing it all up:

"Whoever wins, this city can't lose'. Tell that to the losing half at a quarter to five, Richard.

***

AT RUNNYMEDE, THE players assembled in the lobby before leaving at half past twelve on their Holts coach, the mood relaxed and upbeat. So much so that were soon singing 'Molly Malone' ... 'cockles and mussels, alive, alive oh' ... and a touring song called 'Mardi Gras' ... 'The town's alight, because tonight, the world's a crazy masquerade...' "Phil Hogan brought it to the club after touring Australia," said Mike Smith. "As we approached away grounds on a match day, everybody would start singing the thing. It would build up and up, getting the adrenaline going."

A camera crew was on board. When the reporter asked Mick Crane how his nerves were holding up, he joked: "I aren't nervous cos I'm not playing." Millward, at the front, told them: "I feel very calm really." He didn't look it.

When they reached Wembley, the players caught sight of the thousands of supporters and the mood changed in an instant. "Everybody went quiet," recollects Roy Holdstock. "There was an eerie silence as we sat there looking out. I don't care who you are, when you go down Wembley Way everyone is full of their own thoughts and most have a tear in their eye. I know I did."

"We knew what was coming," said Millward. "We knew the schedule and had been told what to expect but, even so, it was like being in a fairytale."

Having an outrider was one of those extra touches that made the occasion so special. "We picked ours up a few miles from Wembley," said Brian Hancock. "The sirens went on and suddenly our journey gathered pace. As we got nearer the traffic was stopped for us and we sailed through red lights. It was an exciting experience." As a result, it didn't take long for the team buses to arrive. Clive Sullivan was one of the first off, met by his children, Anthony and Lisa, and soon after, the Hull bus pulled in too. By 1.00pm, its players were in their dressing room, settling in, reading telegrams they'd been sent, before a visit from the royal equerry.

"He was very formal," said Sammy Lloyd. "We stood there, a bit awkward, while he explained how we should behave when we met her. 'When you chaps are introduced to Her Majesty and she offers her hand, one does not shake it, one simply accepts it and bows one's head slightly, like so.' We all nodded and looked at Paul Woods, hoping he was listening and wouldn't stick the nut on her."

And, according to Hull KR's Roy Holdstock, Hull FC had an extra guest. Not for the first time before a Challenge Cup final, a mascot was smuggled into the room in a kit bag: "We'd been told normal team mascots were not allowed, but the FC players thought theirs brought them good luck. I was disappointed when I found out. My son, David, was the Rovers mascot and he couldn't walk out with us, so it was a bit disappointing to see Hull bringing theirs in. I know that Colin Hutton was fuming about it as well."

***

UP IN THE Banqueting Room, guests finished dessert and coffee was served. "I was often very nervous at this time of the day," admitted David Oxley, "hoping everything went well." With his Royal Guest comfortable, he took his coffee outside and stood, alone, on the balcony between the Twin Towers from where he had a clear view down Wembley Way. The sight of tens of thousands of fellow Hull folk arriving together, banners waving, klaxons sounding, stunned him. "Any doubts I might have had about trouble disappeared. At that point, I thought: 'We are going to be okay'."

Down below, the players emerged for their pre-match walkabout, the stadium nearly half-full. And now the nerves were really jangling. While the band of the Welsh Guards marched in formation, they strolled tentatively into the arena to a huge roar. For the *Hull Daily Mail* men, officially off duty but able to walk out with their respective teams, it was a highlight of their week, if not their lives.

"I will thank Roger forever for what he did for me that day," said John Sexton. "As you left the dressing room, the tunnel ran slightly uphill so all you could see, at first, was a thin strip of light at the top which got bigger as you got closer to the pitch. Even though there were perhaps 30,000 in the ground at that time, emerging into that noise was like nothing I'd ever experienced. It literally made the hairs stand up on the back of your neck."

Among the players, Tim Wilby remembered advice he had been given as part of the Leeds squad in 1977. "When I'd been on the pitch before that match, John Atkinson told me I'd get a chance to play there one day. He said: 'When you do, enjoy it all. Walk around like you own the place; wave to the crowd as if you know everyone personally.' I did that and my nerves disappeared. I was ready for the challenge."

Graham Bray played there for Featherstone in 1974. "I thought I'd be okay in the walkabout. I wasn't expecting to be overawed by the atmosphere but it was incredible. Nothing prepares you for it, not even being there before. Quite a few lads said the same. The noise was incredible."

Sammy Lloyd, strutting around the edge, chewed gum. "I'd really love to kick a few today," he told a reporter, "but if they go, they go and, if they don't, they don't."

"I saw my parents straight away," said Roy Holdstock. "Then, when I looked up a tier, I saw my sister who'd flown over from Jersey. So that was a brilliant start to the day."

As for the coach: "All I could think was 'come on, get a grip of yourself, you've got to get your backside into that dressing room. You're player-coach and have to start talking to a team about winning a rugby match'," said Millward and, sure enough, with just over an hour to kick-off, he got down to business. As his players settled into their preparations inside, Roger paced the floor. "We've experienced it now," he said. "Let's quieten down. We're going out there right in us minds, not like kids. Be careful with yourselves."

"Roger was a cat on a hot tin roof," recalled Holdstock, and he was not the only one, Clive Sullivan even more so.

"You'd think a man who captained Britain and played in a World Cup final would be okay," said Dave Hall, "but he was physically sick. I looked at him and thought: 'Bloody hell, this is a massive. I've spoken to dozens of Rovers players over the years about how big a Hull derby is, but nothing came close to that one."

At five-past-two, the BBC's Tony Gubba wandered in. "How's the shoulder?" he asked Phil Lowe.

"Well I partially sprung [it], which made life a little bit difficult for a couple of days," he said. "But I knew on Thursday I'd play. It was a bit sore but the doctor told me the pain was just a reaction from the travelling and the tough training session on Wednesday evening. By Thursday it was fine." Lowe's expression hinted he didn't believe it himself.

Gubba called Millward over next. Standing him next to Big Phil, he asked them both their height and weight. "No offence, Rog," said Gubba, "you're quite small, aren't you?" Millward looked like he could punch him. So did Lowe, if his arm didn't hurt so much.

"And you've never been to Wembley before, have you, Roger? And, no offence, but you're 33 now, aren't you?"

"32, Tony."

"Ok, and are you going to win?" asked Gubba, running out of insults. Without hesitation, Millward answered 'Yes', wanting desperately to kick him out of his dressing room.

***

SOUTH DRESSING ROOM next, this time to wind Arthur Bunting up. "Now, Arthur," said Gubba, "the last time you were here was as a player with Rovers in 1964, wasn't it? And you lost."

"That's right, but don't remind me of that Tony."

"And Hull have been at Wembley twice, in 1959 and 1960, when they lost quite heavily on both occasions. Are you haunted at all by those defeats?" Bunting reminded Gubba of the coach's own record of just one defeat in six derbies, so the reporter tried another angle, suggesting they may have misused the hallowed turf.

"Well, we didn't actually train," Bunting said. "Sammy had a few kicks at goal and we had a few drops at goal. Paul Woods put a few kicks into touch. I didn't realise we hadn't to do that."

"Not even when the little groundsman came on and cleared you off?" continued Gubba.

"I told them not to, but they all went down the other end of the field and I couldn't stop them."

Gubba then found Lloyd and asked him about the pitch walkabout and what he was wearing. "I had a pair of cords on, very tight. I took two or three kicks, most of them were unsuccessful. I hope I've got them out of my system but there was quite a nasty swirling wind, which surprised me."

***

BACK IN HULL, the streets were quiet. Around two o'clock, buses returned to depot and some city centre shops began to close. By 3pm, Paragon Street, Ferensway, Prospect Street, King Edward Street – normally packed with shoppers – were deserted. Traders lost an estimated £500,000 in takings.

But there were still a few people about. A camera crew approached a group of men watching television through a showroom window. "Hull FC or Rovers?" a reporter asked one man. "Neither. I'm watching the wrestling,"he replied.

***

AT 2.30PM, WINDSOR DAVIES and Melvyn Hayes from *It Ain't Half Hot Mum* began the community singing, Hayes in black and white, Davies red and white... 'Congratulations', 'Sailing', 'John Brown's Body', 'Old Faithful' and 'Red Red Robin,' as well as 'You'll Never Walk Alone' and, finally, 'Abide With Me' played by the Band of the Welsh Guards.

In the press box, with around two hundred colleagues, sat Dick Tingle. "Most of the nationals had a couple of people there and there were several from Australia. The place was full. The *Hull Daily Mail* photographers, sent down on Friday, were pitchside."

As the music subsided, the players were in the tunnel, lined up with chairmen and coaches at the head of the line. Little more than two feet away from their opposite number, there was nevertheless no communication. They kept their thoughts – and nerves – to themselves, giving nothing away.

Brian Lockwood recalls how, when facing Rovers there with Widnes a year later, his Chemics coach Doug Laughton was a master of mind-games. "Dougie kept us in the dressing room for ages. The officials had to tell us half a dozen times to come to the tunnel, but he kept everyone waiting. When we did come out, he had us chatting away to the Hull KR lads. 'Alreet, cock' we'd say to them, 'how you doin'? Have a good game, eh?' It totally wound them up. Then we'd start waving to our wives in the crowd, even if we couldn't see them, to look like we were perfectly at home. Rovers were wound up, kicking the tunnel wall and all sorts. I think we won that Cup final in the tunnel."

But there were no such goings-on in 1980. While both coaches and most players would later claim to have felt quite relaxed, every player stared purposefully ahead. Then, bang on time, at 2.48pm precisely, the signal was given and the two chairmen began to walk out. Behind them, Arthur Bunting and Roger Millward, followed by the players.

Those who saw them first were those furthest away, the Hull fans, who raised the roof with their cheers. As the first men cleared the tunnel, streamers rained down. Steve Hubbard was covered in ticker-tape, Tim Wilby brushed off what looked like pink toilet roll. Bill Land, a director since 1953, turned several times to the Rovers fans, wondering perhaps where they had all suddenly come from. To his left, Charlie Watson's involvement with Hull FC went all the way back to 1950. He seemed unmoved, blocking everything out. Arthur Bunting behind him did the same.

Once on the greyhound track, the teams went towards the north side of the ground, in front of the Royal Box, the massed banks of supporters, flags and scarves catching many a man's attention. Millward held a match ball, trying to chew gum, act nonchalant, taking lungfuls of air at the same time.

Said Sammy Lloyd: "People told me there was nothing like coming out at Wembley and they were right. As you left the dressing room, you had a long walk to the pitch, the noise getting louder every step. Some lads' lips started trembling. You remember your family and supporters and everyone hankering for you to do well."

Despite the occasion, Steve Hartley maintained his composure. "All you can see is people's legs," he said, "and it's hard to describe how loud it is, but your mind is on the game. There was about a quarter of an hour between walking out, meeting the Queen Mother and having your name read out. That gave you time to get prepared."

In a crowd of 95,000 is it really possible to recognise individual supporters, even if it is your wife or girlfriend? "Yes," says David Watkinson. "Remember that they were all wearing bright red jumpers, so they stood out a mile!"

As the players lined up again and awaited the guests of honour, some go through exercises, sprinting on the spot or jumping up and down, Steve Hubbard saw a familiar face. "I used to do a lot of building work in York and deal with this particular foreman on a building site. I knew he was a rugby league referee and I knew he sometimes ran the line, but that was all I knew. When I stood opposite the Hull team and then saw the referee and officials, I saw my mate, one of the touch judges!" The first choice had pulled up injured and he'd been drafted in late. "When Graham Bray hit me after I'd scored, it was him who came running on to give us the penalty."

As is customary when a Royal guest attends a cup final, the national anthem is sung immediately. For anyone else, the anthem is played after the guests have met the players. The Royal Standard flew atop the Twin Towers as another nod to the Queen Mother's status and on she came, along with Lord Derby, RL chairman Sumner Baxendale and RL secretary and Hull KR supporter David Oxley. Although few players can remember much about the biggest game of their lives, most can recall what the Queen Mother said to them. She told Mike Smith, for example, that the going seemed to be rather good. Graham Bray had a black eye from a fractured cheekbone, so she asked him about that: "I just mumbled some nonsense to her, that made no sense." Allan Agar leaned forward, put his arm out and said something like: "I hope you'll be wearing red and white at the end of the day, Ma'am." He reckons now that she didn't hear a word: "...but when you watch it back, it looks as if I've whispered into her ear and touched her arse," a boon to piss-taking mates in his local in Featherstone. One thing's for sure, the royal personage was in no hurry.

"I was aware that it was taking a long time," said David Oxley, at the back of the party. "But it was such a privilege to have her there, and she was, after all, eighty years of age. You're never going to tell her to get a move on, are you?"

Three minutes were allocated for the presentation of the teams and it took four and half. "Apparently, the broadcasters and Wembley officials were getting twitchy as everything usually runs like clockwork so people were getting nervous when three o'clock came and she was still on the pitch. Finally, they left pitchside and it was a quick dash for the chairmen who, in observance of protocol, must be in their seats before the Queen Mother reaches hers.

Richard Watson, diehard Hull FC fan and grandson of the Hull chairman that day, recalls how proud his granddad was of his role. "He was someone who'd lived during the war and his generation were much more respectful of royalty than mine. He said she was lovely and was delighted to be sitting next to her during the game. I don't know if they tossed a coin or what, but he felt he had got the best deal because he was to sit next to her in the second half when she presented the cup to the winning captain too. Obviously, my granddad hoped she would be handing it to Steve Norton..."

As the Queen Mother made her way back to her seat, the players were introduced to the crowd, one by one. They followed the instructions in the programme of arrangements: "Each player, when he hears his name, shall run smartly to the position he occupies on the field of play."

Rovers were first, David Hall kicking it off, every name greeted with cheers from the crowd, the biggest reserved for Millward and Norton. Then Fred Lindop, the referee, called the captains to the halfway line for the toss, where 'Knocker' flipped the coin and Millward called heads. It came down tails and Norton opted to receive the ball first and stay in place.

Hull were to attack west to east, both sides defending the ends filled by their own supporters. Meanwhile, on TV, Tony Gubba pushed a microphone in front of the Hull FC mascot. "So, you met the Queen Mother," the reporter said. "What did she say to you?"

"Nowt," replied the youngster.

We were ready for the ultimate Hull derby.

Oranges

15

THE SUN HAD gone in and a gentle wind blew at the backs of the men from Hull KR as Agar kicked off.

Deep in the Hull twenty-five, fullback Woods took it on the full, drove it in and was stopped by Lowe and Rose. Tindall and Stone took turns to attack before Norton, Birdsall and Lloyd exchanged passes and the ball was moved to Pickerill before the scrum-half spilled it on the fourth tackle.

It was the story of the match in miniature: six errors and three penalties in the first five minutes – hardly a classic start. "The occasion got to the players," reflected referee Fred Lindop. "They tried hard but it wasn't a great game. There was a lot at stake."

As the final progressed, it desperately needed a spark of quality. It arrived in minute nine, when Rovers were awarded another penalty. Agar found touch thirty yards out and seconds later they were ahead.

***

Last One Out...

JOHN SEXTON KNEW something was going on when he was asked to stay away from training on Thursday morning. From a distance, the Rovers writer watched the players going through the same training drill. Over and over again. It didn't seem to be going too well, though, invariably ending with the ball on the floor, expletives flying left and centre.

"I wasn't allowed to know what was going on but I knew they were working on something," said Sexton. "Every time they tried it, Steve Hubbard came in to catch the ball and it ended up on the floor. Brian Lockwood went bananas."

What they were working on was a simple little move that had never seen the light of day in England, saved for a special occasion. A potential match-winner, in fact. But it had to be executed perfectly; there was no margin for error.

Given how important it would become during the game and, arguably, in the history of the club, it is surprising how the memories of those involved vary so widely when it comes to the move they called 'oranges'.

What is not in doubt is where it originally came from: Australia. In the summer of 2014, I visited the village of Methley, midway between Castleford and Leeds, to meet the man responsible for bringing the move to Hull KR. "I'd seen Arthur Beetson do it while playing for Eastern Suburbs," said Brian Lockwood. "He used to run at the line, throw a big dummy to a second-rower and then run into the defender, get his arms out of the tackle and pop a pass to his winger, Bill Mullins, who would have followed up alongside. I don't know why it was called 'oranges'."

The move had never been tried by Rovers and, at first, Lockwood only suggested it as a way of breaking up the monotony of training. "I wanted to use Sully as the runner but he said, 'Oh no, no. You're not getting me running that far' and pointed to Steve Hubbard. 'Use him. He's thick.' So we tried it. Arthur was such a strong bloke that he could always get his arms free from the tackle to pop the pass out. I wasn't as strong as him so had to pass before the defender got me. Other than that, the move was exactly the same. I'd throw two big dummies to one of the second-rowers, either Rosey or Lowey, and then take the tackler on. The rest of the defensive line would have peeled away following Lowey and then Hubbard would appear, take the pass and go through the gap. That was the plan, but Hubbard couldn't time his run right. He'd get there too late or too soon or drop it."

Allan Agar has a slightly different version. "Originally, Hubbard wasn't involved. Locky had planned to have Paul Rose going through. Forwards and backs trained separately and it was a move involving just the forwards, Locky, Phil Lowe and Rosey. I stepped in and told him it was a mistake. The move could only work if you've got someone coming through who was fast enough to get around the fullback. So I told him to use Hubbard. With Rosey, he'd have tried to run over the fullback and we wouldn't have scored."

Hubbard also has a slightly different recollection of its origins. "It was a move Roger and Brian used in Australia but it just didn't work. We went through the move about a dozen times, but I dropped the ball every single time."

For Phil Lowe, the key to its success depended on him duping Steve Norton. "Knocker would mark me as he knew I was difficult to stop once I broke through the first tackle and his own defence was strong. I had to time my run perfectly to convince Knocker to go with me. If I went too far without the ball, Knocker would realise it was a dummy run and look to tackle the next man."

Norton agrees with Lowe. "In those days every team had a big running second row forward like Phil. It was one of the main attacking weapons. The only way to stop it was to get up quickly, get in their faces. None of them were as big or as good as Phil though and we knew that if he got going he'd be nearly unstoppable. I was the only one fast enough to get out of the defensive line quick enough but a brain like Brian Lockwood was able to work out that I'd be leaving a big gap behind me. If nobody came up with me to close it, we would be in trouble."

***

WHATEVER THE MOVE'S potential and from wherever the idea originated, by the end of Thursday's session, it seemed to be irrelevant. If they couldn't get it to work on the training ground, what chance of it working at Wembley?

Brian Lockwood thought he had shelved the idea and reminded Millward in the dressing room before the game that they weren't going to do it. But Roger wasn't so quick to abandon a strategy he felt just might unlock the Hull defence. "I said: 'Let's keep it in mind'."

With Hull penalised for offside, Millward prepared to kick for touch. On the TV pictures, Hubbard says something in his ear. Was it 'oranges' or was he offering to take a shot at goal? "No idea," he recalled thirty-five years later. "I can't remember. He probably wouldn't have heard me anyway."

Ball in touch, Millward gives a signal to a teammate out of shot. Is it Lockwood? Once again, I tried to find out. Did Roger give him the signal? "No, I called the move," said Lockwood. "It was always going to be my call if and when we did it. As the game started, I was having it easy. I was getting the ball and getting it away nicely to Lowey or Casey. I thought: 'We could put this move on here, I'll have loads of room.' So once we got the penalty, I said to Hubbard and Lowey: 'Right, it's on'."

Sexton saw it coming and agrees that it was the prop forward who instigated the move. "When the time came and I saw Locky lining it up, I knew it was coming. Once the ball landed in Hubbard's hands, there was never a doubt that he would score." But Rovers hooker, David Watkinson, whose job it was to restart play from the penalty, was trying to call the whole thing off. "It had never worked and we had a chance to build some pressure. I just thought we were going to drop it."

In the seconds before play resumes, summariser Alex Murphy comments that Millward is hanging back: 'Hull are trying to cut off the supply of blood to the brain.' He had spotted that whatever happened next may involve other playmakers. Phil Lowe, about to pull a huge con trick on Steve Norton, knew how fine the margin was going to be.

"When I started my run, in my peripheral vision I could see Knocker coming with me and didn't dare look straight at him. His eyes were following me and he'd have known I was throwing him a dummy. I just had to keep going and, when the gap appeared behind me, hope that Steve would take the pass and go. It was a relief when I saw that it had worked."

It is all over in seconds. If Lowe glances at Norton he may switch target and nab Hubbard. If Hubbard mistimes his run by an instant the ball will hit the deck, Hull will regain possession and the opportunity will be lost. Neither of those things happen. Norton realises too late what is going on and can't change his direction in time, while Lloyd is too late to plug the gap, Hubbard already in position. No doubt mindful of the numerous times the winger dropped the ball in training, Lockwood practically puts the ball in his hands.

Watkinson remembers that: "Knocker was screaming his head off." Birdsall, Newlove and Pickerill give chase but the momentum is with Hubbard, in the clear and heading for the line. Only fullback Woods and wingman Bray have any chance of preventing Hubbard from scoring and fail to do so. 'Oranges' worked to perfection, Hubbard using reflexes and intuition he hadn't practised because they hadn't got that far!

***

IN AUGUST 2015, TWO weeks before Hull KR were due back at Wembley for the first time in nearly thirty years, the ex-winger was at his bar in a hip part of Hull's waterfront, enjoying a coffee with Hull KR's latest record-breaking winger, Josh Mantellato, riffing about Wembley and goal-kicking. Josh thrilled to hear tips on how the wind circulates at Wembley and how quickly the whole occasion flies past.

Exchanging pleasantries, I wished Josh well (while secretly hoping his day would be miserable) then Hubbard and I adjourned to a quiet corner and turned the clock back.

"The move was only ever designed to get me into space. It wasn't necessarily about scoring but once you're in the clear, you just do what you can to get over the line. I was about fifteen or sixteen stone, big for a winger back then, so was going to take some stopping. People have asked what it feels like to cross the line at Wembley but you're not thinking about it. All your instincts kick in."

There are many ways to place a ball over the whitewash and, as tacklers close in, success or failure can rest on your choice at that critical moment. Hubbard, five yards out with men either side, slid over in more of a flop than a dive, ball held out in front in both hands. Bray reached him first and unsuccessfully tried to dislodge the ball with his left arm. Then Woods got there, sliding in legs first before rolling over both Bray and Hubbard and finishing clumsily on his backside. The former, meanwhile, in attempting to punch the ball from the scorer's grasp, managed only to land a couple of blows to Hubbard's face, the winger jumping to his knees to defend himself before, just as quickly, falling back down again, supposedly in pain but kidding no-one. "Roger told me to do it. Sure enough, we got a penalty that I kicked from under the posts. Keith Tindall still ribs me that I should have got an Oscar for that!" And the touch judge that rushed on to signal foul play was his building site workmate.

It was Wembley's first 'seven-point try,' mistakenly attributed to the usual FC fall guy, Paul Woods, by Murphy in the BBC commentary box. "I read it was for him coming in with his knees," said Bray, "but I definitely threw a punch. And it was a good one – a right hook."

Hubbard recalls that Bray paid him a visit in the Rovers dressing room, to apologise for punching him and to explain that he had merely been trying to knock the ball free.

"No, that didn't happen," insists Bray. "I never went to see him and I wasn't trying to knock the ball free either. It was just frustration. It was a well-worked try but it should never have been scored. If Graham Evans had been my centre partner, I'm sure he would have picked him out."

Millward wasn't bothered about the detail of the move just the feeling of satisfaction that it worked so well. "It was unbelievable. It was our first attacking penalty and so sweet."

"I was lucky to get the man of the match award," says Lockwood. "Allan Agar was the best player on the field that day. I got the Lance Todd Trophy for that one pass."

***

HIGH UP OVER the Wembley pitch, Eddie Waring describes numerous replays from different angles.

"It certainly was an amazing try and it came almost from nothing," he said. Not quite, Eddie. Not quite.

Ronnie, Fred and the Tryless Second Half

16

THE TRY UNSETTLED Hull and they lost their discipline badly. None more so than Ronnie Wileman. On the second tackle following the restart, he conceded a penalty for offside and then, in the next set, launched a high-shot at Lockwood for which he was fortunate not to be penalised. On the third tackle, he hit Millward.

"Sometimes people move past you and you're not sure what happened," said Fred Lindop. "It looked a bit late but, I'll be honest, I didn't know it was as bad as it was. We hadn't the advantage of looking at a big screen. You've got one second to make a decision and I didn't see it properly."

But the touch judge on Rovers' left touchline saw it perfectly, flagging straight away. Lindop pulled Wileman and delivered a fierce finger-wagging, pointing to the dressing room. Wileman, fiddling with his shorts, looked guilty.

"He's very, very lucky to stay on the field," says Alex Murphy on the BBC. "I know they've been told to mark Roger but I don't think they should mark him that closely."

Ironically, Millward had warned his players about high tackles. He'd reminded them about what happened in 1970.

Lindop's last Challenge Cup final had been between Castleford and Wigan that year, the latter's biggest threat the goalkicking of Colin Tyrer, whom Hepworth flattened. They had to carry Tyrer off, but Lindop let Hepworth remain on the field and Cas went on to win the game.

"Lindop would not make the same mistake again," Millward wrote in his autobiography, "so I warned my players that if anyone stepped out of line, he'd be sent off. But then, when Ronnie hit me, he still didn't send him off!"

The tackle broke Millward's jaw; for the third time in six months. In commentary, Waring notes that he looks dazed and the man himself admitted it took 20 minutes to regain his senses. "Everything was a blur up to then," he said. But Hull FC continued to lose the plot. Straight from the restart, Stone aimed a punch at Holdstock, directly in front of Lindop who awarded the penalty, 20 yards out and almost directly in front of the posts. Hubbard had no trouble kicking it and the stoppage gave Cliff Wallis more time to assess the extent of Millward's injury. On the Hull bench, Bunting was furious.

Shortly afterwards, Birdsall grappled a rampaging Phil Lowe to the floor on Rovers' right. In doing so, he gave Lowe too much attention and the touch judge raced back on, flag aloft, pointing at the culprit. Yet another penalty to Rovers – their eighth – with still only 17 minutes gone. The game was already slipping away from Hull FC, though Rovers were unable to take full advantage. Watkinson fumbled on Rovers' next set and then Lockwood was penalised for playing on after being called held. The game continued in stop-start fashion with handling errors galore and penalties for infringements, high tackles and technical offences, but the stoppages let Millward find his way back into the game.

Last One Out...

On 25 minutes, Lloyd missed a chance to score Hull's first points when he pulled a penalty attempt to the left of the posts after being tackled late by Lowe, just one of a string of penalties finally giving Hull a foothold in the game. They continued to build and Tindall, Stone and Birdsall drove it in. Norton tried some magic but the advance fizzled out as Birdsall was tackled on the last. In those pre-handover days, the game restarted with a scrum midway between the posts and Rovers' right-hand touchline. They had head and ball but, as Agar put it in, both hookers struck simultaneously and Watkinson kicked the ball straight out towards Pickerill, who scooped it up. Newlove, on the open side, had already seen a potential overlap on the blind and ran around the back, Pickerill shielding the run and popping him the ball. In a flash, there was an overlap, allowing Newlove to race away on a diagonal line to the corner. With Wilby and Prendiville outside him, he carved a three-on-two, Smith and Hubbard outnumbered, and the 35-year-old knew how to exploit the advantage. Running at Smith, he commited the centre to the tackle, before a simple ball to Wilby on his left. The centre, at 6ft 4", had the size and strength to squeeze between Hubbard and Casey to touch down.

On the back of a bit of possession and pressure, Hull were suddenly right back in it but Lloyd, after struggling to set the ball up four times, missed the conversion: 7-3.

Errors continued to dominate the half's remaining 12 minutes and, in the final minute, Lockwood sets Rovers up with a good attacking position. The ball came to Millward who, with just seconds remaining, stepped to his left and dropped a goal from bang in front, thirty yards out.

***

FIFTEEN MINUTES LATER, the teams, unchanged, returned to the arena. This time, there was no pomp or ceremony as they sauntered raggedly back, stepping over hoardings advertising Rizla and the *Daily Mirror*, Girobank and the TGWU. En route, they passed the marching bands of the Welsh Guards and a pitch invader dressed as Max Wall.

Hull began the second half as they did the first. Norton put Birdsall through a gap but Newlove's pass to Wileman went behind him, slowing the move. At the next play the ball, Newlove knocked on as yet another attack came to nothing.

Nevertheless, Hull regained possession when Wileman won the scrum against the head and were awarded yet another penalty for a scrum infringement. From thirty yards out, slightly to the right of the posts, Lloyd missed by several yards though and the score remained 8-3.

As both sides settled down, the game opened up a little with more try-scoring opportunities in fifteen minutes than the entire first half put together. Ref Lindop, however, was determined it would not become a try-fest.

Six minutes in, Pickerill was penalised for feeding. Agar and Casey probed the left before the ball was switched right. As Rovers' attacking line spread out, Norton raced out of the line to cut off the attack but Millward stepped inside and fed Hartley. League's top try-scorer the previous year, he hadn't been overjoyed by his treatment at Hull KR. One week stand-off, next at centre, depending whether the coach himself was fit to play. It hadn't affected his form though and his blistering pace made him the biggest threat in the back line.

"We feared Hartley more than anybody, including Roger," admitted Bunting.

Hull's greatest fear was what Hartley might do if he got the opportunity to use his pace on Wembley's wide open pitch. The outcome, for Hull FC, might be devastating.

Last One Out...

On 46 minutes, having found himself in open space and, seconds later, sashaying around Newlove and Woods, he placed the ball down between the posts for a try. Effortless. But Lindop, in perfect position, pulled him back for a forward pass. "I didn't know it had been disallowed," said Hartley. "I couldn't hear the whistle and only knew when I turned around. It was marginal. In those days, anything level was usually chalked off. Nowadays I think it would have been given."

But, after surviving Rovers' early pressure, Hull began to build their own attack. Norton set Walters racing into space who fed Wilby. Hull continued to probe down the left and, as Rovers scrambled to hold back the black and white tide, moved it right, quick hands, to Walters. With Sullivan off his wing and Rovers' in disarray, Bray then had a straight run to the line, but as he crossed it, Lindop had already blown his whistle for obstruction. Agony!

The TV replay is clear. Fullback David Hall sets off to shut Bray down, bundle him into touch. Sammy Lloyd, who has found himself in the Rovers defensive line, sees Hall bearing down and instinctively takes a step into his path. He might have got away with it had his left arm not been raised, making the obstruction more obvious. "I remember that very well," said Lindop. "It happened right in front of me."

Alex Murphy said: "That's what you call a top class referee, in the right position at the right time."

Last word on the matter goes to Arthur Bunting, with a master's eye for detail. "It wasn't an obstruction. You have to look at the way Hall runs into Sammy. He tried to go in front of him. Why did he go that way around?"

Lloyd was given an opportunity to make amends a few minutes later – another penalty within kicking range, close to the spot from where he'd missed ten minutes earlier. This time he made no mistake, sending the ball straight between the posts and closing the gap to 8-5 against a backdrop of incessant and deafening noise from the Hull supporters, who sensed that their team was getting on top in the game.

Suddenly, it was all Hull. First Wileman made a thirty-yard break up the middle and then Newlove put Wilby into space down the left, building wave after wave of attack and handling the ball much better. In response, Agar sought to regain control for Rovers, hogging the ball, pinning Hull back with several astute kicks, gradually tightening up the match. Nevertheless, as it moved into its last quarter, Hull continued to look the most likely side to score next.

As sporting commentators are inclined to do, Murphy and Waring ventured to sum up the game, explaining to viewers how the contest would most likely be won or lost.

Murphy was particularly troubled as to whether Millward was going to use his substitute bench, referencing Phil Lowe's lack of involvement as well as the captain's own injury problem. Eddie Waring, however, in the 61st minute of his penultimate Challenge Cup final, offered the following thought: "I think it's going to be now ... the chance that's come ... with the chance that's taken at the right moment ... Because they've been rather the same position for quite a while ... all around the half way line."

***

IN THE 65th minute, Hull were once again pressuring the Rovers line with Pickerill, Stone and Norton to the fore. Hull briefly lost momentum but the broken play was exploited by a well-timed run from Keith Tindall, who latched on to Norton's pass and found himself in the clear, head back, racing over for the try that would level the scores.

Tindall remembers it like it was yesterday. "I always used to come off around the back of Knocker and couldn't believe I was in so much space. I just thought, 'I'm in, I'm in'. All the Hull fans in front of me ... tens of thousands of Hull fans ... and I'm going to score." Play though was called back and Tindall looked distraught ... heartbroken.

"We were lucky there," admitted Rovers hooker David Watkinson. "When I saw Tindall racing through, that was the first time I thought we weren't in control."

When Tindall and I met in 2016, I told him how Alex Murphy called it a good yard forward. "Never! When I took that ball off Knocker I took it there [indicating that the pass was taken just above his hip]. Lindop was stood behind the play and from there it always looks like its drifting forward. I remember slowing it down on video loads of times." The 64-year-old paused, the only Hull-born player in the Hull FC line-up. "I'd had a good game. My mum had flown in from Australia and everything. If I'd scored, you never know, I might have won the Lance To..." His voice trailed off. The sentence, if not the thought, unfinished.

But just a few moments later, a Hull player was over again. This time Ronnie Wileman spotted the smallest of gaps between the legs of defenders as he played the ball on the try-line before being flipped onto his back by Holdstock, Smith and Agar. Held up. The third disallowed try in 13 minutes with Hull fans beginning to realise it was not their day, some already placing responsibility at the hands of the referee.

Having soaked up wave after wave of attack, Rovers went on the counter and took play deep into the Hull half, Casey, Rose and Lockwood linking well. The game opened up, players on both sides handling the ball more comfortably as the tie belatedly sprang to life.

Rovers moved the ball to the right and the play broke

down momentarily, but then Smith noticed Bray off his wing and found Hubbard who went for the corner. His diagonal run took him away from Pickerill and Woods but the full-back's tackle brought him down and the ball was grounded short. Momentum though carried him over the line. Yet again, Lindop was decisive, ruling out a score. "The rules are clear," Lindop insisted. "Contact must be made with the ball above the waist, but Hubbard fell on the ball with his legs."

Still today, Steve Hubbard is adamant he scored. "I had a perfectly good try disallowed. I slid over the line. If that had been given, not only would it have finished the game off, I would have ended the season as top try-scorer instead of sharing it with Keith Fielding. I might even have won the Lance Todd."

Murphy: "I personally think that's a try. He's grounded but his bodyweight takes him over."

***

FIVE DISALLOWED TRIES to go with the controversial non-sending off incident in the first half. There were plenty of talking points, so many might-have-beens and maybes, I put to Fred Lindop in 2016. "It were full of 'em, lad," he replied.

Ten minutes left and finally movement on the benches. Hull's fresh legs belonged to the 33-year-olds, Hancock and Farrar. While Lloyd attempted another unsuccessful attempt at goal, they prepared to replace Newlove and Stone. Rovers brought off Rose and, finally, on went John Millington.

"Rosey should have come off earlier," says Millo. "He had made lots of mistakes and wasn't having a good game. I was very nervous on the bench but, once I got my first touch and my first tackle, it was just another game. Until I looked up into the stands!"

"Millo came on and immediately told all the lads there were eight minutes left," said Millward. "We couldn't believe it. I thought there was ages left. It had absolutely flown by."

By then, Agar was dominating for Rovers, increasing in confidence, taking a scoot from acting halfback to get Rovers out of their own half. With five to go, Lloyd was penalised for tackling Millward without the ball. Hubbard lined up his kick towards the Hull fans and sent it straight through to bring about the most famous scoreline in Hull Kingston Rovers' history: 10-5. The Rovers fans, sensing victory, burst into 'You'll Never Walk Alone'.

But Hull weren't quite finished yet and, with two and a half minutes left, Prendiville, starved of possession all game, fielded the restart and went for broke. From deep in his own half, he backed himself to round Hubbard and found himself briefly in space before being tackled by Agar.

Hull threw caution to the wind. Norton, Hancock and Walters moved the ball right until it reached Bray, just inside his own half. Sullivan was out of position and Bray sniffed a chance, but Sullivan also had years of experience. Make that decades. Sully gave him the space and invited him into it, Bray motoring, crossing halfway and heading for the corner.

"If it hadn't been so late in the game," says Bray, "I'd have probably gone on the inside but I knew there wasn't long and just had to go for it. Clive wasn't as quick as he used to be but had a good brain. He gave me just enough room to tempt me."

Though not as fast as he once was Sullivan was still no slouch. Keeping pace with the Hull man, he timed his tackle to perfection. Just as it seemed Bray might make it, Sully launched himself. Textbook: around the waist, head tight to backside. As Sully slid down the wingman's legs he came crashing to ground and was rolled into touch. With less than a minute remaining, it was as good as over. "And the old maestro himself. Clive Sullivan. Still a good tackler. Still a good footballer." This time Eddie summed it up perfectly.

Bray knew the game was lost, but reached over to Sully and gently tapped him on the head. "I remember that as plain as day," he says. "He was a gentleman was Clive."

On the other side of the field, Hubbard was also on the floor. "I stood on Agar's leg and went over." In the seconds after Agar tackled Prendiville, Hubbard hit the ground feet away from the BBC microphone, clearly heard moaning in pain. "It looked bad and my wife, watching from the other side of the stadium, was worried. But she was sat next to the wife of our club surgeon who reassured her: 'I think he's alright, he's moving his head'!" While a stretcher – or hospital trolley by the look of it – was called on, physio Cliff Wallis wrapped a dirty bandage around Hubbard's legs. It is doubtful he had ever been carried from a field in such style.

"I thought there was still about 20 minutes to go," said the patient. "At Wembley, you lose any sense of where you are and how long you've been playing for. I was devastated but by the time I got into the tunnel it was all over."

***

IN THE FINAL minute, Hull won a penalty which Woods kicked to touch. Wileman to Farrar, next tackle Tindall and then the hooter sounded. No grubber kick, no up and under, it was all over. The Rovers celebrations began.

The centre of attention, inevitably, was Roger Millward. He leapt into the arms of David Hall, both then mobbed by Sullivan. It was an appropriate tableau. Two rugby league legends from Wales and West Yorkshire, together with Hall, a born-and-bred Hull bloke.

Roger and Sammy

17

"HULL BANK ON Lloyd" proclaimed a home-made banner at Wembley yesterday. And the boast came true as Hull FC beat fierce local rivals 18-7, thanks in no small part to the boot of Sammy Lloyd.

Hull's goal-kicking phenomenon, whose two towering touchline penalties had carried the black and whites to their epic semi-final victory over Widnes, had been calmness itself during the pre-match amble around the pitch.

"I'd love to kick a few today," he told a BBC reporter, "but if they go, they go and if they don't, they don't."

Fast forward a couple of hours and Lloyd's phlegmatic approach to the biggest game of his career had proved justified as his perfect six from six had not only earned his team their first ever Challenge Cup win at Wembley but Lloyd the Lance Todd Trophy.

Lloyd's – and Hull's – first points came early in the first half from a coolly taken penalty kick and, although Hubbard's cute try and penalty goal had given Rovers a temporary lead, Hull were soon level when Wilby powered over in the 23rd minute. And they were ahead when Lloyd slotted over the conversion after the ball had *repeatedly fallen over in the build-up. Before that, Hull had been dramatically reduced to twelve men when hooker Wileman was dismissed for a high tackle on Millward, who was forced from the field and played no further part in a game that he, his teammates and the tens of thousands of Rovers supporters will want to forget.*

It would take a heart of stone not to feel some sadness that Millward's biggest day ended in such heart-breaking fashion.

After Hubbard landed another penalty, the game was deadlocked at 7-7 at half-time, but Hull were soon in the lead and took command when Lloyd's early penalty was followed by a try from Bray, although Lloyd had been fortunate in the build-up not to be penalised for an obstruction on Hall. To rub salt in Rovers' wounds, Lloyd then nonchalantly goaled the conversion from the touchline. It was one of those days.

Two further Lloyd penalties followed as Hull tightened their grip on the game and, long before the end, the Hull fans in the West Stand (opposite the players entrance with the royal box to their left) waved their flags and sang: "There's only one Sammy Lloyd".

Oh, what might have been...

***

"I SPENT MANY years dealing with the disappointment of 1980," reckons Sammy Lloyd. "For five years I had a staple answer to being asked how it felt, without ever really telling anyone how gut-wrenching it was. Nobody dreams about leaving the pitch at Wembley as a loser, do they?"

In a decade when rugby league was blessed with some of its greatest ever goal-kickers, Geoff 'Sammy' Lloyd was arguably the best of the lot. By the end of the '70s, he was in possession of most records at Castleford and Hull. Such was his potency, especially from long range, that teams feared making any kind of infringement inside their own half. But by 1980, aged 30, he was on borrowed time. He'd been at Hull a year longer than planned and injuries had limited his appearances – "I kept breaking my arm and had to play with heavy strapping on. There were all these young bucks trying to take a shot at me." But neither injury or age could diminish his imperious boot.

The two towering touchline penalty kicks in the semi at Station Road sent Hull to Wembley and earned Lloyd man of the match. If the Cup final was going to be close, there was a good chance that Lloyd's kicking would tip it Hull's way.

His first significant moment came after twenty-five minutes, with Hull 7-0 down. Lloyd himself was caught off the ball by Len Casey just inside Rovers' half. Lindop gave the penalty and Lloyd stepped forward. It was a tough kick, particularly against the wind, and after calmly tee-ing it up he pulled it at least six or seven yards to the left.

The second followed Tim Wilby's try. Eight yards from touch, this time he struggled to place the ball and it fell over three times. "My boot sponsors, Puma, were delighted," he'd later joke. "They got a few extra seconds of coverage." That one sailed wide to the right. Early in the second half, trailing 8-3, came the easiest of the lot – midway between the posts and touchline, around twenty-eight yards out.

***

THE ROGERTHORPE MANOR Hotel, a few miles outside of Pontefract, was quiet one Sunday morning in the summer of 2014. Hull FC, under Lee Radford, sat tenth in Super League and England's footballers were already home from the World Cup. "They get paid too much money, no passion," said a member of bar staff, though whether he was on about Hull or Wayne Rooney's lot was unclear. I took my coffee to a corner table to await the arrival of Sammy Lloyd. Even at 64 he cut an impressive figure. The distinctive arched eyebrows were now as grey as the hair on his head, but you could never mistake him for anything but an ex-sportsman.

I had decided to take along a laptop with a recording of the game on it. As our conversation came around to the subject of goal kicks, I tentatively asked if he would like to view it all again; he did.

As we crouched over a computer screen watching a 34-year old recording, listening to commentary that was scratchy even in 1980, Sammy nervously watched his former self go through the usual preparations. Steps back, then to the left; wipes his right boot on the back of his left sock. A short run up, that signature little hop and step as he addressed the ball. There was silence in the ground – and in the bar – as we watched the ball sail hopelessly wide. Even three decades later, the miss still shocked as Sammy sucked in his breath: "Bloody hell, it was miles off."

A tinny Alex Murphy, alongside Eddie Waring, said: "Sammy is usually the most reliable kicker of all, but he is just not doing it today."

Ten minutes later, Hull were awarded another penalty in almost exactly the same spot. After three successive misses, did Lloyd have second thoughts about whether to go for goal again? There were other options. Hull could have run the ball or someone else could have had a go (Prendiville? Woods? Birdsall? Though none were in the same class as Lloyd).

"No. I never considered it," Sammy replied without hesitation. "I relished taking kicks, particularly when the pressure was on. If anything, that improved my accuracy." There was certainly pressure on that fourth kick but, this time, Lloyd was on target and Hull drew closer at 8-5.

With five minutes to go, and still trailing 8-5, there was

another opportunity in around the same place as the previous two kicks. It was pushed to the right again, almost a facsimile of the third kick at goal, half an hour earlier. As the ball flew right, Lloyd stared at the posts in disbelief. The BBC cameras, cruelly, lingered on the kicker as he finally turned away and prepared for the restart. On the tape, he stares at the ground, bites his bottom lip. A teammate asks if he's okay. Lloyd nods before looking at the turf again.

In total, he missed four out of five – eight points going astray in a game that was lost by five.

And then there were the conceded penalties. On 53 minutes, Lloyd's obstruction on David Hall denied a try for Bray. Lloyd felt he had no choice, Hall thought Bray would've scored regardless.

I'm with Hall. Although he was closing in fast, Bray was flying. His momentum may well have carried him over. The worst that would have happened would have been a scrum five yards out, Hull head and ball. Lloyd's decision may have cost Hull another three, possibly five, points.

Five minutes from the end, there was Lloyd again, pulling on Roger Millward's shirt twenty yards out with Rovers on the attack. It's an unnecessary foul, borne out of frustration. Lindop duly awarded the penalty and Hubbard lined up the kick that stretched the lead to five points. Then came another telling and sad episode. While Murphy went on about Lloyd's senseless foul, Hull's veteran ex-captain Brian Hancock strode over to Lloyd, threw an arm around him and attempted to console the player, but the hand was gently brushed away.

It would be implausible, however, to argue that Lloyd choked. Anyone who saw those touchline kicks at the end of the semi-final could have no doubts that here was a guy who could handle pressure. But there were many who felt that

Lloyd could never recover, such had been his disappointment and so public had been his downfall.

He was heartbroken, anxious about the fans' reaction. "How can I face them after this?" he told a reporter. "This was the biggest day of my life and I've fluffed it. It might be better if I moved."

A story did the rounds that, after the game, Lloyd went back out onto the pitch armed with a ball and marched to the spots from where he had missed each kick. In front of an all-but empty stadium and with tears streaming down his cheeks, Lloyd banged over every kick. Is that true?

"No, it's not. Some say I did it in my stocking feet but it's all rubbish. I've heard someone else say that I did it in my carpet slippers. I mean, why the hell would I have taken my bloody slippers to Wembley? No, it's not true. We all went to the bar to get drunk."

Nowadays, Lloyd is philosophical. "As I've got older and listened to great people who have faced disappointment in lots of different sports, I've learned that you've got to stand up, dust yourself down and get on with it. Life's about today, right now. It's not about yesterday and trying to relive things. I don't relive my victories let alone my defeats. The past is gone. No matter what you do, you can't change it.

"I had wise words from so many people. Dave Allen, the comedian, came up to speak to me after the game. He said that if you want to know what it's like to be disappointed try being a comedian at the Glasgow Empire! That made me laugh and there were lots of comments like that. I realised that disappointment can make you. The disappointment made me a much more grounded individual during my life."

The healing process began the next day with an emotional reception when the team returned to Hull. "On our tour around Hull and back to the Boulevard, I expected them to jeer and boo me, but the reaction was truly unbelievable. The streets were packed and the Boulevard was absolutely chocker, but it's all kind of foggy because we were all totally hammered. And were, for a long, long time."

Despite the homecoming, Lloyd briefly considered retirement and a move to York was also on the cards, but he knew he would only find salvation if he could demonstrate that Wembley 1980 would not be the game that defined him. He completed two further seasons with Hull FC and, at Wembley in 1982, put in an impeccable goal-kicking display to earn Hull a draw. In the final minutes, with the chance to win the game, his conversion sailed high over the Wembley posts. Many, including Lloyd, still argue that the ball went between them. In a parallel world, Lloyd has kicked the last-minute conversion to win the cup for Hull at Wembley, it's just that the touch judges didn't agree.

Hull were back at Wembley again in 2016. During the build-up, Lloyd, an enthusiastic musician, teamed up with the current playing squad to record a song, 'Come on you 'Ull'. There he is in the video, in black and white, backed by a local band and hundreds of FC fans. Two days after Hull won at Wembley for the very first time, he was on stage in Queen's Gardens for a victorious homecoming this time, performing the song to a tremendous reception. Despite all the years, they still love Sammy Lloyd in Hull.

***

BY 1980, ROGER MILLWARD was one of the biggest names in the world of rugby league. Twenty-nine caps for Great Britain, seventeen for England, three full tours, three world cups and a season with Cronulla. Over 400 appearances in sixteen years as a professional. Worldwide acclaim as one of the finest players of his generation. And now, in the last two seasons, a Floodlit Trophy and League Championship, making him not only Rovers' most successful player but their most successful coach as well. A hugely successful career in every respect. Except one.

He'd never won the Cup, nor played at Wembley. Each year, the competition came around and sixteen times he'd been knocked out. A semi-final in 1977 was as close as he got. 'Poor little Roger', his teammates teased.

As his coaching reputation grew, his strengths as a player were on the wane. After a decade and a half as principal playmaker during the sport's most rugged and aggressive era, Millward's 5ft 4" frame was worn and torn. Repeated injuries blighted the Championship-winning 1978-79 season. Millward went on tour but tore knee ligaments in a warm-up game in Queensland. Three weeks later, it was no better and he went under the knife. Rumours circulated that he was finished and that Cronulla wanted him as coach. From a hospital bed in Sydney, he assured Rovers' board that he'd be coming home and playing on for one more year.

As we have seen, prior to Wembley, Millward spent much of it in recuperation, first from a leg injury sustained in that exhilarating derby and then that twice-broken jaw. The story became one of whether, if Rovers made the final, he would be fit enough to play in it, though all doubts were put aside after the magnificent semi-final display against Halifax, when he was chaired off the Headingley pitch as man of the match. And when he did finally get to run out beneath those famous Twin Towers, he did so fourteen years after joining Hull KR and sixteen years after his first professional game for Castleford.

Roger Millward died in May 2016. Around two years before that sad day, I bumped into him at a rugby league event in Hull, introduced myself, got his number and gave him a call. On a cool but bright Sunday morning, I went to see one of the game's all-time greats at his home in Kippax.

Roger had not been in good health for some time and I hoped he would not be too inconvenienced by my visit. I needn't have worried. The courtesy and hospitality of the Millwards began before I even reached their house. I arrived in town a little early, stopped to buy them a box of chocolate biscuits. While standing in the Co-op, waiting to pay, my phone rang. It was Roger, or rather his wife, Carol. "Is that Vince?" she asked. "Roger just asked me to ring you to check you hadn't got stuck in all those roadworks in town. Do you want me to come and meet you, love?" I assured her I was fine and would be with them in minutes. "Okay," she said. "Roger's looking forward to meeting you. I'll stick kettle on."

Very soon, I was in Roger Millward's lounge, sipping coffee and listening as he took me back to 1980. There was no doubt that – by the spring of 1980 – the Challenge Cup had assumed massive proportions.

"The cup was always a target and every time the ties came around, there was an extra bit of excitement," he said. "The cup was special because the prize was so great, but you also knew that you would only get one chance each year. I'd been all over the world with my country, done everything I could have done in rugby league, but there was just one thing short ... Wembley. Every year, I would go down there anyway to watch. All the pubs and clubs in Kippax would run trips. I first went in 1952, as a five-year-old, with my mam and dad. We'd get the bus Saturday morning, there and back in a day, home at two or three in the morning – every year."

I wondered if it bothered him while watching, knowing yet another year had slipped by. In 1979, the RFL invited him as a special guest, on the top table like some form of consolation prize. As years went by, it must have got worse? "No doubt about it, but you just had to try even harder next year."

For Millward, though, getting to Wembley was never going to be enough. He also had to win. In the build-up, no man in either camp was more intense and focussed, in the view of some teammates to the point of obsession. "It was all new to us," the man himself explained in his autobiography. "Everything seemed very fresh and strange and I became a bit uptight and was 'having a go' at some of the players." When Allan Agar quietly told him to calm it, he took it on board. "There were experienced guys in that squad like Allan, Brian and Clive, who helped me as much as I helped them."

***

THE EARLY STAGES went like a dream. Not only were Hull FC struggling to cope with the occasion, but the set move his players struggled with in training had worked to perfection. With less than ten minutes gone, Rovers were 5-0 up. But only moments later, Millward's day changed abruptly.

From a penalty on the restart, Hall found touch and Rovers resumed on halfway. Lockwood and Holdstock drove the ball in. On the third tackle, Agar switched it left to Milllward who dropped it back inside to Lowe, a nothing play. The Hull defence, sitting back, watched it and Lowe was tackled comfortably by Birdsall. Roger, however, lay prostrate on the ground, the victim of Ronnie Wileman's right arm.

The touch judge ran on but there was surprisingly little reaction from Millward's teammates. Agar's initial reaction was to run in and protect his captain. "I'm waving my arms around telling everyone to calm down," he recalls, "when actually everyone was already quite calm. It was strange."

Last One Out...

Cliff Wallis raced on with a wet sponge while Lindop pulled Wileman out of the line and delivered his stern, finger-pointing lecture. On TV, Eddie Waring and Alex Murphy, lost for words, said little. Did Roger himself know it was broken?

"Well I knew summat wasn't right 'cos my jaw wasn't where it should be!" he said in Kippax. Given that this was the third time in six months he was no stranger to the feeling, but this was Wembley. He'd only been going eleven minutes. Did he feel the tackle was premeditated?

"It was definitely late but I used to joke that Ronnie got there as soon as he could," he said, trotting out a line he had probably used a thousand times over the years.

It would have come as no surprise to Millward that he would be singled out for rough stuff. He'd faced that kind of treatment all his career. He later wrote: "I've no axe to grind with Ronnie Wileman. Once you're out there, you do what you think is right – and what Ronnie decided to do was what he thought was the right thing to do at that particular time. At least he respected me and saw me as the main danger."

"I wanted someone to smack Roger all the time," reflected Hull Captain Steve Norton, many years later. "He's that good. Roger is like a God to me, but he was playing for Hull KR and it's the Cup final. But Rovers also had some big lads and so they were just as entitled to smack me if they thought I was a key player. Even though I was a big mate of Roger's, it didn't break my heart when Ronnie hit him."

Arthur Bunting is still troubled by the suggestion that Millward's injury was part of a gameplan. "I'm sure there are people who think players were under orders to take Roger out, but I would never condone that. Anyway, we were glad to see him at six. He was still a good player but, to be honest, past his best. We were more afraid of Steve Hartley."

"Ronnie got an absolute bollocking at half-time,"

reveals Keith Tindall. "All our tactics had been planned with Roger in mind. We'd prepared how we were going to handle him as the first receiver. But once he got injured, he dropped back and it changed the way they played. Agar came into the game much more, and we hadn't prepared for that, so Arthur wasn't happy. I was sat next to Ronnie in the dressing room so I could hear it. But nothing much bothered Ronnie."

Did Millward contemplate coming off the pitch?

"No, not really, but I couldn't let Hull or my own players know how much pain I was in. If they'd looked, they would have seen that my jaw was protruding to the side but that didn't last long because a couple of minutes later, I went in to tackle Knocker. I missed one of his legs but the other caught the side of my jaw and knocked it back into place. So I thanked him for that and carried on. You're playing at Wembley and you're so full of everything that you don't think of the pain. You just get on with it."

So Millward played on but left little impression on the game, barring that timely drop-goal just before the break. Rovers had Hogan on the bench. If he moved to centre, Hartley to stand-off, it wouldn't have been impossible to cover that position. Within a few minutes, Millward dropped deep into a more defensive position behind the line. At a break in play, the cameras focussed on him, standing hands on his hips as Hartley checked how he was, waving a physio onto the pitch again. Millward waved him back off though, despite clearly being in serious trouble.

Having stuck it out, Roger went home with the team on Sunday, toured the city and celebrated with the supporters at Hull City Hall and Craven Park. And at the end of a long, emotional and extremely painful weekend, he and Carol stayed with the Huttons at the Zetland Arms, before going to get his jaw checked out in hospital on the Monday.

***

ROGER MILLWARD ATTEMPTED a comeback the following season. Returning to action for the 'A' team at Batley, he broke his jaw for a fourth time. Doctors asked him, 'Is that it?' but it wasn't a question. A few days later, he retired, aged 33.

"They always say that you know when to retire," he said. "And 'A' team football at Batley ... what a way to go."

He continued to coach Hull KR and led them through the most sustained period of success in club history, winning two league titles, the John Player Trophy, Premiership Trophy and Yorkshire Cup as well as twice returning to Wembley as a coach. Much later, in 2007, cancerous cells were found in the small cracks left behind in his jaw. Eight years later, on the thirty-fifth anniversary of the 1980 Challenge Cup final, Millward told the *Hull Daily Mail*: "I've suffered for it, but I wouldn't change anything."

No one could erase the memory of leading the victorious Hull Kingston Rovers team up the thirty-nine steps to the Empire Stadium's Royal Box, to receive the trophy from the Queen Mother, followed, appropriately, by Clive Sullivan.

BBC Radio Humberside reporter Peter Ward, sensing that the moment was as much about Millward as the Hull KR club itself, captured the moment perfectly.

"Roger Millward coming across the front ... Roger Millward, a Rovers scarf around his neck ... and it's his, he's got it. It's in his arms. The Cup. It's Roger Millward's. And my goodness me, the crowd know it as well. He holds it high above his head. The pinnacle of a career that has been glorious in every way."

Upon his death, by way of tribute, Hull Kingston Rovers retired the number six shirt.

Post Match

18

AS THE HOOTER sounded, few supporters turned for the exits. Hull fans, devastated by defeat, nevertheless begin to sing. First, 'Old Faithful' then that eternal anthem of loyalty in the face of defeat, 'We'll Support You Ever More'. Mindful that, a year ago, their team was in the Second Division, they knew how far it had come, disappointment mixed with pride.

Rovers fans, of course, were definitely going nowhere.

The players, winners and losers, embraced. Millward was centre of attention, teammates and opponents seeking him out to offer congratulations, Keith Hepworth embracing him in one nice moment. The man whose presence in the Cas team prompted Millward to move to Hull KR.

With remarkable understatement, Roger Millward later described his own emotions: "Being surrounded by 72,000 Australians after you've just whalloped 'em at the Sydney Cricket Ground is a nice feeling. Being at Wembley as player coach when you're just about to go up and get that trophy is also a nice feeling."

Last One Out...

With Sullivan and then Millington behind him, having reached the summit Millward hoisted the silverware, though Sully took the base and Millo, unexpectedly, a winners flag presented by sponsor State Express. That ended up auctioned as part of Millington and Hartley's benefit year although, eventually, did find its way back to the club and even now makes occasional appearances at the ground or club shop.

Rovers fan Roger Pugh was at the game with friends from the Goodfellowship pub. "We managed to get tickets ten rows behind the Royal Box and could see the trophy lifted but that's all we could see. None of the players at all."

And then came the traditional lap of honour, ten minutes of pure impromptu joy. Grown men danced. Roger Millward wore a plastic cowboy hat, Steve Hartley flowers. Followed by pressmen and ballboys, the players, squad men included, ambled around waving, hugging and occasionally grabbing hold of the trophy, before running a few yards and lifting it to the crowd. Millward, every twenty yards or so, found himself on someone's shoulders – man of the moment but also the smallest. No one tried to lift Lowe or Millington.

"We were followed around by a Wembley official," Hartley remembers. "Some lads went on to the greyhound track to pick up scarves and hats and flags and he kept telling us to stay on the pitch and keep moving."

John Sexton worked his way down and couldn't resist joining in the celebrations. "I'll always remember coming across Len Casey and John Millington. When they saw me, they shouted 'Secko! Secko!' and began hugging me. We were all jumping up and down and, at that time, I was as much a supporter as anyone on the terraces."

Sexton then saw Mick Crane with whom he shared a keen interest in horse racing. "Craney didn't play so I wasn't sure what to say to him. Something like: 'That was fantastic, wasn't it Mick?' To which he replied, 'Aye, John, but do you know what won the 2000 Guinneas?'"

Steve Hubbard, stretchered off, lay stranded in the Wembley tunnel. "They stuck a black and white monitor on the end of my trolley, a microphone under my nose and Frank Bough started asking me questions. All I wanted to do was get out there and join the lads, or else get my ankle fixed. I can't remember what I said to Bough but remember Stuart Lunt, our doctor, coming to get me. He called me a 'lazy bugger' and told me to get up and go and get my medal."

Unbeknownst to either man, Hubbard's teammate, Paul Harkin, had already collected it on his behalf and the Royal party, duties over, were preparing to withdraw to their Retiring Room. On seeing Hubbard emerge from the tunnel hobbling on the arm of the club doctor, Harkin did an about turn, raced up the steps and handed the medal back to the Queen Mother. "Do you mind waiting for my mate," he is said to have asked her. And she did!

Like most rugby folk who encountered the royal guest that day, Hubbard was more than a little smitten. "She was very nice and asked how I was. I thought it was lovely that she waited until I could get up there. In fact, my auntie later wrote and thanked her for waiting to give me my medal and we got back a lovely letter wishing us all well and hoping that I made a speedy recovery." Hubbard's injury didn't prevent him from joining in the celebrations. "I hobbled down the steps and managed to get around on the lap of honour. It was amazing and I don't remember feeling any pain at all."

Amid the celebrations, one man had his eye on a match ball as a souvenir. "Straight after the game," said Allan Agar, I said to the ballboys: 'I'll give anyone who gets me one a tenner'. By the time I got to the tunnel, there were six lined up. I got all the Rovers players to sign mine and still have it.

Later on, Roger said he ought to have it and he was right. We were given a players' handbook the week before and one of the things it said was that the winning captain should get to keep the match ball. But he never bothered to ask."

As the lap of honour eventually came to an end, the players passed Frank Bough, waiting patiently in the tunnel to speak to key players, particularly Millward. With a broken jaw and holding a red and white teddy, he wasn't able to say much but still managed to get himself into trouble.

"I mentioned that I would probably go and get drunk – even if I had to drink through a straw," recalled Millward in his autobiography. "But a few days later, I received a letter from a woman complaining about my 'drinking habits', which she obviously didn't approve of. She also took me to task for using 'Humberside' and not 'East Yorkshire'."

***

AS IS THE custom, the defeated team follow the victors up to receive their medals and do their own cursory lap. Tindall and Lloyd looked utterly distraught. With that completed, no Hull player was keen to hang around and, unsurprisingly, they were in their dressing room long before Rovers, who continued to milk the acclaim on the pitch.

The BBC cameras cruelly followed the losers inside and the inquest began into how the game was lost. There was no doubt in the mind of Arthur Bunting. "We lost it in the first 20 minutes," he told Tony Gubba. "We had a penalty count of about 9-2 after 20 minutes. I don't blame the referee for that because we did silly things; things which are not in our nature. Once we settled down, we looked the better team."

Only Phil Lowe and Clive Sullivan played in more Hull derbies than Brian Hancock and nobody was better qualified to pass judgement as he did, much later, in 2014: "It wasn't like a proper derby," he said. "Normally, when we played Rovers it was like, 'We've got to beat 'em at all costs' but at Wembley it was 'we need to enjoy this.' The atmosphere was a bit too nice for my liking." Hancock wasn't the only one that felt that way, but we'll come to them later.

In the north dressing room, meanwhile, celebrations rolled on. Lockwood, first man back, summed up the relief for the television viewers: "A fine afternoon's work, but I'm glad that's over with." Millington right behind him, bottle of Hull Brewery bitter in hand and Cup lid on his head, began to sing: "When the red, red robin, goes bob, bob, bobbing along…." Centre stage was Hubbard on the massage table. Someone planted the cup on top of him and he was soon drenched: "Millington poured a full bottle of champagne over my head. I never realised how much champagne stings your eyes but it was the best shampoo I've ever had." He was surrounded by photographers, his image destined for the back pages the next morning. In contrast to Sully and Roger, Lowey and Rosey, Hubbard had played less than sixty games for Rovers, but already had league and cup winners' medals.

There were scars of battle everywhere. Aside from Millward and Hubbard, Rose had a vicious looking gash on his thigh and Lowe, who had somehow managed to get through eighty minutes with a busted shoulder, needed Watkinson to take his shirt off for him. There was no rest for physio Cliff Wallis. "I was chaotically busy, checking the injuries, slapping ice packs on Steve's ankle, having another look at Roger's jaw," he said.

Those that could manage it were soon taking it in turns to dive into the giant Wembley baths while Brian Lockwood, as the Lance Todd Trophy Winner, was due on telly.

"I was asked to go and do an interview with Eddie

Waring," he said. "But, by then, I'd been in the changing room drinking champagne for half an hour and, as everyone will tell you, I can't hold my drink, so when I went into the studio I was already half cut. Eddie was in there, so was Alex Murphy. Eddie started by saying that I'd equalled Alex's record of the most wins at Wembley. Straight away, I said, 'No, I think that's wrong Eddie. I've beaten it, haven't I?' Well, Alex jumped out of his seat shouting. 'No, no, Brian,' he said, 'I've won here three times as well.' It was hilarious."

Back in the dressing room, Watkinson, supping champagne, told a reporter: "It's a better feeling in here than it will be in there," as he gestured to the south dressing room.

***

HE WAS RIGHT. Steve Norton remembers that there were plenty of long faces. "After the game, some of our lads were moping around feeling sorry for themselves, saying they'd let the fans down. I was as disappointed as anyone but we had to remember we'd done well to get there. A few years before, we'd been relegated and were in the Second Division. The club was on the up, there was plenty to be pleased about. The directors had put loads of champagne in the dressing room for after the game. Not just a few bottles either. There were great big jeroboams. I told the lads that we had plenty to celebrate and cracked some open."

Clive Pickerill remembers it differently. "I'd never seen Knocker so disappointed. Never. Absolutely devastated."

Soon, most players were in the communal Wembley bath, supping champagne from plastic glasses as the sound of 'Old Faithful' echoed around.

***

230

AS FOR ME, I had never been more disappointed and upset in my young life. As soon as the final hooter went, I burst into tears and couldn't stop. I wasn't on my own. Grown men around me were doing the same. As were some Rovers supporters who found themselves in the Hull end. One put his arm around me and said, "It's okay, son, it's okay. You should be proud of them."

We stayed to watch the players come around to us, and watched them until they'd gone all the way down the tunnel on the opposite side of the ground. We saw Millward get the Cup, but I wasn't interested in that. Not even slightly.

As we walked down the stairs at the back of the stand, somebody had a small radio and a group of supporters huddled around it, listening to the football scores. There was a cheer when we heard that City had beaten Southend 1-0, saving them from relegation. A victory for West Hull. The crowd, 3,823, helped by hundreds of free tickets given to schoolboys, six hundred more than the club's lowest ever attendance.

Back in the Alexandra pub on Hessle Road, feelings were raw. A Yorkshire TV crew recorded the reaction. "If I could see the referee I would tell him what I thought of him 'cos he's robbed the Hessle Road lads," said one elderly Hull supporter. "I don't want to be here when they come back," said another. "I wish I could have the day off."

The players, meanwhile, were off to a boozer of their own, Wembley's Long Bar. Emerging from the tunnel one last time, they walked around the edge of the pitch. Sammy Lloyd stood chatting with Dick Tingle as the groundsman watered the pitch. Most stared up at the vast empty stands, trying to take it all in.

Inside, players of both teams mingled, grabbed food. It is a cup final tradition – the victors are magnanimous, the vanquished gracious – but it didn't last long. Everyone wanted to get back to their hotel, to see their wives and start the party. "I know we went up to the bar but I couldn't tell you who was there or what happened," said John Millington.

One young man who has cause to remember his trip to the long bar was Richard Watson, 17-year-old grandson of Hull FC chairman, Charlie. "I got to sit in the Queen Mum's chair and had a piss in her toilet!" he said. "At the end of the game, my dad took me and my brother in to see grandad. We also saw some players, Alex Murphy and Billy Boston, but it was a bit boring really. Until my dad took us through this little doorway and into a tunnel. It was a bit run down to be honest, but we soon realised that we were walking into the Royal Box. What I remember most is that, although it was quite wide, there weren't any seats in there. But they had put in some old wicker chairs, with cushions. The sort you might have in your garden. Anyway, me and my brother took it in turns to sit in her chair and then we went down another few steps and into the Retiring Room, which had its own little toilet. Well, I couldn't resist and had a little wee in it. That was my claim to fame from the 1980 Challenge Cup final."

By six o'clock, it was time to go. Wembley by then almost empty. Almost empty, but not quite.

As the rest of his workmates drifted away, Hull fan Paul Hogan and his pal Paul Jennison decided there was no hurry. "We just sat down on the concrete steps and then Paul pulled out a bottle of Southern Comfort, which was still half full," remembers Hogan. "Because most of our group were from East Hull, the tickets were in the Rovers end, but that didn't matter – we black and whites wore our colours and there were no problems. It was impossible to rush out of the stadium so we stayed and finished our bottle, promising that next year we would stand in the Hull end."

Just before boarding their bus, some Rovers players wandered back down onto the pitch. "The place was empty," said physio Wallis. "It was a really strange feeling after all the excitement."

Roy Holdstock suddenly remembered that he had a job to do. "I'd promised some of the lads from Greatfield Estate that I'd take them back some of the Wembley turf. So I went on with a black bin bag and started picking up divots. After a couple of minutes, I'd filled about a third of it when someone shouted 'Oy! What are you doing?' So I dumped the bag, ran off and jumped on the bus."

By then, most supporters were on their way home. Those travelling on the Wembley Specials headed straight back to the train station for the long journey north. "I have no idea where we caught our train from," said Tony Daddy. "It wasn't far from Wembley and it was absolutely rammed with Hull and Rovers supporters. We were on one platform, they were on another. I was absolutely heartbroken, it was the worst day of my life. But to have to stand across the track from thousands of celebrating Rovers fans made it even worse. They were chanting, taunting us. One or two Hull fans couldn't stand it and made to go across the tracks. Nothing happened but it could have been a bit nasty. The trip home wasn't much better, although the train was mostly full of Hull fans. We had to keep stopping to let the Express trains pull past and didn't get back until gone midnight."

It was worse still for Pete Smedley and his dad. "Our car ran out of petrol. It was a hire car and dad didn't read the gauge right. Halfway back, it started chugging and then the engine stopped. So dad found a jerry can in the boot and set off walking five or six miles to the next services. He was gone about two hours while me and my brother stayed in the car."

Paul Hogan and Paul Jennison, having finished their

Last One Out...

Southern Comfort, managed to meet up with the rest of their group outside Wembley station. "We jumped on a tube to Kings Cross. It was mayhem and our train to York was full, every man for himself. So much for reserved seats! We got home about 4.00am, just as it was starting to get light."

***

AT A QUARTER past seven, the Rovers team bus pulled in at Runnymede, with wives and girlfriends in tow. Just time, Lockwood remembers, for some private celebrations before dinner. "Once the women arrived, some of the lads couldn't wait to get back up to their rooms. They'd been away since Wednesday! I remember walking down the hotel corridor and seeing suitcases outside the bedroom doors. They'd dragged them into their rooms so quickly they hadn't even bothered to take their cases in."

Dinner was impressive. Hull Brewery had donated several cases of champagne and no expense was spared by the club either as the players sat down to a lavish meal, wine and beer flowing freely. Even after four days, the service still amused many of the players, as Brian Lockwood recalls. "The waiters were coming around to serve us vegetables and so on. One asked my wife Ann, 'Do you want fooking chips with that, madam?' 'I beg your pardon?' she said, shocked. I had to explain to her that, for four days, Len Casey, Phil Lowe and Paul Rose had been telling him to '...get some more fooking chips over here,' so he thought that was the name for them."

There were a few formalities. Bill Land raised a toast to Roger Millward, then John Millington led three cheers for the player-coach, still in distress with his broken jaw. John Sexton proposed the toast to the winning team, but remembers that the party soon fell flat.

"When you lose a cup final, you can't get any lower and so, within a few hours, you manage to pick yourself up and often end up having a great party. Dick Tingle told me that was what happened at the Hull FC hotel. Whereas the winners are euphoric at five o'clock and it can't really get any better than that, so you start to come down. Our party was as miserable as any I've ever been to!"

Steve Hubbard agreed. "I don't think it was much of a party, to be honest. By the end of the night, there were only a few of the lads still up. I think Roger stayed up, and Millo and Sully, but that was about it. Everybody was mentally shattered, completely drained. In my recollection of the night, I was in bed by about ten o'clock."

In Enfield, though, the party went deep into the night. "The club organised a big dinner and everybody was there," says Tim Wilby. "Directors, secretaries, vice-presidents, cleaners, ground staff, first team, reserve team, colts ... everyone. All with their nearest and dearest. It really was a club thing not just a first-team occasion."

Across London, supporters were either celebrating or drowning their sorrows. Seventy-odd regulars of the 'Halfway Hotel' were back in the West End. "Despite the defeat, we all headed back to the Prince of Wales," recalls Pete Allen. "We had a great sing-along to 'Knees Up, Mother Brown', 'Any Old Iron', 'The Lambeth Walk' and all the other traditional London songs. It was all great fun, until it turned a bit ugly when they ran out of draught beer at ten o'clock."

The parents of Roy Holdstock and David Hall chose the East End. "After the game, I'd managed to find my mam in the crowd. I'd given her a kiss through the fence and gave her my medal," explained Hodstock. "My dad told me that she'd been a nightmare, waving the medal around and saying: 'Look what my son won today at Wembley'."

Last One Out...

· Bryan Leason and the Rovers Supporters Club swiftly changed their plans. "We gave up our usual trip into the West End and instead opted for serious celebrations in the Ski Lodge, the hotel's basement bar, where the champagne corks were popping at regular intervals. 'You'll Never Walk Alone' was constantly played on the jukebox and we had our own rendition of 'Red, Red Robin' ringing around the bar."

***

THE MORNING AFTER, the Rovers players woke in fits and starts. "It was a really strange feeling," remembers Allan Agar. "It wasn't just the end of the weekend but the end of the season. All of a sudden I think we all just wanted to go home to see the supporters."

The bus wasn't due to leave until 12.30 and most took advantage of a lie-in. Except Dave Hall, who fancied a beer. Going down to the bar, he found the shutters up, a little old lady still cleaning up from the night before.

"Shit," he muttered.

"David, are you after a livener by any chance?" came a voice from nowhere. Rovers director Percy Johnson was perched on a stool behind a pot plant.

"I am, Percy, yes."

"Well those shutters will be coming up in five minutes, David and I will gladly buy you one."

And he did.

"Our directors were absolutely fabulous," said Roy Holdstock. "They were working class blokes who enjoyed the success every bit as much as we did. Great blokes."

Soon came the small matter of settling the bill. Each player had been given the opportunity to charge bar tabs and other sundries to their hotel room, to be settled on checking out. Some used an advance from their Wembley bonus to pay for it, but some had been even more inventive.

Roy Holdstock explains: "We had a community room at the hotel where we had our team meetings and, unknown to the club, some of the lads found out that you could charge things to the 'community room'. Well once word got out, everyone was at it. We were booking everything to that room. The final bill was something like £900!"

As well as the 'community room' bill, directors were hit in the pocket. As the players drifted out of reception to board their bus, Max Gold was among the last to check out. "How much?" he was heard to say. "I've never even played golf!"

But there was no delaying the coach at its appointed departure time and the journey home was swift. Some players recollect bumping into the Hull team at Leicester Forest services, while others were too busy celebrating to notice much at all. "Me and Steve Hartley drank a bottle of whiskey on the way home," said Mike Smith, "but we were still so high that we didn't even get drunk."

The first stop was at Newport, West of Hull, where the players and directors swapped buses for the open-top version that would tour the city. Here, they definitely bumped into the Hull squad.

Hull's journey had been very similar with plenty of alcohol to numb the pain. "I think we all felt for them," said Dave Hall. "We knew what it meant to us. The following year, we went there again and lost and I was absolutely gutted. Even so, it didn't stop Millo from giving them a load of shit. He hated everything black and white, did Millo."

"No, I felt sorry for them," insists John Millington. "I even gave them some of our beer!"

By a quarter-to-five on Sunday afternoon, the Rovers open-top bus had reached the edge of Hull. As it began its tour through the north of the city, the crowd began to grow and grow. "I'd never seen anything like it," recalls Allan Agar. "I won the Cup with Featherstone in 1983 and the entire town came out for that one, but it still wasn't anything compared to when we won the cup in Hull. There were just thousands of people as far as you could see along the entire route, and there were even some Hull FC supporters amongst the Rovers fans welcoming us home. My best memory of the whole weekend was the homecoming."

Bernard Watson, veteran of the Leeds Cup-winning team of 1968, agreed, telling everyone that "...there were many more out for Rovers than for Leeds."

Surrounded by thousands of fanatical supporters, the bus could barely navigate its way through. Along the route, eager cyclists tried to keep pace, riding along the pavements or darting out in front of the vehicle. At the busiest points, crowds of supporters surged off the pavement encircling the bus and bringing it to a standstill. People used every possible vantage point, the upstairs windows of homes, shops or offices were all taken and there was barely a lamppost in East Hull that did not have a daredevil Rovers fans clinging to it in full red and white regalia.

It was a breathtaking sight for the players, most of whom had never seen anything like it. Brian Lockwood had been a cup winner with Castleford and tried to prepare his teammates for the experience. "On the way home, I told Len Casey it would be the best thing he would ever experience in rugby league. He said, 'No, going on tour to Australia must be the best.' I said, 'A tour lasts a few months, you'll be enjoying this all year!' Well, once we turned onto Holderness Road and saw the thousands of supporters everywhere, all in red and white and singing and cheering, Len turned to me and said, 'Eh, Locky, you were right. This is the best thing'."

The tour took much longer than planned. It was 6.30 by the time the city centre was reached, pulling up in front of the Willis Ludlow store, across the road from the City Hall. One by one, the players stepped off the bus, some a little worse for wear, and slipped into a side entrance. Last off was Roger Millward, holding the Challenge Cup.

Beneath the old balcony, the crowd were beside themselves. "We're on the march, we're Roger's army," they sang, the numbers boosted suddenly by hundreds of supporters that had followed the parade into the city centre.

The crowd, more than 4,000 strong according to the police, filled Queen Victoria Square entirely, from the steps of Ferens Art Gallery to the Maritime Museum, all the way back to Monument Bridge along the edge of Princes Dock. Some reports suggested that five hundred police were on hand across the city to keep the peace but, in the city centre at least, the mood was joyous and the police stood around, in some cases joining in.

Eventually, and with great ceremony, Roger appeared on the balcony, between the Deputy Lord Mayor and Lady Mayoress, holding the cup, resting it on top of the City Hall balcony for all to see. While chairman Bill Land and the Deputy Lord Mayor, Alex Clarke, tried to quieten the crowd, another chorus of 'You'll never walk alone' broke out.

Eventually, the crowd hushed sufficiently for Alex Clarke to make a short speech, surprisingly eloquent in the circumstances, in which he spoke of the mutual shared pride between club, city and supporters.

And then it was Roger's turn. "On behalf of the lads and myself," he began, "I'd like to thank you for the fantastic support you gave us at the stadium. And I think it's only fair to say, thank you for being good for Humberside."

He would get in more trouble for that.

He then introduced the players one by one. David Hall was first, in top hat and scarf. Hubbard raised his crutches in the air to a huge cheer. Mike Smith appeared subdued in comparison with a stylish flat cap. Hartley and Sully received huge acclaim, as did Agar and on it went...

***

NOBODY ABOARD HULL FC's bus expected much of a reception. "Most of us were drunk," recalls Sammy Lloyd. "We'd not really stopped drinking since the end of the game. I had a bottle of Jack Daniels on the back seat of the coach, which I think I'd just about finished when we got back to Hull. And I was terrified of what reaction would come from the fans on our tour around the city and back to the Boulevard. I expected them to jeer and boo me."

The crowds began to grow as the bus reached Anlaby Road. As it turned and began to edge its way down Airlie Street, it was clear that the numbers had been hugely under -estimated. Beaten and disappointed, emotionally wrought, most FC fans had headed for the one place they could grieve together – the Boulevard.

"We grabbed a lift as far as the ground," remembered Hull FC fan 'Ian P' on a supporters' forum in 2010, "and just managed to get in before the team bus arrived. The scene was awesome; it brings a lump to my throat even now. It was packed, heaving, the pitch was awash with the black and white army. Heaven knows how many were in there that day. I was near the open top bus and I did know several of the team personally then. Taffy was a good mate due to his wife [Gillian] and my girlfriend hitting it off when he came north. I was talking to him at the back of the bus and Sammy, poor Sammy, would not come off it. He thought he'd let everyone down, but the crowd were baying for him. It took several other players and those fans close enough to persuade him to come out. He did and the Boulevard erupted."

The bus eventually pulled up behind the 'best stand', allowing the players to briefly escape to the dressing rooms. There, they prepared to make their appearance.

Richard Watson, with his dad and brother, had returned home to Wakefield on Saturday night, but the chairman's grandson was in Hull when the team came home.

"I was sat up in the best stand near the directors' box as the announcer called the players out. One by one they came out of the dressing room, up the little steps on onto the pitch. The crowd just went mad as they appeared, singing all the songs. 'Old Faithful' and 'We'll Support You Ever More,' just on and on. There were no stewards or anything like that and the announcer had asked supporters not to invade the pitch, but that was always going to be ignored and so, no sooner had the players come onto the field than hundreds poured over the barriers. You couldn't see the players at all. Just little groups of supporters with a player in the middle."

Tony Daddy was also there. "It was rammed, there must have been 20,000 people there. I was in the Threepenny Stand with my mates, all in our Wembley gear, flags and banners and so on. The players came out of the tunnel and on to the pitch but, within a few seconds, everyone just poured on and mobbed them. There were mounted horses but we managed to fight our way through to shake players' hands and commiserate with them. It cheered me up a bit, to be honest, to be there amongst the FC family I suppose, the players, supporters, directors and everyone."

"I remember the mounted horses," said Hull winger, Graham Bray. "They were supposed to be there to protect us but one stood on my foot. Bloody painful, I can tell you."

Last One Out...

After an hour or so, and a couple of drinks in the Supporters Club, everyone gradually drifted away from the Boulevard, finally heading home. After the reception at the City Hall, the Rovers players headed back to Craven Park for another party, this one a little more upbeat than the one at Runnymede.

"Our Supporters Club wasn't much more than a tin hut," said club treasurer Bryan Leason, "but it had a brilliant atmosphere and that night it was absolutely terrific. It was already full when I got there around half past seven and then we all made way for the players when they turned up about 9 o'clock. Our artist that night was Liz Dawn from *Coronation Street* and she said: 'Can I come back next week?'

The following days saw some emotional moments for several players as they reflected on the achievement. On Sunday evening, Brian Lockwood went to see his mam and dad for what he hoped would be a warm reunion. Lockwood takes up the story. "My dad never praised me. Even when I first started playing for Castleford, I'd come home after I'd won the man of the match award and I'd go see them. My mam would say 'You played really well, love' and my dad would sort of nod his head and say 'Eyyyup'. I'd say, 'Alright dad, did you enjoy the game?' I'd be desperate for him to say something good about how I'd played or how proud he'd been. But he'd always say something critical like, 'Thee took thee eye off t'ball. I was watching thee, and thee took thee eye off t'ball.' I used to come away thinking 'There's no pleasing him. I can't make him happy'. I'd come home upset about it. It was always like that. So, after I'd got back from London, I went to see my mam and dad who'd both gone to the game on a trip. My mam gave me a hug and told me how proud she was and then I asked my dad if he'd enjoyed the game. He looked up and nodded, said 'Eyyup' and that were it. But then my mam said, 'He cried, Brian. When he saw your name on that big screen, that you'd won Lance Todd Trophy, he cried!' So I looked at my dad and he said, 'I did not! I did not!' But I knew it was true."

***

ROVERS' CELEBRATIONS DIDN'T end on Sunday night. It was a Bank Holiday weekend and, by Monday lunchtime, many of the team were out again, this time joined by their mates and many of the reserve and colts players who had not made it into the Wembley squad. One was Steve Crooks who would play at Wembley for Rovers in 1981 and go on to coach both Hull teams during the 1990s. The celebration party found themselves in The Holderness Tavern.

"We used the Holderness quite regularly at that time and were well known by the landlord, but that didn't count for anything once it came to three o'clock. No matter who we were, the pub shut at three o'clock. At that time in Hull, there would have been a dozen or so places that you could go to if you wanted to carry on drinking, social clubs and the like. A few of the lads were members at Belmont Club around the corner on Newbridge Road, so we all piled down there. There would have been twenty or thirty of us, with the Cup."

But the victors didn't get the reception they hoped for at the East Hull social club. "Only them that are members can come in," said the irascible doorman, Charlie.

Crooks and the rest of the entourage couldn't take him seriously as they stood there with the Rugby League Challenge Cup, believing, probably quite rightly, that just about every licensed premises, at least in the East of the City, would have paid to have the Rovers squad descend upon them at the end of that weekend.

"Someone tried to persuade him," remembers Crooks, "'C'mon Charlie, let us in,' they were saying, while one of the lads who was a member duly went inside to try and persuade the club steward to let us in. Eventually he did so and, within half an hour, everyone had phoned their mates, wives, girlfriends and kids to tell them to get down to Belmont Club and have their photos taken with the team and cup. There were hundreds in there that afternoon and hardly any were members. And, by the end of it all, Charlie was still sat in his chair on the door, livid."

Others continued to celebrate. Brothers-in-law Roy Holdstock and Dave Hall went to The Falcon. "My family are all Rovers fans but Dave's family are staunch black and white," said Holdstock. "When we went in you wouldn't believe the reception we got. All the Rovers fans were over the moon to see us, as you'd expect. But Dave's family were all Hull fans and they congratulated us as well, hugged us and told us how proud of us they were. That brought home how special the whole occasion had become for everyone."

As the dust settled, tributes poured in. The behaviour of Hull supporters had exceeded everyone's expectations. It had become the story of the weekend. In a crowd of 95,000, an estimated 60,000 people, divided by a bitter rivalry, had journeyed to the other end of the country for up to four days, had shared buses, trains, hire cars, hotels, pubs, clubs and Wembley Stadium and the whole unlikely, often drunken, entourage had caused not a single significant incident of misbehaviour. Police confirmed just four arrests, each for a mild instance of drunkenness. It was staggering. There'd been trouble at recent derbies, no point denying it. With segregation impossible, there were obvious concerns. Yet it turned out that, once they left Hull, rugby league supporters realised they had more in common with each other, than set them apart. They also found that their shared respect for their city and their sport counted for a great deal more than anyone expected.

Weeks later, England football supporters ran amok in Turin, goalkeeper Ray Clemence was blinded by teargas, Kevin Keegan expressed his 'shame'. In contrast, Hull in 1980 gave rugby league a huge boost at the start of a new decade.

David Oxley, typically, managed to sum it up nicely at the time. "It has been a fabulous weekend for the city and it couldn't have come at a better time. The industrial and employment scene is rather bleak but the two rugby league teams have brought sunshine and smiles to the faces of their fans. And what wonderful fans both sides have – there were 60,000 of them that made the trip to Wembley and there wasn't a single incident. They're a credit to the game, a credit to the city and to the two teams that mean so much to them."

And they were good at the box-office too. A sell-out 95,000 brought receipts of £448,000 (although, in 1988, several hundred unsold and unused tickets appeared in Wakefield to suggest that the game wasn't, after all, sold out) with each club pocketing 15 per cent after the bills had been paid.

A shame then, that it hadn't been the best of matches. Hancock reckoned the atmosphere had not been fierce enough and Rovers hooker David Watkinson agreed. The cup final was only his second derby, but he would go on to play in twenty. "For one thing, both teams were away from home. And at Wembley the supporters were a long way away. They weren't on top of us like they would have been in Hull, especially at the Boulevard. So it wasn't a derby as such, not the usual blood and guts. "

The pressure had been almost unbearable. The weight of expectation. Some players spoke of barely being able to breathe. Little wonder performances were affected. "There was such a lot of pressure on us," recalls Watkinson. "In a normal game, you can make mistakes and you've got next week to put things right, but at Wembley the pressure was stifling. It was a dour affair but there was so much at stake."

Fred Lindop had more experience of Hull derby games than most of the players. His reflections on the passion felt towards rugby league in the city are worth recounting in full.

"I made my debut as an official at the Boulevard. I was to be a touch judge for an 'A' team game in the mid-'60s. I caught the train from Leeds to Paragon Station and walked down Anlaby Road to the Boulevard. As I entered the ground, I could sense tension even though it was a reserve fixture. I was certainly apprehensive and, when I saw a policeman I told him, 'Am I glad to see you today, officer!' He replied 'You bugger off, you're on your own today,' and walked away and left me! That was my introduction to the Boulevard. I always had a respect for the people of Hull because of their love of rugby league and of their clubs and civic pride. I generally got on well with players of both and so was often the sacrificial lamb given the derby to officiate. Nobody else wanted them! The 1980 final wasn't a great game, but the players gave their all and I just think that probably the occasion got to them."

"There's always pressure in a derby game but this was different," believes Dave Hall. "We just could not lose. Some players nowadays talk about the pressure of the derby and that it's more important than the two points and they're right, but I remind them what we played in. A final at Wembley. Against Hull FC. It might never happen again. Now that's pressure."

By Tuesday, life began to return to normal for most people. Workers on the Humber Bridge finally decided to return to work after a two-week stoppage. Although most went back on Tuesday, it was Thursday or Friday before everyone had re-appeared. John Millington was back at BP. "I'd had a bet with my mate, Billy. Whoever's team lost would climb to the top of the highest tower at Saltend and put the winner's flag up there. So I went back to work, just to see him put that red and white flag at the top of that tower."

Roy Holdstock wasn't ready to go back though. "I was self-employed at the time, working with my dad. He'd ring me up every morning, 'Are we doing any work today?', he'd ask and I'd say 'No, no'. We were out every other night and spent most of the summer taking the cup around. I didn't do any work for three weeks."

"I couldn't face it," says Tony Daddy. "I worked at an engineering plant on Sutton Fields and it was half Hull, half Rovers. I just couldn't drag myself in on the Tuesday morning so I went to doctors, invented some illness and didn't go back to work for a fortnight. When I did finally go back, it was horrible. Absolutely horrible."

I was back at Endike Juniors on Tuesday to face the taunts from my red and white schoolmates. I already had my excuses lined up. It was the referee's fault. We were robbed. Deep down, I knew we just hadn't done well enough. But, we would be back, I told them. We'd win it next year.

***

WITH THE SEASON over, some players chose the moment to call it a day. John Newlove's retirement, at 35, was no great surprise. Nor was Allan Agar's, who was expected to join the Rovers coaching staff.

There was more of a shock when Arthur Bunting also announced plans to quit. Couldn't balance the job with business commitments, he said. But, the very next day, Bunting met with the board, the problem was solved and a new three-year deal was announced.

On Wednesday night, Brian Lockwood drove over to Salford for the Lance Todd presentation dinner. But he was in for a shock. "The Lance Todd trophy had been nicked! I only found out on the Wednesday that the one they'd given me at Wembley had been a replica because the original had been stolen sometime during the previous year. When I turned up at Salford's clubhouse they told me they hadn't had time to get it engraved, so the one they gave me had nothing on it. But it was a lovely dinner. Lots of the previous winners were there and they were introduced to the crowd in chronological order. The most recent winner presents it to the current winner, so I was given it by David Topliss."

The *Hull Daily Mail* compositors were still on strike but the *Hull Times* hit the streets on Friday with their man Peter Shilling on the front page, along with his 'mate' Mac Stone, clutching a slip of paper that clearly read "Hull KR 10-5 Hull FC". Remarkably the mystery man had got it right after all, also predicting that there would be just two tries scored. He didn't, however, pick Lockwood for the Lance Todd. But then, neither did anyone who was there.

At the end of the week, most of the Hull squad were getting away. "Throughout the season, someone kept a kitty," explained Tim Wilby. "Anyone who won a man of match award put their money in, players' fines, donations, raffles, sweepstakes. Everything went into the pot to be spent on the end-of-season, players-only trip away. We caught the ferry from Hull and spent four days in Amsterdam."

"I don't remember that," says Graham Bray. "That may have been later, after I left Hull."

"I don't recall going to Amsterdam," said Keith Tindall.

"I remember the civic reception, but don't remember a trip on the ferry." It's just possible that Wilby went on his own.

***

IT HAD ALWAYS been the intention to hold a joint civic reception for both teams regardless of the result. And so everyone reassembled at Hull's Guildhall on May 12th. But the old divides still ran just below the surface.

"I don't know who the dignitaries were," says Brian Lockwood, "but I well remember one of them standing up and making a speech about what an occasion it had been and how, if it hadn't been for the referee, Hull would have won. I hadn't expected someone in his position to say that. Clive Sullivan looked at me and we both said: 'We're not having this,' so got up and walked out of the hall. Later on, there was another one – a lady, something to do with the council – who said that the black and whites would have won if it hadn't been for the 'bastard referee'. I was stood with my wife at the time and I just said, 'Come on, love, we're going home'. I really hadn't expected people from the council to say stuff like that."

During the evening, the whole game was shown again on a projector screen. Fred Lindop was there, keen to check his own performance. "It was the first time I had seen the recording of all the incidents, but I never had any doubts about my decisions," he said. "I did not realise at the time I had disallowed five tries but felt I was 100 per cent correct."

During the week that followed, most of the other players drifted back to work, including Mike Smith. At times, it was tough. "I found myself sweeping up and told someone, 'this time last week, I was shaking hands with the Queen Mother and now I'm shaking hands with a yard brush.'"

Legacy – From 10-5 to 1-1

19

THE NEXT HULL derby took place on 22nd June at the Circle – a benefit cricket match for Paul Rose and Keith Boxall, in front of just over a thousand supporters.

Rovers batted first, Steve Crooks scoring 46, Sully, 30. Lazenby picked up three wickets with his seamers and the wily spin of director Roy Waudby claimed two more victims. Rovers scored 186 in thirty overs before the heavens opened and the players spent the rest of the afternoon dodging the rain and posing for photographs with the Challenge Cup.

"We took it turns to take it out that summer," recalls Steve Hartley. The club turned no organisation down – Brough Golf Club ... Boothferry Park ... a car and motorcycle show at Beverley racecourse, where Roger rubbed shoulders with Chris Quinten from *Coronation Street* this time ... Malet Lambert's school summer fête ... Phil Lowe's pub in Sproatley ... schools ... shops ... Chris Lawson's heating business on Anlaby Road, a stone's throw from the Boulevard. Not many turned up to that one.

***

JOHN SEXTON, IN a thoughtful piece in the *Sports Mail*, reflected on a season that would only be remembered for one day: May 3rd. It had been an otherwise disappointing season for the Robins.

Although they had made it to two cup finals, they'd made no impact in the other three competitions. And their league form was mediocre at best. After a reasonable start, a home defeat to Leeds in November was the first of five successive home defeats. It opened up a gap between Rovers and the leaders that they never managed to close.

Nobody in 1980 would have spoken about Rovers' attractive style of rugby as a 'brand', but whatever their methods the Robins continued to entertain despite their league position. Sullivan (17), Lowe (15) and Agar (14) all recorded impressive try-scoring returns, but the biggest beneficiary was Steve Hubbard, who broke a host of club records during the season.

His 30 tries in 39 games put him joint top of the try-scoring charts with Keith Fielding and he ended the season as highest point-scorer in all divisions with 366, breaking Neil Fox's club record. Not bad for a man making his first full season as a Rovers player.

It wasn't enough though to earn him either the club's or the sport's Young Player of the Year award. Those honours both went to teammate Roy Holdstock who, although still only 25, won the awards a full eight years after his debut at a time when some players may have been thinking about a testimonial season.

By the end of May, Millward had agreed a new three-year deal and immediately started the process of rebuilding his team. He began with a clear out. Dunn, Watson, Leighton, Tyreman and Madley were all moved on. Two American guest players were sent home and four former Colts players let go. Of the more senior players, Agar had hoped for a coaching role, but his phone never rang. Rovers appointed Ged Dunn instead and Agar went to Wakefield. Lockwood's departure was more protracted, with a hint of acrimony. There was a feeling around Craven Park that Millward felt undermined by Lockwood, that Lockwood saw himself in the coaching seat.

Lockwood was not short of offers and had been courted by Oldham, Salford and Wigan as soon as the season ended but, at that stage, he hoped to remain at Craven Park. "I wanted to play with Rovers and would have been happy to have ended my career at Craven Park, but four or five weeks went by and they gave me no indication that they wanted me. I thought they were trying to find a way to tell me."

Bill Land saw it differently. "We have just won the Challenge Cup," he told the press at the time. "Surely he doesn't expect me to go around to every player and say 'will you be playing for us next year?' It is just expected that they will be. They can't just take themselves off and sign for another club without telling anyone." The relationship was over. Within a few weeks, Lockwood signed for Oldham.

A few months later, he left there too. Having been at a progressive club like Hull KR, he had no truck with what he saw as an amateur outfit and signed for Widnes. It proved a shrewd move. The Chemics went to Wembley yet again in '81 where they beat, of all teams, Hull KR to make it four cup final victories for Lockwood. He was back again in '82 to play Hull FC. Widnes drew but lost the replay, leaving Lockwood with six unbeaten Wembleys (including the 1973 Test), an impressive record until Shaun Edwards came along.

Sully wasn't finished either. When the 1980-81 season began, he lined up alongside Lockwood at Oldham, but a broken arm cut short his stay and he was back at the Boulevard the following year, helping the team through a congested fixture list. The season ended with Sullivan's second Challenge Cup final appearance, at 39, in the replay at Leeds.

And on he went, into his third decade as a player. Briefly, he coached at Doncaster, but returned yet again to the Boulevard to join the coaching staff, making the occasional appearance when injuries struck. He played his final game, in April 1985, as a substitute at Bradford. He was 42.

Six months later, though, Clive Sullivan died from liver cancer. "It had been a bad winter," recalls Ros Sullivan, "and Clive helped them out. In the last game he played he got winded somehow and my mam always said that might have been the cause of his cancer."

Ros goes onto to describe her own best memories of her husband's legendary career. "Of all the highlights, the World Cup, *This is Your Life*, MBE, there is nothing to beat that weekend at Wembley in 1980. For Clive, I'm not sure what he would say was the highlight ... he was so proud of getting the MBE. And a big thing for him was being made captain of Great Britain. He was very, very proud of being Welsh and playing for Wales. He would be absolutely astounded at what has happened since he died and how people still talk about him. My daughter says there's never a week goes by when someone doesn't mention her dad. He'd be amazed that people still remember him. For me, whenever I listen to the travel news and hear them mention the road they named after him it feels very strange, but makes me very proud."

***

Last One Out...

ALL WAS QUIET at the Boulevard for a few weeks until, at the end of May, season tickets suddenly went on sale, two months early. The sum of £18 would get you a standing pass, £27 to sit down. And the directors made no secret of why. They needed money to hunt down new signings.

As the cash poured in (£5,000 on the first day alone), Hull went in search of players, pestering Leigh relentlessly for John Woods and then turning their attention to Wakefield, and David Topliss. You can't have him, insisted Wakefield, but do you want Trevor Skerrett? And so, for a world record £40,000, Hull signed one of the toughest props in the game.

Hull had previously broken the world transfer record in 1978 to bring Steve Norton to the Boulevard for £25,000. Rovers then topped it to sign Hogan for £33,000 from Barrow, before besting it again in 1980 to re-sign Casey for £38,000. Hull's signing of Skerrett held the record for less than twelve months until Rovers smashed it yet again, the last time a Hull club would shell out a world record transfer fee, when they paid Wigan £72,500 for George Fairbairn.

All this activity made Hull-born players nervous. "I thought that was the end of me when Hull signed Skerrett," admitted Keith Tindall, "but it wasn't actually."

The truth was that Bunting just wanted more players. He knew that if they were to compete for trophies on all fronts he needed strength in depth. In 1980, Hull used thirty-four players in a forty-three-game season but, outside of his first thirteen, the quality was thin.

And it wasn't like they were short of cash. The fans had bought into the ambitions of the club in a huge way and had come flooding back to the Boulevard. The average home attendance exceeded 10,000 and players became accustomed to playing in front of large, noisy crowds. There were twenty league attendances above 10,000 during the season and twelve of those were at the Boulevard; a further three were games that also involved Hull FC.

So, as the cash flowed in, Bunting spent it just as quickly. Not only were win bonuses frequent and generous, the club paid out over £30,000 on travelling expenses during the campaign (an astonishing £150,000 in today's money).

But, despite Hull's third place finish, their victories tended to be hard-fought low-scoring affairs, the highest try-scorer (Prendiville) managing just sixteen touchdowns. After smashing every record in the book the year before, Lloyd suffered a frustrating season, managing only twenty-one appearances in which he kicked fifty-three goals.

The times were changing fast at the Boulevard. The Hull team of 1980 had been assembled quickly, in just a couple of years. And it was dismantled almost as quickly. By the autumn, Hull were planning ahead in a big way. In October, Boothferry Park hosted a Hull versus New Zealand tour game. Prior to that, director Dick Gemmell met with Kiwi stars Dane O'Hara and Gary Kemble and proposed a deal. They were blown away by the noise generated by the FC fans and agreed to sign, bringing about a new era for the club. And it got better. 'Are you interested in my mate as well?' asked Kemble. 'He's called James Leuluai.'

***

NOTTINGHAM FOREST BEAT Hamburg and kept the European Cup. Ian Botham was captain of England and Brian Jacks won *Superstars*. Seb Coe was at Costello, running the fastest 800m of the year. The Challenge Cup was there too and so were the protestors. 'Don't go to Moscow', they told Coe.

On the corner of Beverley Road, they opened Jacksons' Club, the biggest privately-owned club in the country. *Grease* and *Saturday Night Fever* were now a double bill at Cecil. The Human League were in town, so were Gene Pitney, Frankie Valli and Suzi Quatro and, on 9th June, Bruce Lee was finally arrested for three murders, before going on to confess to a whole string of them. In the city centre, dredging work had begun in the Humber and Railway docks. If work went to plan, the new marina was expected to open in 1982.

Hull's landscape was changing. On 13th June, the one-and-a-half kilometre middle road section of the Humber Bridge was completed and a crowd gathered on the Hessle riverbank to watch. There were cheers when the final deck was lifted into place. It was still hoped that the work would be completed before the end of 1980 and that the bridge would open to vehicles in early 1981, but some continued to doubt its value, claiming it would take forty years and £500m to pay off the debt to the Government.

In July, the trawler *Cordella* pulled into Albert Dock, a week early, its hold practically empty. Hull's fishermen never received the help and support promised. The EEC's Fisheries Policy was finally revised in 1982, but it was too late for Hull. The ship owners were compensated for the loss but the trawlermen got nothing. They had been 'casually' employed for all those years, not entitled to redundancy until, in 2012, Alan Johnson, MP for West Hull, secured some compensation for the surviving claimants, who got £1,000 each.

***

IN RUGBY LEAGUE, the Challenge Cup final was the second all-Hull final of the season. The following year, they met in the Premership Trophy final and, in 1982, the John Player Trophy final. In 1984-85, they met in two more, the Yorkshire Cup and John Player Trophy again. Six finals in just over five years, a remarkable sequence that sums up the stranglehold the two clubs had over the sport. But then it ended and there have been no more all-Hull finals since.

Hull supporter Dave Willson is also a maths teacher. He calculates that, in any particular season, there is a 0.23 per cent chance of the two clubs meeting in the Challenge Cup final. "Working on an assumption that, whenever and whoever they play, there is a 50 per cent chance of them winning and progressing, that stacks up to a once-every-five-hundred-year event."

If that seems like an unrealistic long-shot, ask yourself how close have we ever got to it happening since?

But it nearly did, just five years later. Both teams made the semis. Rovers were champions but it was Hull, with their all-star team of Australians and New Zealanders, Norton, Crooks and Schofield, that pulled in the crowds. Watched by a total of 60,000 supporters, three epic semi-finals played out over ten days in Leeds. Hull needed a replay to beat Cas at Headingley, but Rovers fell to the eventual winners, Wigan, at Elland Road.

And that was it. The squads broke up, crowds tumbled and, in 1986, the two Hull teams finished seventh and eighth in the league. In the first round of the cup, they were drawn together again. Rovers won before less than 9,000 supporters.

A lucky draw eased Rovers into the semis where they overturned Leeds after a replay. Smith and Watkinson were the only survivors from 1980 in Rovers' Wembley team, but they couldn't prevent Castleford winning the cup.

It was another twenty-nine years before Rovers made it to Wembley. But they won't want to be reminded of that game in a hurry.

***

Last One Out...

HULL'S CUP RECORD wasn't much better. Until 2016, Hull had been back to Wembley five times since 1980 and still hadn't won. 'You'll Never Win at Wembley', became the song to haunt generations of Hull FC fans.

Within the same era, Rovers won every trophy in the game, including three league titles. But nobody was interested in any of that. Wembley, 1980, is all that counts. So, have they overdone it?

"It is still one of those games that people ask you about once they realise that you're a Rovers supporter," reckons Roger Pugh, whose official club history, *The Robins*, begins with a chapter on the 1980 final. "We wouldn't have dreamed that the game would have become so important, but yet it is the only time that Rovers have won the cup and it was also the last first-team game played by Roger, as well as Lockwood, Agar and Sullivan. But, should we be referring to it today except in the context of it being Roger's final game? Probably not."

"The legacy of the 1980s has probably been more of a burden for Hull than Rovers," believes Tony Collins. "Rovers have always seen themselves as the underdogs who are usually satisfied if we can stay in Super League, whereas Hull should be and expect to be a top-four team. That era has been more of a millstone for Hull than Rovers. But, in the city, it's still very important and people still talk about it and will talk about it for years."

Steve Hartley sees no end to the legacy of 1980. "I still talk to people who weren't even born in 1980 and they know the teams and know about the humour and the banter. I never thought that we'd still be talking about it thirty-six years on, but I think we still will be in another thirty-six years."

Steve Hubbard talks most often of the try he scored, "I think that made an awful lot of people happy and an awful lot of people sad. I've been called everything from a pig to a dog for scoring it. I've been on building sites where people have thrown bricks at me. Although I think they've meant it as a joke."

It's doubtful whether any member of the Hull FC team felt the disappointment as keenly as Keith Tindall, the only Hull-born player in the side.

"It was the biggest disappointment of my life. Nobody ever lets me forget it. The biggest disappointment was that we got over the line three times. Any one of those tries and one or two of Sammy's goals and we'd have won. It never leaves you. Rovers supporters have never stopped going on about it and they never will. It'll go to the grave with me."

***

NOBODY DOUBTS THAT the game, the weekend and the occasion will last long into the memory of Hull folk, but what about the game in general.

Did it have any impact? A legacy, even?

"Without a doubt," believes David Howes, who knows a thing or two about these things. "The 1980 final was an event and, through its success, it gave confidence to the sport as a whole. After 1980, we began to use events as a way of marketing the game through the media. Some influential people in the game told us that we were mad to take internationals to Old Trafford and to Wembley, but we got over 50,000 at Old Trafford in 1986. The 1980 Challenge Cup final showed that was possible."

You wouldn't expect Tony Collins to play down the 1980 final, but this is his view. "I think it raised the profile of the game in the same way that the 1982 Kangaroo tour did. It gave the game a spring in its step and killed off any doubts that it couldn't survive, or was in retreat." And the impact on the city at a time of such historic change?

"It's easy to exaggerate how depressed the city was. There was still a lot of fight in it. Economically, the fishing industry was gone and there were lots of problems in many other industries as well, but day to day I don't think people were as depressed as you might imagine. I think Wembley encapsulated how people felt. It was a chance to let ourselves be heard and get on the national stage and say 'Here we are! We are Hull.'"

Thirty-six Years of Hurt

Epilogue

JUNE 1980. STILL celebrating, still basking, the Rovers board set their minds to commemorating their success. Bill Land announced that the social club being constructed at Craven Park would be called the '10-5 Club'.

And it's still there. Although it's now called the '10-5 Suite' and at a different ground, Rovers having moved in 1989.

In later years, Rovers fans would be ridiculed for this decision. Hull fans claiming it marked them out as a small-time club, but Rovers fans got their own back. In spades.

It is unclear when Rovers supporters first began to sing the 'You'll Never Win at Wembley' song. It certainly wasn't during the 1980s. It probably emerged in the 1990s when the fortunes of both clubs were in decline. Rovers fans clinging to the singular success that Hull fans had never enjoyed.

It hurt Hull supporters and it got worse as time went on. No matter how much success Hull FC might have enjoyed, Rovers fans would always have 1980. And, because of 1980, Rovers fans could almost forget their own less-than-impressive Wembley cup final record (P5, W1). Clearly, even after thirty-six years, the occasion still resonates, largely because Rovers won and Hull had never won since.

When Hull FC won the Challenge Cup at Wembley in 2016, the outpouring of relief and emotion from the players and supporters owed as much to the fact that it would finally bring an end to 'that song' as any satisfaction at actually winning the thing.

"In a funny way," Sammy Lloyd told me on the day that Hull brought the Cup back to Hull, "the way the weekend has unfolded has massively removed a lot of the remaining pain of the past years." For you and tens of thousands of other Hull FC fans, Sammy.

And so, the story of the 1980 final really came to an end on 27th August 2016.

Thirty-six years of hurt that began on the final whistle in May 1980 were brought to an end. And, just as I had in May 1980, I found myself in tears. From the moment that Jamie Shaul scored in the 73rd minute, I couldn't stop. And, when I looked around me, there were dozens, hundreds of others just like me.

Hull FC had won at Wembley. It was 1-1.

Acknowledgements

I WROTE THIS book because nobody else had written it. The late 1970s and early 1980s were a uniquely special time in the history of rugby league in Hull, but few people had ever attempted to record much of it.

So it seemed like a book was long overdue.

But as I began my research, focusing on the spring of 1980, I found myself going further and further back, to the start of the season, to the record-breaking season before that and then, to fully appreciate 1980, I realised I had to return to the middle of the decade, when Wembley was but an impossible dream.

From the mid-1970s, the perspective was different.

Hull was different. It still had a fishing industry, there was still optimism about the future, about Humberside and the Humber Bridge. So that was part of the story that couldn't be ignored either. And so, as I set out to write about rugby league, I found that the city kept coming into the foreground. It wouldn't keep away.

***

THE NARRATIVE RELIES extensively on the recollections of those who were there, mainly the players. Some quotes were taken from interviews they did at the time, usually reported in the *Hull Daily Mail*. Most, however, come from interviews I have carried out over the past four years. Therefore, there would be no book were it not for the players who took part. At the outset, I didn't know any of them.

My first port of call was Mike Page, the ex-Hull FC director, and only member of either club's Wembley party whose number I had in my phone. I rang him and we met in the Marquis of Granby in Hessle in late 2013. He turned up with Arthur Bunting. 'Give me a ring and come round for a chat,' said Arthur. By the end of the night, I also had telephone numbers for Brian Hancock and Brian Lockwood.

Early in 2014, I bumped into Chico Jackson, chair of Hull FC's Ex-Players' Association. Through him, I managed to contact Kenny Foulkes, Charlie Birdsall, Sammy Lloyd and Tim Wilby. I remembered that I also had Dick Tingle's number, so I went to see him and, at the end of our meeting, he gave me John Sexton's contact details.

Lee Crooks gave me Knocker's number, and Paul Prendiville's. And then Mike Page got in touch again; he had Steve Hubbard's too. Allan Agar turned up to a Gareth Ellis testimonial event I went to, so I introduced myself and arranged to go over to see him. He later gave me David Watkinson's number.

I saw Roger Millward at another event, introduced myself and went to Kippax to interview him. Then there was an event at Hull's History Centre, celebrating Clive Sullivan. His wife, Ros, was there and we arranged to meet. So was

Acknowledgements

Colin Hutton, who I went to see at his home. At the end of our chat, he put me in touch with Phil Lowe.

But I still hadn't spoken to many Rovers players, particularly the locally-born players who I knew were still scattered around East Hull. And so I looked up their Ex-Players' Association chairman, Wayne Parker, who helped me get in touch with David Hall, Roy Holdstock and John Millington. I went to meet Hall and Holdstock and they turned up with Mike Smith. Millo could not have been more accommodating, digging out some of his mementoes, as well as sharing his stories.

I knew that one or two ex-Hull players still visited the KC Stadium, so I took to using the Kingston Suite bar, where I bumped into Keith Tindall and Barry Edwards, another long-standing member of the Ex-Players' Association who put me in touch with David Doyle-Davidson and Vince Farrar. Farrar, it also turned out, had Graham Bray's number. By chance, I realised that I knew Jean Pickerill, wife of Clive, and so I managed to speak to him. Somewhere along the way, I happened upon Steve Hartley.

And so I managed to speak to twenty-two of the thirty players who played at Wembley as well as several that didn't; Steve Crooks, Keith Boxall, Barry Edwards. I spoke to both of Hull's coaches and both *Hull Daily Mail* journalists.

Without exception, these men, and very often their wives and partners, treated me with the greatest courtesy and were unfailingly generous with their time, very often trusting me with their memorabilia, medals and trophies. This project has been an absolute labour of love and the greatest pleasure has been from getting to know those men.

I am extremely grateful to them, hope they find some pleasure in reading the story and apologise if I have made any errors in the telling of it.

Last One Out...

Roger Kahn is quoted elsewhere in this book and, as I got to know those men of 1980, I was reminded again of how he once described an ageing baseball team: "...it is fiercely difficult for the athlete to grow old, but to age with dignity, and with courage, cuts close to what it is to be a man."

***

I WOULD ALSO like to thank David Howes and David Oxley for their candid accounts of a pivotal era in the history of rugby league, and Fred Lindop for his time and memories (along with Ben Thaler, who put me in touch with him).

Amongst supporters and club officials, Chico Jackson, Wayne Parker, Tony Daddy, Pete Smedley, Richard Watson, Tony and Andrea Roberts, Paul Hogan, Pete Allen, Bryan Leason, Roger Pugh, David Sherwood and, of course, Fred Lewis, whose sign inspired the title, all deserve gratitude (as does Jeff Barmby for helping me to discover Fred).

I am indebted to Terry Turner, Terry Dance and Walla Longden for help with understanding Hull's industrial landscape during the late 1970s, and also to Tony Collins for his contribution and insights into the clubs' historical rivalry.

The vast majority of the factual content comes from the words of Tingle, Sexton and the *Hull Daily Mail*, whose archives were a crucial source of evidence. I am also grateful to the *Hull Daily Mail* for their permission to reproduce many of the photographs that appear in the book, and to James Smailes in particular for helping me to obtain them. The staff at the Hull History Centre, British Library in London and Heritage Quay in Huddersfield aided my research significantly. The television documentaries made around the time of the final, *All Hull Let Loose* and *A City Divided* were informative, as well as entertaining.

Acknowledgements

Very often, accounts differed from one person to another, which is to be expected of events more than three decades ago. Nevertheless, I have presented the memories of participants as they were told to me. There were varying recollections, for instance, of the meeting in Sully's room. Brian Lockwood recalled it vividly, others believed it might have happened at another time. Some others again had no recollection of such a meeting. "We were in bed early," remembers Millo. But nobody doubted that the feelings I have tried to portray were genuine and true. It is the memories that matter; who am I to tell someone it might have happened differently?

I am grateful to Phil Caplan and Tony Hannan of Scratching Shed Publishing for their expertise and guidance in transforming a hefty, meandering manuscript into the book you are now holding.

I'm grateful too to fellow rugby supporters who read rough drafts of this book and provided invaluable guidance – Wayne Fewster, Andrew Jolley, Steve Ostler and my dad, John Groak, in particular, for all of his support and advice throughout this project. And to both my parents, for all of their love and support and for taking me on that pub trip in 1980 which left a scar that took thirty-six years to heal!

Finally, thank you to Claire for taking an interest in fishing and the Humber Bridge, and carrying on with our life while I traipsed around Castleford and East Hull meeting middle-aged men she'd never heard of. Oh, and for checking the grammar. And to Dylan and to Ebony who will hopefully, one day, read this and understand why I wrote it.

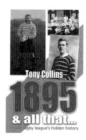

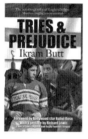
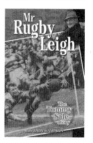

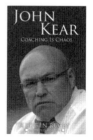

Be inspired.

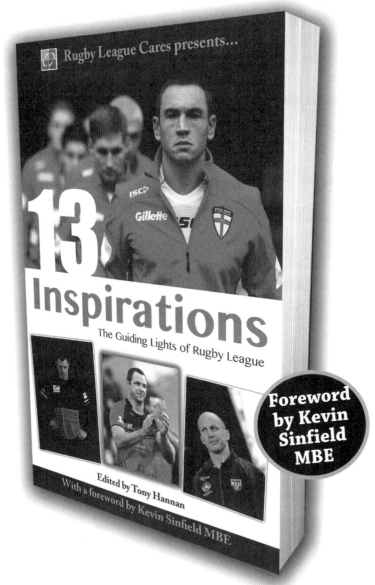

Rugby League Cares presents...

13 Inspirations
The Guiding Lights of Rugby League

Edited by Tony Hannan
With a foreword by Kevin Sinfield MBE

Foreword by Kevin Sinfield MBE

With contributions from many of the leading writers and personalities in the game, **13 Inspirations** is a lively literary collection in praise of the guiding lights of rugby league.

In aid of Rugby League Cares

The Robins

An Official History of Hull Kingston Rovers

Roger Pugh

Historian Roger Pugh takes us back to the founding fathers of a club whose name has become synonymous with rugby league, and traces their story up to the present day.

This is a fascinating odyssey of initial growth in the nineteenth century against all the odds; heady early successes; a fight against debt and economic depression; the transition to 'nearly men'; glorious renaissance and a breakthrough to the top; and more latterly the slide into obscurity, administration before rescue and return.

With a foreword by Colin Hutton and preface from chairman Neil Hudgell, *The Robins* also has pocket profiles of iconic players through the eras, a focus on the great matches, a list of club honours and records, a directory of players, officials and coaches, and other insightful analysis.

Putting the Robins in their social context, this meticulously researched volume will appeal not only to fans of the red and whites of East Hull, but also sporting historians and those who love a tale of defiance and pride.

www.scratchingshedpublishing.com

At the outset of a glorious and varied career, Bev Risman faced two major dilemmas.

Should he represent his ancestral homeland Wales or England, his country of birth? Ought he to play rugby league or rugby union?

Son of league icon Gus, Risman made his name in the fifteen-a-side code, playing for England and touring with the 1959 British Lions.

After initially moving to rugby league with Leigh, he enjoyed huge success at Leeds, with whom he played in the famous Watersplash Challenge Cup final.

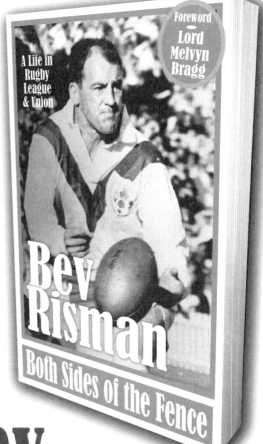

A Life in Rugby League & Union

Foreword
Lord Melvyn Bragg

Bev Risman

Both Sides of the Fence

Rugby dynasty and destiny

With a foreword by Lord Melvyn Bragg, *Both Sides of the Fence* offers insight into decades of great change. A fascinating autobiography, it lays open the events and personalities that dominated both codes of rugby.

"A highly readable memoir..."
The Guardian

Investigate our other titles and
stay up to date with all our latest releases at
www.scratchingshedpublishing.co.uk